Long before microwave cooking existed, Corning was saving you time and energy. It's their specialty. Only with glass cookware can you tastefully prepare, stylishly serve and conveniently store food all in one dish. Now, Corning offers you a total concept of convenience by combining the qualities of microwave energy with the advantages of their products. The results are greater versatility and flexibility in meal preparation to match the needs of your lifestyle. Since most foods will cook in less than half the time of a conventional oven, more speed is attached to your dish in going from the oven to the table. With the microwave and Corning, you can:

- prepare, cook and serve in one dish in only minutes.
- quickly defrost and cook frozen foods.
- reheat stored leftovers in a matter of seconds.
- use fewer pots and pans by serving food on the same plates you cook on.
- make "on-the-spot" meals for your "on-the-go" family easy by cooking meals in minutes right from the refrigerator or freezer.

Heat-resistant glass and glass-ceramic products such as PYREX® ware, CORELLE® livingware and CORNING WARE® cookware can be used and re-used in every type of microwave oven for any length of cooking time without melting, warping or imparting flavor. Corning products are available in a variety of shapes, including round and oval, which provides the best transmittal of microwaves extremely important to microwave cooking. The durability and attractiveness of their products lets you serve in the same dish you prepared in virtually eliminating clean-up time.

Information concerning specific Corning products recommended for Microwave is available. CORNING WARE® cookware products are detailed on pages 16-20 and PYREX® ware are detailed on pages 243-244.

If you find menu planning a little difficult with microwave cooking, *Mastering Microwave Cooking* will assist you in discovering time-saving recipes for all types of food. It offers a plentiful choice of recipes everything from appetizer to dessert with assurance of culinary success. A special section on Micromate® browning dishes has been included on pages 245-246 in the back of the book. Now, with the Corning Micromate® browning dishes you don't have to forego anything to save time. Your steaks, chops, and roasts will be browned just to your liking and this section will tell you how.

Corning and the micro_____ ___ _____ kitchen convenience. They_____ gredients for your active, o__

D1132829

ABOUT THE AUTHORS

MARIA LUISA SCOTT and JACK DENTON SCOTT are among the most experienced in microwave cooking in the country. They have been working with the medium for over eight years and were asked by *Reader's Digest* to present the story of the microwave oven to its millions of readers. The Scotts are magnificent cooks, and have worked closely with one of the world's greatest living French chefs, Antoine Gilly, winner of the world's outstanding awards of chefdom. In collaboration with Antoine Gilly, the Scotts wrote *Feast of France*. The *Wall Street Journal* called it one of the best cookbooks ever written. In addition to cooking as a hobby, Jack Denton Scott is a successful writer, with novels, travel books, natural history, adventure and children's books to his credit. Maria Luisa Scott, aside from being a superb cook, is a copy editor, typist, researcher and severe critic. Among the Scotts' other books are *The Complete Book of Pasta*, which was ten years in the making and is now considered a classic, *Informal Dinners for Easy Entertainment*, which includes easy, but elegant recipes where the food can be eaten informally without the use of a knife, and *Fork Dinners*, the first cookbook to concentrate on the new informality sweeping the country where the guest is served dinner with a plate for one hand, and a fork for the other hand. The Scotts' other recent book is *Cook Like a Peasant, Eat Like a King*, which has been hailed as a great collection of simple country recipes from around the world.

MASTERING MICROWAVE COOKING

MARIA LUISA SCOTT
AND
JACK DENTON SCOTT

ILLUSTRATED BY
DORIS CAGGIANO

BANTAM BOOKS
TORONTO · NEW YORK · LONDON

MASTERING MICROWAVE COOKING

A Bantam Book / December 1976

2nd printing .... *June 1977*	*8th printing* .... *May 1978*
3rd printing .... *June 1977*	*9th printing* .... *July 1978*
4th printing .. *November 1977*	*10th printing* ...... *August 1978*
5th printing .... *December 1977*	*11th printing* ..*December 1978*
6th printing ...... *January 1978*	*12th printing* .. *February 1979*
7th printing .... *April 1978*	*13th printing* .... *May 1979*

14th printing

15th printing

16th printing

17th printing

18th printing

19th printing

20th printing

21st printing

ISBN 0–553–13019–6

Published simultaneously in the United States and Canada

Bantam Books are published by Bantam Books, Inc. Its trademark, consisting of the words "Bantam Books" and the por-
trayal of a bantam, is registered in U.S. Patent and Trademark
Office and in other countries. Marca Registrada. Bantam
Books, Inc., 666 Fifth Avenue, New York, New York 10019.

PRINTED IN THE UNITED STATES OF AMERICA

CONTENTS

FOREWORD

We have been cooking with a microwave oven for about eight years. We acquired one not long after it was made available for household use, and have watched it progress from an innovative and astonishing speed machine to the most convenient and effective cooking medium yet devised.

Every day sees new advances. Some of the best engineering brains in the world are at work on microwave ovens, making them even more efficient and flexible than they are right now.

And they are flexible. The microwave oven formerly was famed only for its speed. Place food into it and, depending upon size and amount, wham! it was cooked literally in seconds. Right now speed is still important, but there is much more. As you will learn from the illustrations in Part II of the various ovens that are offered, precise cooking is possible. Microwave ovens now have variable power and automatic defrosting. Some are even computerized, which means that so-called epicurean cooking is possible. Everything from a soufflé to a stew can be prepared and, with some models, food can go directly from the freezer into the oven for defrosting and cooking in one continuous operation.

We have cooked and tested nearly every variety of food in our microwave ovens (we are now on our third!). And except for some of our own misjudgments and blunderings, we have seldom found it wanting. For our taste, large beef roasts and large fresh ham roasts are just satisfactory, a little chewy, and we have a few other reservations which we will discuss later. But these are minor complaints, as compared to what we find wanting in electric and gas ranges.

All cooking methods, of course, have cookbooks. Microwave cooking already has its share. To date, however, most seem to look gingerly at the microwave oven, treating it more as a supplementary medium than an all-purpose stove that fulfills over 80 percent of all cooking needs.

Many of the books disguise good ingredients with mixes and phony sauces, treating the medium as an elementary one that can handle only the simple or, sometimes, the absurd. Those cookbooks seem to concentrate on convenience foods and quickies made with mixes. All of this camouflaging and mincing around is not necessary. This is a *stove,* in our opinion, the best ever created.

We also point out that all cookbooks merely are guides. Just as a licensed guide takes you through the dark gloom of a forest and puts you on a sunny path leading to your cabin, so does the cookbook writer try to lead you through the complexities of cooking. That other guide does not tell you how to walk or talk, nor advise what shoes to wear; neither can the cookbook writer give you style, good judgment and a sense of timing, nor endow you with imagination.

It all lies in the eye of the beholder. A good example of the individuality of cooking was the experience of our sister/sister-in-law, Mina Thompson. She had promised to bake some cakes for a charitable affair, and asked ten friends to help. Wanting to offer everyone the same dessert, she gave each friend the same recipe. The ten women showed up with what appeared to be ten different kinds of cakes. Each had given it her own touch, using different varieties and qualities of ingredients. Each person handles a recipe differently.

Arno Schmidt, Executive Chef of the Waldorf-Astoria Hotel in New York City and one of the most respected chefs in the country, made a few observations on this aspect of cooking that are worth quoting:

Every so often, I am asked to give a precise recipe for a particular dish. I am happy to oblige because there are really no secrets in cooking. However, I balk at the word "precise."

In baking, it is imperative to scale out accurately all ingredients and if you know how to put them together, how to bake them, and how to decorate, you can be quite sure that you will have a consistent product.

Cooking is different because we deal with fickle Mother Nature. We have come a long way in breeding the right animals, in selecting the proper seeds, and grading the lemons and the chickens. Still, whatever we use has to grow and depends upon sunshine and rain, the loving care of a farmer, and a conscientious grocer to bring it to your doorstep.

No wonder that seemingly similar foods taste and act differently depending upon endless factors. A pinch of freshly dried herbs can be stronger than a whole teaspoon of stale herbs. One cup of new leeks can taste stronger than two cups of old ones. Two pieces of meat, both the same grade and approximately the same weight and cooked about the same way, will not necessarily be completely identical when you get them on your plate.

In addition to that, in cooking there are so many variables like the type of pot you use, the type of heat, how much you prepare at a given time, and so on. For example, it might take one chicken a certain time to cook in your oven, but put five chickens in and you will see that it will take considerably longer.

Now add human nature. Two chefs following the same recipe will invariably come up with different products. I, myself, cook best what I like most. Taste in humans is acquired and what is too salty for one is flat for the next. For that reason, cooking is not a science because science strives for precision. Cooking is a craft which can rise, on occasion, to an art, and it takes skill, talent and creativity.

And so it is with the microwave oven. It will be as good as you are. As with other cooking, you must experiment and learn to use microwaves in your own style.

We cooked the recipes in this book to please ourselves. Some may not be cooked long enough for you, nor may they have the right seasonings for your taste. This is merely a matter of adjustment. You cook them and season them as you want, using what you read in this book as a framework and guide. If you want to adapt one of your own recipes for the microwave oven, plan to cook it in about a fourth the time you are accustomed to. Try to find a recipe in this book that is similar and use that as a guide. However, *be sure* to read the Introductions to Part I and Part II and the chapter introductions before using these recipes.

With the microwave oven, cooking has finally come of age, just as flying has, although it has taken the oven somewhat longer to be accepted. These days, few of us want to fly in a prop plane. We prefer the comfortable, timesaving jet. The microwave oven has also pushed us into a fast and convenient world of the future, where we speed with ease through cooking routines. Once you use a microwave oven, you'll never want to be without one again.

Jack Denton Scott
Maria Luisa Scott

PART I
About Microwave Ovens

If you are just becoming aware of microwave cooking, and even if you are not, you may have questions about this "new" method of cooking. A "space-age stove" for many, it still has an air of mystery, although it shouldn't, since the same shortwave energy powering the microwave oven is used in sunlamps, medical equipment and television sets.

However, you don't have to understand all the mechanics to appreciate the many advantages of microwave cooking. One of the most important is the great saving in energy, plus the economical fact that food doesn't shrink as much as it does in conventional cooking. There is more nutrition in food cooked with microwaves, and also more flavor. Food can be cooked and served in the same utensil, saving on dishwashing. The oven is simple to clean because food doesn't bake on it, and it just needs to be wiped out with a damp cloth. Leftovers taste as fresh as the day they were cooked. But, of course, first and foremost, microwave cooking is very fast.

How was the microwave oven invented?

Microwave cooking is not new. Discovered by accident in 1945, when a Raytheon scientist placed a chocolate bar beside a radar vacuum tube he was testing, it quickly and successfully was put to commercial use in 1947. The first model, Radarange, cost about $3,000, but was offered only to hotels and restaurants. Twenty years passed before a home model using standard household circuits was offered to the public in 1967 as the Amana Radarange, which today in a highly advanced model, is a popular TV performer. By the early 1970s a dozen other companies were manufacturing microwave ovens.

Public acceptance, however, was slow. Many considered it an expensive gadget and were awed by its speed, but not enough to purchase it. Most brushed it off as a fast fad. But not all. About 900,000 people worldwide bought the microwave oven in 1970, were pleased with its performance and spread its magic by word of mouth.

By 1975, there were eight million microwave ovens in use worldwide, about two million in the United States alone, and the microwave industry projects, on the basis of present sales and consumer interest, that by 1980 there will be 33,700,000 units in use worldwide. As you read this, about 10 percent of American families will be cooking with microwaves. In mid-1976, microwave oven sales were up 150 percent over the previous year, and still rising.

How does the oven work?

How can "waves" *cook?* Rub your hands together briskly. What is the result? Heat. Friction. That, more or less, is the way microwaves work. When they enter food, they cause the liquid or moisture molecules to vibrate 2,450 million times a second. That astoundingly fast friction forces the food to heat. The greater the moisture content, the faster the food will cook.

These waves do not use the *direct* application of heat, as all other cooking methods do. Electromagnetic waves from the magnetron power source (or tube, not unlike the one in your television set) are instantly absorbed *into* the food, becoming heat.

These microwaves are waves of energy (with short wavelengths— from approximately one tenth inch to forty inches; and high frequencies—300 million to 100 billion cycles per second), very much like those sent out by television and radio stations. They travel at the speed of light, about 186,000 miles per second; thus, when you summon them, they are there instantly.

Stated simply, the cooking occurs in five stages:

(1) The magnetron tube sends microwaves into the oven cavity.

(2) The metallic oven walls, floor and ceiling reflect the waves (just as light is reflected by a mirror), bouncing them back and forth in irregular patterns.

(3) These energy waves then strike a "stirrer" in the oven, a slowly revolving metal fan which reflects the power bouncing off the walls, ceiling, back and bottom of the oven, distributing it so that it enters the food from all sides to cook evenly.

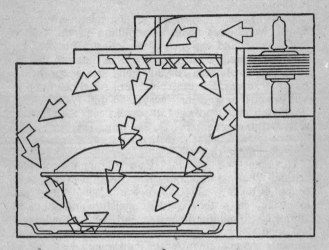

(4) A dish of the proper material transmits the waves, allowing them to pass into the food. Microwaves pass through glass, paper, ceramic, plastic, without effect (a fact that seems to amaze everybody). The objects do warm up, but only because the heat transfers from the food to them. We will discuss utensils later in this section.

(5) Food *absorbs* the microwaves, causing the food molecules to rub together so fast that friction results, heating the food. There is some misunderstanding about this function of microwaves, even among those who have been cooking with the waves for some time. Many believe that the food cooks from the inside out. Not so. It is cooked throughout at the same time, with more cooking on the exterior of the food. The waves penetrate only about one half to one and one half inches, depending upon the density of the food, and then the rest of the heating occurs through conduction or transference.

This means, with proper timing, a roast can be cooked so that it is brown on the outside, and rare, medium or well-done on the inside.

To state it in simplest terms, in microwave cooking, (1) metal reflects, (2) the proper dish transmits and (3) food absorbs microwaves.

Why are microwave ovens becoming so popular?

Several factors are behind the boom, but energy and its spiraling cost probably is the main reason. Microwave ovens save about 75 percent in energy compared to conventional methods. In fact, a microwave oven can pay for itself in a few years.

A family of four using a microwave oven 80 percent of the time and an electric stove 20 percent of the time would have an annual cost of just $7.98. Using a new electric stove, and no microwave oven, that same family would pay $28.59 annually. An old electric stove would cost $42.18 to operate for one year. It has been estimated that by cooking an entire meal for four by microwave, the cost would be about that of toasting one piece of bread in an electric toaster.

Here are some specific, city by city readings on microwave energy savings.

ANNUAL ENERGY COST SAVINGS CITY-BY-CITY WITH MICROWAVE OVENS

City	Cost Per Kilowatt Hour[1]	Household Using Only Electric Range[2]	Household With a Microwave Oven[3]	Annual Savings	15-Year Savings[4]
Albany, NY	3.4¢	$ 40.97	$15.94	$25.03	$375.45
Albuquerque, NM	3.3	39.77	15.47	24.30	364.50
Anchorage, AK	2.4	28.92	11.25	17.67	265.05
Asheville, NC	4.0	48.20	18.76	29.44	441.60
Atlanta, GA	3.0	36.15	14.07	22.08	331.20
Augusta, ME	3.4	40.97	15.94	25.03	375.45
Baltimore, MD	4.7	56.64	22.05	34.59	518.85
Baton Rouge, LA	2.5	30.13	11.73	18.40	276.00
Bennington, VT	5.0	60.25	23.45	36.80	552.00
Billings, MT	2.5	30.13	11.73	18.40	276.00
Bismarck, ND	3.0	36.15	14.07	22.08	331.20
Boise, ID	2.3	27.72	10.78	16.94	254.10
Boston, MA	4.6	55.43	21.58	33.85	507.75
Bridgeport, CT	4.4	53.02	20.63	32.39	485.85
Buffalo, NY	3.4	40.97	15.94	25.03	375.45
Burlington, VT	2.6	31.33	12.20	19.13	286.95
Camden, NJ	4.6	55.43	21.58	33.85	507.75

City					
Carmel, CA	2.9	34.95	13.60	21.35	320.25
Carson City, NV	3.4	40.97	15.94	25.03	375.45
Charles Town, WV	3.5	42.18	16.42	25.76	386.40
Charleston, SC	4.5	54.23	21.11	33.12	496.80
Charlotte, NC	3.0	36.15	14.07	22.08	331.20
Chattanooga, TN	2.4	28.92	11.25	17.67	265.05
Cheyenne, WY	2.2	26.51	10.32	16.19	242.85
Chicago, IL	2.9	34.95	13.60	21.35	320.25
Cincinnati, OH	3.0	36.15	14.07	22.08	331.20
Cleveland, OH	3.8	45.79	17.82	27.97	419.55
Columbus, OH	3.6	43.38	16.89	26.49	397.35
Concord, NH	3.7	44.59	17.36	27.23	408.45
Cumberland, MD	3.7	44.59	17.36	27.23	408.45
Dallas, TX	2.5	30.13	11.73	18.40	276.00
Denver, CO	2.7	32.54	12.67	19.87	298.05
Detroit, MI	2.8	33.74	13.13	20.61	309.15
Dover, DE	6.1	73.51	28.61	44.90	673.50
Duluth, MN	4.0	48.20	18.76	29.44	441.60
El Paso, TX	2.7	32.54	12.67	19.87	298.05
Fairbanks, AK	5.2	62.66	24.39	38.27	574.05
Flagstaff, AZ	3.8	45.79	17.82	27.97	419.55
Fort Worth, TX	2.2	26.51	10.32	16.19	242.85
Gary, IN	3.0	36.15	14.07	22.08	331.20
Glenwood Springs, CO	2.3	27.72	10.78	16.94	254.10
Grand Rapids, MI	3.5	42.18	16.42	25.76	386.40

City	Cost Per Kilowatt Hour[1]	Household Using Only Electric Range[2]	Household With a Microwave Oven[3]	Annual Savings	15-Year Savings[4]
Green Bay, WI	3.5¢	$ 42.18	$16.42	$25.76	$386.40
Harrisburg, PA	3.7	44.59	17.36	27.23	408.45
Hartford, CT	4.0	48.20	18.76	29.44	441.60
Honolulu, HI	4.5	54.23	21.11	33.12	496.80
Houston, TX	2.7	32.54	12.67	19.87	298.05
Iowa City, IA	3.0	36.15	14.07	22.08	331.20
Jackson, MS	3.3	39.77	15.47	24.30	364.50
Jacksonville, FL	4.3	51.82	20.16	31.66	474.90
Kansas City, KS	2.5	30.13	11.73	18.40	276.00
Kansas City, MO	3.4	40.97	15.94	25.03	375.45
Las Vegas, NV	2.8	33.74	13.13	20.61	309.15
Lexington, KY	2.9	34.95	13.60	21.35	320.25
Little Rock, AR	3.3	39.77	15.47	24.30	364.50
Los Angeles, CA	3.3	39.77	15.47	24.30	364.50
Louisville, KY	2.5	30.13	11.73	18.40	276.00
Macon, GA	3.0	36.15	14.07	22.08	331.20
Madison, WI	2.7	32.54	12.67	19.87	298.05
Martinsburg, WV	3.6	43.38	16.89	26.49	397.35
Miami, FL	3.6	43.38	16.89	26.49	397.35
Minneapolis, MN	3.6	43.38	16.89	26.49	397.35
Montgomery, AL	3.6	43.38	16.89	26.49	397.35

Muncie, IN	2.8	33.74	13.13	20.61	309.15
Nashville, TN	2.6	31.33	12.20	19.13	286.95
New Orleans, LA	2.7	32.54	12.67	19.87	298.05
New York, NY	8.7*	104.83	40.79	64.04	960.60
Newark, NJ	4.6	55.43	21.58	33.85	507.75
Norfolk, VA	4.4	53.02	20.63	32.39	485.85
North Platte, NE	2.6	31.33	12.20	19.13	286.95
Oklahoma City, OK	2.0	24.10	9.38	14.72	220.80
Omaha, NE	2.9	34.95	13.60	21.35	320.25
Peoria, IL	3.2	38.56	15.01	23.55	353.25
Philadelphia, PA	4.7	56.64	22.05	34.59	518.85
Phoenix, AZ	4.3	51.82	20.16	31.66	474.90
Pittsburgh, PA	3.8	45.79	17.82	27.97	419.55
Portland, ME	3.4	40.97	15.94	25.03	375.45
Portland, OR	1.8	21.69	8.44	13.25	198.75
Providence, RI	4.3	51.82	20.16	31.66	474.90
Rapid City, SD	2.7	32.54	12.67	19.87	298.05
Richmond, VA	4.4	53.02	20.63	32.39	485.85
Sacramento, CA	2.1	25.31	9.85	15.46	231.90
St. Louis, MO	3.0	36.15	14.07	22.08	331.20
Salt Lake City, UT	2.4	28.92	11.25	17.67	265.05
San Diego, CA	3.6	43.38	16.89	26.49	397.35
San Francisco, CA	2.7	32.54	12.67	19.87	298.05
Sauk Centre, MN	2.3	27.72	10.78	16.94	254.10
Seattle, WA	1.0	12.05	4.69	7.36	110.40

City	Cost Per Kilowatt Hour[1]	Household Using Only Electric Range[3]	Household With a Microwave Oven[3]	Annual Savings	15-Year Savings[4]
Sioux City, IA	3.2¢	$ 38.56	$15.01	$23.55	$353.25
Spartanburg, SC	2.9	34.95	13.60	21.35	320.25
Springfield, IL	2.8	33.74	13.13	20.61	309.15
Springfield, MA	4.5	54.23	21.11	33.12	496.80
Tampa, FL	3.2	38.56	15.01	23.55	353.25
Traverse City, MI	2.8	33.74	13.13	20.61	309.15
Tucumcari, NM	3.0	36.15	14.07	22.08	331.20
Tulsa, OK	2.2	26.51	10.32	16.19	242.85
Walla Walla, WA	1.9	22.90	8.91	13.99	209.85
Washington, DC	3.5	42.18	16.42	25.76	386.40
Wichita, KS	2.0	24.10	9.38	14.72	220.80
Wilmington, DE	4.7	56.64	22.05	34.59	518.85

[1]Cost per Kilowatt Hour (KWH) based on monthly use billing of 500-750 KWH and does not include local taxes, surcharges, or special services.
[2]Based on family of four using a 1965 electric range for 1205 KWH per year.
[3]Based on using the microwave oven 80% of the time at 228 KWH per year and the conventional electric range 20% of the time at 241 KWH per year.
[4]Based on 15-year life expectancy of the ovens at present KWH rates.
Sources: "Typical Electric Bills," Federal Power Commission, 1975.
  *Consolidated Edison Power Company, New York, May, 1976.
  –Litton Microwave Cooking Products, May, 1976.

William W. George, president of Litton Microwave Cooking, the world's largest manufacturer of microwave ovens, believes that the steadily rising cost of energy makes the microwave message so strong that "by 1985, about 40 million microwave cooking appliances will be in use in the United States. This is about one out of every two homes. This would mean a nationwide energy reduction that year of 32.3 billion kilowatt hours of electricity, and a yearly cost savings of $1.1 billion at current energy rates."

Today, with so many couples both being wage earners, the microwave oven also is the magical answer to feeding the family nourishing hot food in mere minutes with minimum effort.

Consider: The oven cooks all foods in about a quarter of the time of any other method. Some take even less than that: a potato in four minutes, an acorn squash in seven, both of which take about an hour to bake in the conventional oven. With this speed it peels hours off kitchen chores.

It will cook a large turkey to perfection at six or seven minutes a pound, whereas a conventional oven takes 35 minutes a pound. A family-size roast of beef takes only 40 minutes, a broiler chicken 15 minutes. You can scramble an egg in 45 seconds; bake a cake in 5 minutes, a cupcake in 30 seconds; heat a roll in 10 seconds; defrost and cook a lobster tail in 5½ minutes. A one-pound steak, frozen solid, is ready to cook in 3 to 5 minutes. Microwaves defrost frozen foods faster and more efficiently than any other medium. This means that you can come home from work and pop that frozen meal into the microwave oven and have it piping hot on the table in minutes.

We want to point out another wonderful aspect of the microwave oven that seems to have little made of it: No heat! What a joy during the sweltering dog days of summer to have "cool" cooking for the entire meal. No hot kitchen, no exhausted cook.

Not long before we started work on this book, the East Coast had a heat wave, with temperatures in the mid-nineties, the air humid as a tropical forest. We found it no chore to cook a dinner in the microwave oven, cool drink in hand, in minutes. A roast chicken, a dish of fresh broccoli in white wine, a baked potato dripping with sweet butter, a green salad, and a classic cheesecake (all recipes are in this book). It took little more than a half hour and there was no kitchen hot as a smelting furnace to take the pleasure out of it.

The five steps we used in cooking this dinner may prove instructive. (1) The 15-minute chicken came out of the oven and "sat" wrapped in aluminum foil for the carry-over cooking time. (2) The broccoli then was cooked in 3½ minutes. (3) It was "setting," covered, while the potatoes cooked in about 7 minutes. (4) While the potatoes were setting, the cheesecake was cooked in 7 minutes. (5) While it was setting for the carry-over cooking time, we whipped up a green salad. No wasted movements, and the entire dinner on that hot night required only 32½ almost effortless heat-free minutes.

Quite a record, we think. Also, the chicken was cooked on the serving platter, the broccoli in the dish in which it would be served, the baked potato on a paper towel. The leftover cheesecake in its glass dish went into the freezer. Dishwashing was no chore that night!

Research by Corning Glass Works among many owners of microwave ovens revealed that most of them had purchased their microwave ovens because they believed that it was easy, casual cookery, that all they would have to do would be to place a dish of food in the oven, press a button, and presto! in seconds, or minutes, it was ready without any further effort on their parts.

It *is* the *easiest* way to cook. But it is not completely *casual*. Not much effort is required. But *some* is. Dishes must be rotated. Food must be stirred. Accumulated liquid must be removed. You can't totally neglect what is cooking in the oven.

What are some of the drawbacks?

Although the microwave oven is better than any other cooking medium, it is not perfect. Because the air in the microwave oven remains at room temperature during the cooking period, some types of baking are not satisfactory. The very hot air in the conventional oven puts a nice crust on bread, and browns pastry. This will not happen in the microwave oven.

Also, anything that remains in the oven less than 15 minutes will not brown. This means steaks, chops, hamburgers, and other small pieces of meat will not brown. Or rather, past tense, *did* not brown. Today, the ingenious browning skillet browns and grills everything beautifully. (The skillets are discussed later in this section.)

Also, the less tender cuts of meat don't do too well, unless your oven has the slo-cook or simmer setting. Otherwise, full speed ahead.

We also have found that the microwave oven is perfect for cooking for two, or for four and six, but we use caution beyond that number. When you prepare large quantities of food, say for eight to ten or even more, then the cooking times are much longer and you also have to do more manipulation, turning, rotating, stirring, etc. You may find the conventional stove better for large feasts.

What kind of utensils can I use with the oven?

You don't have to go out and buy a whole new line of cooking utensils for your microwave oven. But you will not be able to use *any* of your beautiful copper, or enameled cast iron ware. In fact, anything at all with metal is taboo. We often will suggest that you place small strips of aluminum foil on protruding areas, such as the ends of chicken legs and wings and the bone end of a roast, to prevent them from overcooking. How? Metal "reflects" microwaves.

If you use *any* metal object (other than those very small strips of foil) that metal will reflect the microwave energy back to the magnetron tube, which will overheat and soon become inoperative. Like the tube in your television set, the magnetron tube is the most costly part of the microwave oven. If properly cared for, the tube will give many years of service. *So do not use metal.* Don't be tempted, no matter what you hear or are advised.

Also, do not operate your oven empty. Keep a glass of water in it. If it is turned on without food to absorb the waves, they will reflect back to the tube, causing overheating and damage.

In our recipes we repeat that you use a "glass casserole" to alert you to the fact that *glass,* not metal, should be used. Usually we do not state a specific size dish, assuming that your eye will tell you what size cooking utensil to use, as it does in conventional cookery.

We do suggest that you do not use an overly large utensil, unless you are using quite a bit of liquid, then an oversize dish will prevent spillovers, which can happen in a microwave oven. Food, however, cooks better if it is not in a container with lost space. The old French chefs' admonition holds for microwave cooking. "Cook in a pot just large enough to hold what you will cook."

Common sense will tell you not to cook a stew in a shallow dish, place a game hen in a big pot, or a turkey in a small one.

Cookware you can use. Ovenware: Heatproof, Nonmetal dishes are all right, (Pyrex and Temperware dishes). Dinnerware: China without metal trim. Ceramic utensils: Corning Ware cookware is the best and safest of this type and is available in large variety, some of which are listed subsequently. Pyrex ware is also recommended.

All paper is perfect and will save dishwashing chores. You simply discard it. Paper towels, paper plates (not those heavily coated with plastic, as it may melt), napkins, waxed paper, cooking parchment paper, brown-in paper and bags. But do not use the metal tie that comes with most bags. Use string. Also, be sure to poke holes in the bag for the steam to escape.

Plastic is all right. But only for short periods. Use it to heat, not to cook. We find the heat from the food distorts the shape of many plastic containers, and hot food sometimes removes the glaze from most plastic. We have mentioned that plastic wrap can be used as covering for short periods. Pouch packs are all right, mainly for reheating food. Be sure to pierce holes in the bag or it will fill with steam, expand and probably burst. Wood can crack, we don't advise using it. We don't recommend pottery or earthenware. Some have metal in the clay. Wicker and straw baskets are all right just for "seconds," to heat rolls, etc.

If you are uncertain whether a dish is safe for microwave use, here is a simple test you can make:

In the dish you are testing, place a glass of cool water from the tap. Heat for exactly 2 minutes. If the water is almost hot, and the dish cool, that dish is all right. If the dish is just slightly warm around the edges, use it only for a short period of cooking. If the water has remained cool and the dish is hot, *do not use that dish.*

Cookware you absolutely cannot use includes metal pots or pans, or ceramic dishes with metal trim or handles. Do not use closed handle cups in the Corelle livingware line, nor any item in the Centura dinnerware line. Do not use Melamine dishes.

Do not use TV dinner foil trays. Do not use any cooking wrap with foil ends.

Actually, common sense should dictate which dish to use. The food you are cooking should be the determining factor. If you're cooking a food with a thick layer of fat (such as meat) or a high amount of sugar (such as icing or maple syrup), select a dish that can take higher heats. Heat-resistant glass is ideal. Use plastics with caution.

The length of time that food is in the oven is important. When you warm food, it's in the microwave oven a short time, therefore a paper plate or a plastic cup is fine for warming leftovers or heating coffee. But if you're cooking food, such as baking a meat loaf or making gravy, you need a dish that will take hot food for a longer period of time. Once again, heat-resistant glass or glass-ceramic is a good choice.

The type of cooking you do will indicate the kind of dish to use. Sometimes foods require several methods of cooking; this is called complementary cooking. In such cooking, you'll need a dish that can take different types of heat. For instance, if you're browning the food on top of the range before putting it into the microwave oven, you'll need a dish that will take both direct heat and microwaves. Here's a job for a glass-ceramic dish—it saves transferring food from one dish to another and saves dishwashing time. Often, the food can even be served in the same dish. Following is a partial list of Corning Ware cookware, ideal for microwave ovens, giving you an idea of the range of utensils for micro-cookery.

DISH	OUTSIDE DIMENSIONS	INSIDE DIMENSIONS	CAPACITY LEVEL FULL	CAPACITY WORKING
NEW DIMENSION CORNING WARE® COOKWARE			(Working capacity ½″ from top)	
SAUCEPANS:				
No. A-1 1-Quart Covered Saucepan				
Blue Cornflower Emblem Wildflower (-7) Spice O' Life (-8)				
A-1-B Bowl 1 quart size	8¾″ across lugs 7″ opposite lugs 2″ high	6⅝″ between lugs 6⅝″ between sides 1⅞″ deep	1 qt.	24 oz.
Cover A-7-C	2″ high 7″ x 7″ diameter			
Overall height	3⅞″ high			
No. A-1½ 1½-Quart Covered Saucepan				
Blue Cornflower Emblem Wildflower (-7) Spice O' Life (-8)				
A-1½-B Bowl 1½ quart size	8⅝″ across lugs 7″ opposite lugs 2⅞″ high	6⅝″ between lugs 6⅝″ between sides	1½ qts.	38 oz.
Cover A-7-C	2″ high 7″ x 7″ diameter			
Overall height	4⅝″ high			

No. A-2 2-Quart Covered Saucepan

Blue Cornflower Emblem
Wildflower (-7)
Spice O' Life (-8)

A-2-B Bowl	10¼" across lugs	8⅛" between lugs	2 qts. 50 oz.
2 quart size	8½" opposite lugs	8⅛" between sides	
	2½" high	2⅝" deep	
Cover	2⅛" high		
A-9-C	8¾" x 8¾" diameter		
Overall height	4½" high		

No. A-3 3-Quart Covered Saucepan

Blue Cornflower Emblem
Wildflower (-7)
Spice O' Life (-8)

A-3-B Bowl	10¼" across lugs	8⅛" between lugs	3 qts. 81 oz.
3 quart size	8½" opposite lugs	8⅛" between sides	
	3⅞" high	3¾" deep	
Cover	2⅛" high		
A-9-C	8¾" x 8¾" diameter		
Overall height	5⅞" high		

Corning Ware is a Registered Trademark of Corning Glass Works, Corning, N.Y. 14830

DISH	OUTSIDE DIMENSIONS	INSIDE DIMENSIONS	LEVEL FULL	WORKING (Working capacity ½" from top)
NEW DIMENSION CORNING WARE® COOKWARE				
No. A-84 4-Quart Covered Saucepot				
Blue Cornflower Emblem				
Wildflower (-7)				
Spice O' Life (-8)				
			4 qts.	109 oz.
A-84-B Bowl	12" across lugs	9⅞" between lugs		
4 quart size	10¼" opposite lugs	9⅞" between sides		
	3⅜" high	3⅛" deep		
Cover	3" high			
A-12-C	10⅜" x 10⅜" diameter			
Overall height	6" high			
INDIVIDUAL SERVING:				
No. P-150 Two 15 oz. "Grab-It" Bowls (white)				
			17½ oz.	12 oz.
P-150-B Bowl	5⅜" diameter	5" diameter		
15 oz. size	7¼" across top			
	including handle			
	2⅛" height	2" deep		

SKILLETS:

No. A-8 8-Inch Covered Skillet

Blue Cornflower Emblem
Wildflower (-7)
Spice O' Life (-8)

A-8-B Bowl	10¼" across lugs	8⅛" between lugs
1½ quart size	8½" opposite lugs	8⅛" between sides
	2" high	1¾" deep
		1½ qts.
Cover	2⅛" high	
A-9-C	8¾" x 8¾" diameter	
Overall height	4" high	34 oz.

No. A-10 10-Inch Covered Skillet

Blue Cornflower Emblem
Wildflower (-7)
Spice O' Life (-8)

A-10-B Bowl	12" across lugs	9⅞" between lugs
2½ quart size	10¼" opposite lugs	9⅞" between sides
	2¼" high	2" deep
		2½ qts.
Cover	3" high	
A-12-C	10⅜" x 10⅜" diameter	
Overall height	4⅞" high	60 oz.

Corning Ware is a Registered Trademark of Corning Glass Works, Corning, N.Y. 14830

CORNING WARE SETS:

BLUE CORNFLOWER EMBLEM
WILDFLOWER (-7)
SPICE O' LIFE (-8)

No. P-100—Menu-ette Set

1 pt. covered saucepan
1½ pt. covered saucepan
6½" covered skillet

No. A-300—Kitchen Starter Set

1½ qt. covered saucepan
2 qt. covered saucepan
10" covered skillet

No. A-450—Cook 'N' Brew Set

1 qt. covered saucepan
1½ qt. covered saucepan
3 qt. covered saucepan
6 cup teapot

BLUE CORNFLOWER EMBLEM
SPICE O' LIFE (-8)

No. A-500—Chef Master Set

1 qt. covered saucepan
2 qt. covered saucepan
4 qt. covered saucepot
8" covered skillet
10" covered skillet

No. P-260—Bakeware Set

9" Pie plate
8" square utility dish
1½ qt. covered baking dish

No. MW-360 Microwave Set

10" covered browner (white)
2 "Grab-It" Bowls (white)
11½" Oval platter (white)
Microwave cookbook

Corning's offering of its well known Pyrex Ware is so huge that it cannot be reproduced here. But it runs from small custard cups, measuring cups, loaf dishes, oblong and square dishes in many sizes, to bakeware sets with several pieces. There is a Pyrex dish for most microwave needs. So don't worry about having to buy expensive cookware for your microwave oven.

Corning has just introduced a new line of roasters especially for microwave ovens. The large size, 14 inch by 11¼ inch, is designed primarily for use in commercial or combination conventional plus microwave ovens. There is another size, 12¼ by 10¼ inches, which comes in three designs.

We tested these roasters before they were on the market and found them perfect for micro-cooking, sizes and shapes that have long been needed to give cooking flexibility.

The clear sign that microwave cooking has come of age is the fact that other manufacturers are offering special micro-cookware and have more on the drawing boards.

Here is a quick reference chart of utensils that can be used in the microwave oven.

USING DISHES IN YOUR MICROWAVE KITCHEN. . . .

Type of Utensils/Dishes	Microwave Oven	Conventional Oven	Top of Range	Broiler	Freezer	Dishwasher
Heat-Resistant Glass (without metal parts or decorations)	Yes	Yes	No	No	Yes	Yes
Glass-Ceramic (without metals or plastic parts)	Yes	Yes	Yes	Yes	Yes	Yes
Pottery Earthenware Stoneware Fine China/Porcelain	See Manufacturer's Directions or Test	See Manufacturer's Directions	No	No	See Manufacturer's Directions	See Manufacturer's Directions
Paper	Yes (Short time)	No	No	No	Yes	No (Not re-usable)
Straw/Wood	Yes (Short time)	No	No	No	No	No

Plastics	See Manufacturer's Directions (Usually short time only)	No	No	No	No	See Manufacturer's Directions	See Manufacturer's Directions
Metal Cookware/ Bakeware	No	See Manufacturer's Directions	Yes	See Manufacturer's Directions	See Manufacturer's Directions	Yes	See Manufacturer's Directions
Metal Decorations on Glassware, Dinnerware are	No	See Manufacturer's Directions	See Manufacturer's Directions	See Manufacturer's Directions	See Manufacturer's Directions	See Manufacturer's Directions	See Manufacturer's Directions
Glazed Glass-Ceramic Dinnerware	No	Yes	No	No	No	Yes	Yes
Crystal/Cut Glass Antique Glassware	No	No	No	No	No	Not Recommended	See Manufacturer's Directions
Microwave Browning Dish	Yes	Yes	No	No	No	Yes	Yes

With the appearance of browning skillets, micro-browners, or browning dishes (all the same utensil), the microwave oven has become the complete and perfect stove. Now you can brown steaks, chops, hamburgers, fry chicken, make toasted cheese sandwiches, pancakes, fry eggs. The whole world of microwave cookery has been enhanced. We recommend the browning skillet frequently in our recipes.

Like all unique inventions, it is simple. The skillet has a special tin oxide base undercoating. When the empty skillet is preheated in the microwave oven, the special coating interacts with microwave energy and produces heat. The dish has feet, which raise it above the micro-wave oven shelf. This prevents the oven shelf from stealing heat from the dish and possibly breaking.

We have been informed by Corning that browning skillets can be used in all microwave ovens. They did caution, however, that some foreign manufacturers of microwave ovens are using nonthermal glass or plastic trays as bottom shelves. These can become overheated and crack.

All browning skillets come with instructions from the manufacturer, and are as simple to use as a frying pan on your conventional stove. You do not have to use fat in browning skillets to fry, unless you wish. This is good for weight watchers.

To use the skillet, simply place it in the oven and preheat it for the specified number of minutes according to its size. The 6½-inch skillet, for example, is heated only 2½ minutes. You then place the food on it, cover it with its Pyrex glass top or waxed paper to prevent splattering, then cook for the specified time. Food will brown better without the glass top. If you are going to use the browning skillet for several sessions, pour off any liquid in the skillet after browning, then briefly re-heat it each time. That's it.

You do not have to use it as a browner, either. As long as the bottom of the skillet is covered with food, it can be used as a casserole for meats and vegetables, or to cook sauces, or to sauté. We also find it superb for Chinese stir-frying. But do *not* use it on your conventional stove.

PART II

Recipes

IMPORTANT: Read this introduction before using the recipes. The time given at the beginning of each recipe is total cooking time. The speed-cook setting will be recommended most often.

1
How To Use the Recipes

Just as you experimented with your conventional stove, learning its assets and its limitations, becoming aware of its idiosyncrasies, its uneven baking or broiling results, so will you tinker with your microwave oven—and learn. Consider it your reliable kitchen aid that seldom, if ever, lets you down.

You will note that, unlike other cookbooks for this medium, we have listed cooking time at the top of each recipe, so at a glance you can see approximately how much time a recipe takes, and whether we think it should be cooked on high ("speed-cook") and/or simmered or "slo-cooked" at half power.

All recipes in this book were cooked in a 675 watt microwave oven, with all the up-to-date settings including automatic defrost and slo-cook, besides being computerized. In order to assist owners of all models of microwave ovens, we went to Verle Blaha, one of the country's top microwave engineers for help, suggestions, and to discover what kind of ovens were in use in the United States.

He informed us that the magnetron (or oven power tube) manufacturers have designed magnetrons for the following oven power outputs: 300–400 watts; 400–500 watts; 500–600 watts; 600–700 watts; and for commercial use, 700–1000 watts and 1200–1300 watts.

Mr. Blaha has found that 80 percent of all microwave ovens sold in this country fall in the 600–700 watt category, while the remaining 20 percent are divided between the 400–500 watt ovens.

If you already have an oven, you will have received a book of instructions with it which will key you in on cooking times. However, to put everything in one place, here are some helpful hints:

If you own a 500–600 watt oven, add about 15 percent to the cooking times for the recipes in this book.

If your oven is in the 400–500 watt category, about 35 percent should be added.

In other words, if you have a 500–600 watt oven, and you are cooking a recipe in this book that takes one minute, you would cook a total of one minute 9 seconds. If you are cooking food that takes 5 minutes in this book, it would cook 5 minutes 45 seconds. If the recipe cooks 20 minutes here, you would cook 23 minutes.

If your oven is from 400–500 watts, an item that we cook here at 3 minutes would take 4 minutes 3 seconds. Our 20-minute cooking time, for your oven, would be 27 minutes.

Here is a simple test that will quickly help determine if you need extra cooking time in your oven for these recipes. Pour 6 ounces of water run cold from the tap into a glass. Bring it to a boil in the oven. It should take 2 minutes, or perhaps 2 minutes 15 seconds at most. If the water isn't boiling in this time, you will need at least one more minute of cooking time. If it boils more quickly, then, of course, you subtract about a minute.

As you will discover as you use these recipes, cooking times are approximate, and will vary according to power output in your community, and to your own personal tastes.

The common sense rule of thumb is to *undercook* and *test*. This is mainly what you do with your conventional stove, so cooking by microwave shouldn't take much adjustment. Here is a chart to help you translate cooking times. Cooking times in minutes have been rounded off to the nearest half minute.

	600–700 Watt*	500–600 Watt add 15%	400–500 Watt add 35%
TIME	15 sec.	17 sec.	20 sec.
	30 sec.	35 sec.	41 sec.
	1 min.	1 min.	1.5 min.
	2	2.5	2.5
	3	3.5	4.0
	4	4.5	5.5

*Recipes in this book were cooked at this wattage.

600–700 Watt*	500–600 Watt add 15%	400–500 Watt add 35%
5	6.0	7.0
6	7.0	8.0
7	8.0	9.5
8	9.0	11.0
9	10.5	12.0
10	11.5	13.5
11	12.5	15.0
12	14.0	16.0
13	15.0	17.5
14	16.0	19.0
15	17.5	20.5
16	18.5	21.5
17	19.5	23.0
18	20.5	24.5
19	22.0	25.5
20	23.0	27.0
21	24.0	28.5
22	25.5	29.5
23	26.5	31.0
24	27.5	32.5
25	29.0	34.0
26	30.0	35.0
27	31.0	36.5
28	32.0	38.0
29	33.5	39.0
30	34.5	40.5
31	35.5	42.0
32	37.0	43.0
33	38.0	44.5
34	39.0	46.0
35	40.5	47.5
36	41.5	48.5
37	42.5	50.0
38	43.5	51.5
39	45.0	52.5
40	46.0	54.0
41	47.0	55.5
42	48.5	56.5
43	49.5	58.0
44	50.5	59.5
45	52.0	61.0
46	53.0	62.0
47	54.0	63.5
48	55.0	65.0
49	56.5	66.0

600–700 Watt*	500–600 Watt add 15%	400–500 Watt add 35%
50	57.5	67.5
51	58.5	69.0
52	60.0	70.0
53	61.0	71.5
54	62.0	73.0
55	63.5	74.5
56	64.5	75.5
57	65.5	77.0
58	66.5	78.5
59	68.0	79.5
60	69.0	81.0

The great enemy of most kitchen creations is dryness. With conventional heat we often underestimate the amount of liquid to add and overestimate cooking time. One of these hazards, drying out, is almost eliminated with microwaves. This is *moist* cookery. So you do not add as much liquid as you would in conventional cooking. But again we warn, you can overcook and that can be catastrophic. So go easy. Don't be a spendthrift with microwave speed. Like adding too much salt which cannot be removed, neither can you save a chop, chicken or a roast that has been under the microwaves too long. We've used restraint with our recipes, timing them on the short rather than the long side.

You'll be reading this so often that you'll probably be sick of it: Food continues to cook after it is out of the microwave oven, so you *must* allow for that carryover cooking.

Our recipes are mainly for four to six people. If you want to cook for two, cut the recipe and cooking time in half. But watch it carefully, and undercook. For example, although the amount of food may be 50 percent less, it doesn't always follow that the cooking time should also be *exactly* 50 percent less. Play it safe, make it 40 percent less, then add that other 10 percent of cooking time after testing to see if the food is right for your taste.

We have been generous in our amounts, usually allowing half a pound of meat or fish per person. If you wish to reduce that, then, of course, reduce the cooking time.

Read the recipes that you plan to use first. Reading them *twice* is even better. Then plan. For example, if the recipe calls for chopped onions, do the chopping, all the time-consuming chores, first. Then assemble. Gather everything you need in one place so you won't have to hop all over the kitchen.

Place a trivet or a wooden board near the microwave oven on which you can place the hot dish or browning skillet when you take it from the oven. Have hot pot-holders handy, also the spoon or the fork you need for stirring, the spatula for turning food over.

Tips

You do not have to learn how to cook all over again with a microwave oven. But, as with everything, from riding a bicycle to needlepointing a canvas, there are pointers and hard facts that help. Common sense is your best guide.

We find that canned soups make excellent sauces and thickeners. Remember, these commercial soups were originally created by master chefs, and if properly used are an asset to many dishes where tasty thickeners or quick sauces are needed.

This is moist cookery. And very fast. Frequently, liquid does not have time to cook down and thicken. If dishes cooked with liquid do not seem thick enough, also use other thickeners besides soups to get the right consistency. Tomato paste, flour and butter blended, cornstarch, arrowroot, eggs and cream, sour cream, heavy tomato puree are excellent. With a little experimentation, you'll quickly discover what works best for you. As an example, check our recipe for *Sausage alla Pizzaiola,* page 172. Usually that is cooked with tomatoes, not tomato puree. But with microwaves we found the sauce too watery. Tomato puree gave it perfect consistency.

Other books recommend that to prevent splatter you cover food with paper towel. Fine. But first *smell* that paper towel. Often the rolls seem to come impregnated with an unpleasant chemical odor. We do not know what it is, but quite often that chemical odor will be there, and it can be transmitted to the food via microwaves. We once cooked a chicken draped with a paper towel and it ended up tasting as if it had been basted with cough syrup. Waxed paper is safer and an excellent splatter-guard. Plastic wrap is also excellent for quick-cooking foods, keeps the heat in and aids steaming for even cooking. But do not use it for periods of over 3 or 4 minutes, as it is likely to melt, or at least get sticky and gummy.

You will test, rotate, turn or stir the food from time to time. When you open the door, the cooking stops immediately. When you close the door, the time will take up where it left off, so you do not have to add extra time.

If the food isn't hot enough for your taste after the "setting" times that we advise, simply put it back into the oven. But briefly.

Stews and braised meats such as pot roasts are more tender if cooked with the simmer or "slo-cook" setting, which cuts the power 50 percent, and increases the time. However, the slo-cook setting is still fast, cooking in half the time of your conventional stove.

Always place the dish in the center of the oven, thick pieces of food to the outside, thin inside.

If you like food brown and crusty, place it briefly under the broiler of your conventional stove.

Always test for tenderness *after* the "setting" time, for the food will continue to cook for some time after it is out of the oven.

When we say "let set, covered," we mean with aluminum foil, unless otherwise specified.

Test for doneness as you always have, by sight and by touch. A toothpick inserted in the center of a cake will tell if it is done.

As explained, microwaves are drawn to the moisture in food; they take the path of least resistance. Because of the composition of the food itself, there is a higher concentration of heat in certain places. To distribute this heat and assure more even cooking, it often is necessary to change the position of the dish, or of the food itself. Some food should be stirred occasionally, always stir from the outside in. The waves work on the outside first, by stirring "in" the food will cook more evenly.

When heating pastries, or a hot dog in a bun, wrapping them in a napkin reduces moisture and sogginess and distributes the heat more evenly.

Vegetables will cook more effectively if the container is covered. Glass, plastic or paper are good, but we have found, if the cooking time is short, plastic is the best because it holds the steam in more effectively, which means the vegetables will be cooked more evenly.

In stews, or other dishes requiring various meats and vegetables cooked together, try to cut the meats and vegetables so they are similar in size and shape. Otherwise, the smaller pieces will be overdone before the larger ones are cooked.

Temperatures affect cooking. Refrigerated foods take longer than foods cooked at room temperature. Warm foods need mere seconds to become very hot.

Arrangement of food is also important. Even cooking results when all food is placed on the same level. For example, spread out lima beans or peas in a single layer in a large dish. Do not stack food. Always have the thicker parts of food toward the outside, the thinner toward the inside. All of this is spelled out in the pertinent chapters.

Standing time (we call it "setting" time) is needed for all food cooked under microwaves. As we have stated and will state again, allowance must be made in the original timing for this carry-over cooking time. Early in our cooking experience we followed to the letter one cookbook's recipe for roasting two game hens, each weighing one pound. "Twelve minutes breast down, then 12 minutes breast up," plus 10 minutes standing time, were the instructions. To our taste, the birds were badly overcooked. Now we cook them in exactly 12 minutes, and let them set, wrapped in aluminum foil, for 15 minutes. For us, they are perfect. You will have to experiment too.

Types of food and the density of food require different cooking times. Ground meat has less density than

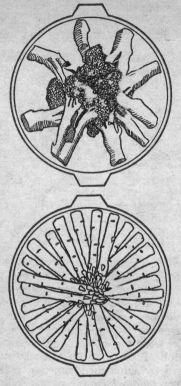

a steak, thus the steak will take longer to cook. Bread and pastry, which are light and porous, take less time than other compact food of the same weight.

As the volume is increased, so is the time. If you place twice the amount of food in a dish, it usually will take almost twice as long to cook it. But you must experiment with this.

Size and shape of food also are important. Boned roasts fare better than those with the bone in because they are more uniformly shaped and will cook more evenly. Trussed poultry cooks more evenly than poultry that is not trussed. Slender, protruding portions will cook more quickly than large, compact areas. Small strips of aluminum foil can be used to cover tips of wings, legs, and the bone end of the leg of lamb, shielding them, reflecting the microwaves and lessening the cooking.

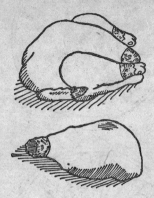

Be warned that herbs are more powerful in this cookery. Their flavors are not diluted and are almost instantly fixed. Too much dill or oregano on your fish or chicken and you will be eating dill or oregano and won't taste the meat or fish.

About defrosting: You will have received an instructional booklet when you bought your microwave oven. Read it carefully. If you have a new oven, then probably you will have an automatic defrosting setting, which means that you merely have to use that setting and the food will defrost, with heating and setting periods automatically alternated.

To perform this manually, for each 8 ounces of frozen cooked food heat one minute and let stand one minute. If possible, always do this with the icy side up so as it melts it will conduct heat downward. Continue until there are just a few ice crystals left. After thawing, heat 1½ minutes per cup of food.

Remember, do not use any foil container. If heating convenience foods such as TV dinners in foil trays, remove them to an appropriate glass container.

The manufacturer of your oven will have included a chart for the defrosting and heating of convenience foods. Many of the food companies are also printing microwave cooking instructions on their packages.

These charts are for your convenience and quick reference. The modern microwave ovens with variable power, built-in computers, sensing probes, etc., operate with almost pinpoint accuracy and come with their own instructional booklets and charts. Regardless, we suggest testing and working on the low side, adding the additional seconds or minutes if needed.

Basic Timings

This chart will give you a good idea of, and will be a quick check point for, most cooking times. We suggest, however, that you read the instructional booklet that came with your oven for other amounts. Be warned that all timings do not increase proportionately when you cook larger amounts of food. It depends upon the kind of food.

Poultry

6 minutes per pound, let stand, covered, 10 minutes

Fish and Shellfish

4 minutes per pound for fish. It is done when easily flaked with a fork.

Shrimp and other shellfish should be just firm, not hard or not soft.

Test both fish and shellfish at 3 minutes, and let both stand, covered, 2 minutes after cooking.

Beef

Roasts, bone in, 2 rib roast, 5 minutes per pound, rare

6 minutes per pound, medium

8 minutes per pound, well done

Let stand, covered, 25 minutes

Same cooking time for 4-rib, but let stand, covered, 40 minutes

Roasts, rolled, sirloin tip, rolled, rump,
   5½ minutes per pound, rare
   7 minutes per pound, medium
   8 minutes per pound, well done
Let stand, covered, 20 minutes

Steaks. Check the instructional booklet that came with the browning skillet, if you will use it, and we advise that you do. One-inch-thick choice steaks take less than one minute on each side. Check at 40 seconds.

Veal

Roasts, 7½ minutes per pound, medium
       9 minutes per pound, well done
Let stand, covered, 20 minutes

Chops. See recipes.

Lamb

Rolled, 7½ minutes per pound, medium
      8½ minutes per pound, well done
Let stand, covered, 25 minutes

Shoulder with bone, 8 minutes per pound, medium
          9 minutes per pound, well done
Let stand, covered, 30 minutes

Leg, pink, French style, 6 minutes per pound
    American style, 8½ minutes per pound, well done
Let stand, covered, 35 minutes

Chops. See recipes.

Pork

Fresh, roasts, loin, shoulder, fresh ham, etc., 9 minutes per pound.
Let stand, covered, 25 minutes

Cured, canned, precooked ham, etc., 5 minutes per pound

Thermometer Readings after Standing Time

All poultry and meats should have a standing time to let the carry-over cooking time finish. If you like to use a meat thermometer (never in the oven, unless it is especially designed for microwave cooking), here is a quick reference chart. While poultry and meats rest, temperature may rise as much as 20 percent. Always use the thermometer *after* the standing time.

MEAT	INTERNAL TEMPERATURES
Beef (rib, rolled rib, rib-eye, tenderloin)	110° to 115° (rare)
	115° to 120° (medium rare)
	130° to 135° (medium)
(boneless rolled rump)	145° to 150° (well done)
Veal (leg, loin, rack, boneless shoulder)	160° (well done)
Lamb (leg, shoulder, boneless cushion, rib)	125° to 130° (medium rare)
	145° to 150° (well done)
Fresh pork (loin, leg, ham)	165° to 170° (well done)
Poultry (chicken, turkey, goose, duck)	160° to 170°

Quick-Reference Charts for Other Cooking, Heating and Defrosting

Defrosting meats: 2 to 3 minutes per pound, depending upon size. Check your defrosting instructional booklet.

Heating precooked meats: 30 seconds per serving, depending upon amount

Heating casseroles: 2 minutes per cup

Fresh vegetables: 6 to 7 minutes for 4 servings

Frozen vegetables: the vegetables prepared in sauces, such as eggplant parmesan, scalloped potatoes, take 5½ to 8 minutes for a 12-ounce package. Stir before serving.

Baked potatoes: 4 minutes for a 7-ounce potato

Warming dinner rolls: 1 to 3, 15 to 30 seconds
4 to 6, 30 to 60 seconds

One 1-pound loaf of frozen sliced bread in wrapping: remove metal twist and heat 1½ minutes, rotating ¼ turn every 30 seconds

Doughnuts: 1 to 3, 15 to 30 seconds
4 to 6, 30 to 45 seconds
Box of 12, heat one minute, rotate box ⅓ turn at 30 seconds

Coffee cake, 13-ounce package: remove aluminum foil, heat, icing side up, 2 minutes, rotate dish ½ turn at one minute. Let stand 2 minutes.

Heating desserts: such as pie, coffee cake, etc., 15 seconds per serving

Heating milk or water: 2 minutes for 6 ounces

Other Uses of the Oven

The microwave oven will prove to be your most versatile piece of kitchen equipment. You'll find many uses as you let your imagination take over. For example, read how we opened clams in the oven, then went on to prepare an unusual appetizer (page 42). Here are a few bonuses, arranged alphabetically by food item, that we discovered:

Appetizers: All appetizers, your own from the refrigerator, or the convenience packages from the grocer, take only seconds to heat, and not much longer to defrost if frozen.

Brown Sugar: Soften that stubborn, hard brown sugar. Place in a small glass bowl with a small slice of apple. Cover with plastic wrap. Heat 15 seconds. The steam from the apple softens the sugar.

Butter: To soften refrigerated butter, unwrap and place ¼ pound or one stick on a glass dish. Heat ¼ minute. Let set 5 minutes before using. If the stick is frozen, heat ½ minute, let set 10 minutes. To melt: heat 1½ minutes. To clarify butter, place ¼ pound in a measuring bowl. Heat 2½ minutes, or until it is melted and boiling. When bubbly, take from the oven. The clear (clarified) butter will float to the top. Pour it off. Discard the rest.

Cheese: Cheese is at its best at room temperature. How often have you forgotten this and brought it out to serve with drinks, finding its personality deadened by the refrigerator? No more. Just pop it into the oven for 15 seconds, or 20, or even 25, depending upon the size of the piece of cheese.

Place a slice of cheese on a piece of apple pie. Heat for 15 seconds, or until it starts to melt.

Cheese sauce for vegetables: Spoon out your choice of processed cheese from the jar into a measuring cup. Heat one minute, or until you can stir it, or until it is soft enough to pour over the vegetables.

Chestnuts: To roast 2 dozen raw chestnuts, slash nuts in four places. Arrange in one layer in a shallow container. Cook one minute, uncovered, stirring at 30 seconds. Nuts should be soft when squeezed. Don't be tempted to cook another minute or they will be overcooked.

Chocolate: To melt: Unwrap a 3-ounce package of squares. Heat in a glass dish 2 minutes. Chocolate curls for pastry: Place unwrapped block of chocolate in the oven. Heat 7 seconds. Scrape the curls off with a vegetable scraper.

Coffee: Don't throw that good perked coffee away. The microwaves will renew it. Store in a measuring cup in the refrigerator. Heat one minute per cup, or until hot.

Crêpes: To make them more flexible and easier to handle, place them in a damp towel and heat until just pliable. Time depends upon the number. If they are frozen, time will double.

Croutons: One quart of bread cubes, arranged in one layer in a suitable dish, are dried in 6 minutes. Stir every 2 minutes.

Dough: Frozen dough defrosts rapidly, so watch it. Try 10 seconds, then 5 seconds more, depending upon the amount. It should be cold, yet pliable.

Egg Whites: Frozen egg whites can be defrosted in the oven.

Fruit: To get more juice from oranges or lemons, heat

one lemon or orange for 15 seconds. To peel peaches, heat a large peach 20 seconds. Let stand 5 minutes. Peel. Warm up chilled refrigerated fruit such as apples, oranges or grapes for 15 seconds. They are juicier and more palatable after the chill is off. Quickly rehydrate dried fruits such as apricots or prunes. Place in a bowl. Barely cover with water (or port wine!). Heat 5 minutes. Let stand 5 minutes.

Herbs: To dry out, place washed and dried fresh herbs on a piece of doubled paper towel. Heat 1½ minutes, or until they can be crumbled. Cool and store in jars with screw tops.

Ice cream: To soften, place one pint package on a dish. Heat 15 seconds. Heat one quart, 30 seconds; half a gallon, 45 seconds.

Frozen ice cream pies and cakes: Slice. Heat each portion 10 seconds, perhaps 15 depending upon size. Fresh pie also heats in this length of time.

To defrost frozen puddings: Heat one 4¾-ounce package 30 seconds. Stir, let stand 5 minutes.

Meat bones: Defrost frozen bones for soup or stock.

Milk: Take the chill off milk. It has no flavor coming right out of the refrigerator. Fifteen seconds should do it.

Nuts: To toast one cup of raw peanuts: In a shallow glass dish, paper or pie plate, arrange the nuts in one layer. Cook, 6½ minutes, uncovered, stirring every 60 seconds. To toast one cup of raw cashews: Arrange in one layer in a shallow container. Cook 9 minutes, uncovered, stirring every 30 seconds. To toast ½ cup of raw whole almonds: Arrange in one layer in shallow container. Cook 7 minutes, uncovered, stirring every 60 seconds.

Spreads and Toppings: Cream cheese (foil wrap removed), cheese, or other appetizer spreads in glass jars (after the metal cover is removed), can be made soft and spreadable in 15 seconds. To warm up maple syrup, remove metal top and heat 40 seconds. Dessert toppings for ice cream can go into the oven right in their glass jars (no metal tops) for 15 to 20 seconds until they are warmed and softened.

Waffles: Heat frozen waffles 35 seconds.

2

Appetizers

An example of the might and the magic of the microwave oven was put into motion one evening when a friend, Roger Gayat, who had moved to Prudence Island, off the coast of Rhode Island, dropped in with three dozen clams that he had gathered that very morning. Fresh clams, from what he claimed were unpolluted waters off his little island were a rare treat and had to be sampled immediately. But fresh clams are stubborn and very difficult to open. The three of us had a unique idea: We placed six clams in the microwave oven for 30 seconds. Sure enough, they obligingly opened their shells wide enough for the female half of this team to expertly insert a clam knife. In seconds we had incomparable clams on the half shell. But more. We also whipped up a tasty appetizer, Clams Oreganato (page 42) and put dinner on the table, all in about 17 minutes.

We had planned to have chicken florentine, but when our friend unexpectedly arrived we learned that this Frenchman, who doesn't cook, but who is married to a Texan who cooks like a Frenchman, had had chicken three times that week. So what to do? No problem. The freezer plus the microwaves produced Pasta Bolognese (page 176). We had on hand some frozen ground sirloin, some chicken livers and a little *filetto* sauce, a tomato sauce with white onions and basil. We defrosted three ground meat patties in 40 seconds, a half pound of chicken livers in 30 seconds, the pasta sauce in 3 minutes. We sautéed garlic in olive oil under the microwaves, added and cooked the ground sirloin for 2 minutes, then stirred in the pasta sauce. Two minutes later, the chicken livers were added and cooked for one minute. The sauce set, covered, while we cooked the pasta under microwaves. *Ecco!* In slightly more than 15 minutes, dinner was ready.

Here is the clam appetizer that proved that it pays to experiment with microwaves:

CLAMS OREGANATO
[Speed-cook; 4 minutes]

2 garlic cloves, minced
2 tablespoons olive oil
2 small ripe tomatoes, peeled, seeded, and chopped
½ teaspoon salt
¼ teaspoon pepper
1 teaspoon dried oregano
2 tablespoons chopped fresh parsley
2 tablespoons coarsely chopped pine nuts
1 tablespoon minced raisins
3 dozen shucked cherrystone clams, minced (reserve 3 tablespoons of the liquid)
8 tablespoons grated Parmesan cheese
8 tablespoons bread crumbs

In a glass casserole, cook the garlic in the oil one minute. Stir in the tomatoes, salt, pepper, oregano, parsley, pine nuts and raisins. Cook 2 minutes. Stir in the clams and the clam liquid. Cook one minute. Blend well. Spoon equal portions into 8 scallop shells, large clam shells or ramekins. Sprinkle each serving with one tablespoon of cheese and one of bread crumbs. Place under the broiler of a conventional stove 2 minutes, or until the cheese has melted and the bread crumbs are crusty-brown. *Serves 8.*

ELEANOR STONE'S MINI PIZZAS
[Speed-cook; 40 seconds]

Two 7-ounce cans tomato paste
1 tablespoon Italian seasoning
1 teaspoon dried oregano
30 slices Pepperidge party rye bread, toasted
½ pound Genoa salami, chopped
1 cup grated Parmesan cheese or slivered mozzarella cheese

In a small bowl, blend the tomato paste, Italian seasoning and oregano. Spread each toasted bread slice with the tomato-paste mixture. Sprinkle on a layer of salami, then one of cheese. Place paper towels in the oven and arrange 10 slices in a circle on the towels. Cook for 40 seconds, or until the cheese begins to bubble and melt. Cook the remaining slices 10 at a time. Serve hot. These freeze well and can be popped under the microwaves right from the freezer. If you do this, increase the cooking time to 55 seconds. *Serves 10.*

MAURICE BROCKWAY'S DATE-BACON DELIGHTS
[Speed-cook; 7 minutes]

20 pitted dates
Bourbon
10 slices bacon, cut in half

Soak the dates in bourbon to cover for a least 24 hours; 48 is better. Drain. Wrap each date in one half-slice of bacon and fasten with a toothpick. On a plate, or a paper plate, place 4 layers of paper towels. Arrange the date-bacon rolls on the towels and cover with one layer of paper towels. Cook in the center of the oven 3 minutes. Turn the rolls over. Rotate the plate a half turn. Cook 4 minutes. Blot off any remaining fat. Serve immediately. *Serves 8 to 10.*

CREVETTES
[Speed-cook; 3½ minutes]

½ cup mayonnaise
2 tablespoons catsup
2 tablespoons brandy
1 tablespoon minced onion
1 garlic clove, crushed
1 tablespoon chopped fresh parsley
1 tablespoon Old Bay seafood seasoning
1 teaspoon salt
⅓ cup beer
⅓ cup water
1 pound small, fresh shrimp, shelled and deveined
4 crisp inner leaves of Boston lettuce

In a large bowl, blend the mayonnaise, catsup, brandy, onion, garlic and parsley. Set aside. In a glass measuring cup, blend the seafood seasoning, salt, beer and water. Cook 2 minutes, or until boiling. Pour the hot liquid into a glass pie plate large enough to hold the shrimp in one layer. Add the shrimp and cook in the center of the oven 45 seconds. Turn the shrimp. Cook 45 seconds. Turn the shrimp again and let set, covered, for 2 minutes. They should be pink and firm, but not hard—be careful not to overcook. When the shrimp are cool, add them to the mayonnaise sauce and mix well. Refrigerate 2 hours. Remove the garlic clove. Serve on lettuce leaves on individual plates. To multiply number of servings, cook the shrimp in one-pound batches for every 4 guests. *Serves 4.*

RALPH GUIDETTI'S MUSHROOMS TRIFOLATI
[Speed-cook; 6 minutes]

This is a tasty, "different" Italian first course or appetizer, to our knowledge not found anywhere in this country except at Guidetti's Restaurant in Wingdale, New York.

4 half-inch-thick slices white bread (crusts removed)
  fried in butter or toasted and buttered
4 large garlic cloves, minced
⅓ cup olive oil
1 pound mushrooms, thinly sliced
Salt and pepper to taste
¼ cup dry white wine
Juice of 2 lemons
3 tablespoons chopped fresh parsley

In a glass casserole, cook the garlic in the olive oil in the center of the oven for one minute or until soft. Stir in the mushrooms and season with salt and pepper. Cook 2 minutes, stirring after one minute. Stir in the wine. Cook 2 minutes, stirring after one minute. Stir in the lemon juice and parsley and cook one minute. Remove from the oven. Stir and let set, covered, 3 minutes. The mushrooms should look "wilted." Spoon them with some of the sauce over the fried or toasted bread slices and serve hot. *Serves 4.*

KIELBASA SAUSAGE CANAPÉS

[Speed-cook; 3 minutes 20 seconds]

½ cup (¼ pound) butter, softened
3 tablespoons Kosciusko mustard (or one of your choice)
24 slices Pepperidge party rye· bread, toasted
½ pound smoked kielbasa sausage in one piece, skinned

In a small bowl, blend the butter and mustard. Spread the toasted bread with the mustard-butter. Place the sausage on 3 layers of paper towel in the center of the oven. Cook 2 minutes. Turn the sausage over and cook one minute. Remove from oven. Let set, covered, for 3 minutes. Cut the sausage into ¼-inch-thick slices (or any thickness you prefer). Place a round of sausage on each slice of bread, then heat under microwaves, 12 at a time, for 20 seconds. Serve immediately, while the sausage is warm. *Serves 8.*

SPANISH SHRIMP

[Speed-cook; 3½ minutes]

4 tablespoons butter
1 garlic clove, minced
⅓ cup dry sherry
1 pound small shrimp, shelled and deveined
Salt and pepper to taste
2 tablespoons chopped fresh parsley
Toast strips

In a glass pie plate large enough to hold the shrimp in one layer, melt the butter. Add the garlic and cook in the center of the oven for one minute, or until the garlic is soft. Stir in the sherry. Arrange the shrimp in a layer and sprinkle with salt and pepper. Cook 45 seconds. Turn the shrimp. Cook 45 seconds and turn again. Sprinkle with the parsley and cook one minute. Let set, covered, 2 minutes. Shrimp should be pink and firm, but not hard. Serve the shrimp warm in the sauce, in ramekins. Pass the toast strips so that guests can soak up the shrimp sauce. Number of servings can be multiplied; cook one-pound batches. *Serves 4.*

SHRIMP IN VERMOUTH
[Speed-cook; 10 minutes]

Vermouth, a fortified wine, becomes vermouth when a number of secret herbs are added, giving it its unique flavor. It is superb for cooking seafood.

½ cup dry white vermouth
⅓ cup clam broth
2 small white onions, thinly sliced
1 small celery rib, thinly sliced
1 small carrot, thinly sliced
¼ teaspoon dried thyme
6 whole black peppercorns
1 tablespoon chopped fresh parsley
1 pound small shrimp, shelled and deveined

In a glass casserole, combine all the ingredients except the shrimp. Cook, covered, in the center of the oven 5 minutes. Stir in the shrimp. Cook, uncovered, 3 minutes. Stir. Cook 2 minutes. Let set, covered, 5 minutes. The shrimps should be pink and firm, but not hard. Serve them on toothpicks. *Serves 4.*

POACHED SCALLOPS
[Speed-cook; 6 minutes]

½ cup dry white wine
¼ cup water
1 medium-sized white onion, sliced
3 sprigs parsley
⅛ teaspoon dried tarragon
1½ pounds scallops
Salt to taste
Crisp leaves of Boston lettuce
½ cup Green Mayonnaise (below)
2 hard-cooked eggs, sliced
2 tablespoons chopped fresh parsley

In a glass casserole, combine the wine, water, onion, parsley sprigs and tarragon. Cook in the center of the oven 2 minutes. Stir in the scallops and sprinkle lightly with salt. Cook 2 minutes; stir; cook 2 minutes. Stir, then let set, covered, 5 minutes. The scallops should be firm but not hard. Let the scallops cool in their liquid. Do not refrigerate. Drain and serve in individual dishes on lettuce leaves with a dollop of Green Mayonnaise atop, garnished with egg slices and chopped parsley. *Serves 6 to 8.*

Green Mayonnaise

In a bowl, blend well ½ cup mayonnaise, 1½ tablespoons chopped fresh parsley and 1½ tablespoons chopped watercress.

TUNA BAUSERMAN
[Speed-cook; 3 minutes]

William Bauserman has topped the oysters Rockefeller people with this one. We like it as a first course, but it also makes an excellent appetizer.

- 1 cup finely chopped fresh spinach
- ¼ cup finely chopped fresh parsley
- 2 tablespoons finely chopped watercress
- 2 tablespoons minced celery
- ½ teaspoon salt
- ¼ teaspoon dried tarragon
- Pinch of cayenne pepper
- Pinch of paprika
- ½ cup mayonnaise
- ¼ cup butter, melted
- 3 tablespoons lemon juice
- Two 7-ounce cans tuna, drained and flaked
- 2 tablespoons buttered-bread crumbs

In a glass casserole, mix all of the ingredients except the tuna and buttered bread crumbs. Cook in the center of the oven 3 minutes, stirring after each minute. Stir in the tuna, blending well. Spoon into 6 scallop shells or ramekins. Sprinkle with the bread crumbs and place under the broiler of a conventional stove until the bread crumbs are crisp and the sauce bubbles. *Serves 6.*

3

Soups

"The army," said Napoleon, "doesn't travel on its stomach. It travels on soup."

With a microwave oven you can feed an army or just your own family in no time at all. But it isn't only speed that is an asset. Soups are especially savory cooked under microwaves. The rapid penetration of seasonings in soups is unequalled by any other method of cookery. Flavors are released and fixed in a flash. Vegetables in your homemade soup will have a much fresher taste than the old-fashioned soups that simmered for hours, losing flavor, freshness and vitamins along the way. Microwave cooking insures that these vitamins are retained.

Frozen soups can be heated in minutes. Canned soups, poured into the serving bowl or cup, are ready in 2 minutes.

Use an extra-large glass bowl or casserole when making soups, especially those with a lot of liquid. This will prevent spillovers. Common sense and your own judgment will see to this—you won't try to make a quart of soup in a 1½-quart dish.

Microwaves will tempt you to be inventive. Mix canned soups, or speedily create your own version of minestrone or Chinese egg-drop. Convert your old soup recipes into new taste delights, in a fourth of the time, and with a freshness and flavor that no other method of cooking can match.

EGG AND LEMON SOUP
[Speed-cook; 11 minutes]

5 cups hot beef broth
6 tablespoons rice
3 small eggs
¼ cup lemon juice
Salt and pepper to taste
1 tablespoon chopped fresh parsley

In a glass bowl, bring one cup of the hot broth to a boil. Add the rice and cook in the center of the oven 4 minutes. Let set, covered, 5 minutes. The rice should be tender but firm. In a glass casserole, bring the remaining hot broth to a boil (this will take about 5 minutes). Stir the rice into the boiling broth. In a bowl, beat the eggs until they are light and fluffy. Adding a small amount at a time, beat the lemon juice into the eggs. Gradually beat one cup of the hot soup into the egg-lemon juice mixture. Stir this diluted egg mixture into the casserole with the hot broth and rice. Season with salt and pepper. Cook 2 minutes, or until it begins to simmer, stirring after one minute. Let set, covered, 5 minutes. Sprinkle each serving with parsley. *Serves 4.*

CHEDDAR CHEESE SOUP
[Speed-cook; 14 minutes]

4 slices bacon
2 tablespoons butter
1 medium-size white onion, minced
2 tablespoons flour
2 cups warm milk
1½ cups warm chicken broth
1½ cups grated sharp cheddar cheese
¼ teaspoon paprika
Salt and pepper to taste

Place 2 paper towels on a plate. Space the bacon evenly on it. Cover with a paper towel. Cook in the center of the oven 4 minutes, rotating the plate a half turn after 2 minutes. Pat the fat from the bacon with a paper towel.

Let cool, then crumble. Set aside. In a glass casserole, in the center of the oven, melt the butter. Add the onion and cook 3 minutes, or until soft, stirring after 1½ minutes. Stir in the flour. Cook one minute, stirring until you have a smooth paste. Stir in the warm milk, a little at a time, stirring constantly until you have a smooth sauce. Stir in the warm broth. Cook 3 minutes, or until the sauce begins to thicken, stirring every 30 seconds. Strain the sauce and return to the casserole. Stir in the cheese, paprika, salt and pepper. Cook 3 minutes, or until the cheese melts and the soup is simmering, stirring after 1½ minutes. Let set, covered, 5 minutes. Serve in hot soup bowls, garnishing each serving with the crumbled bacon. *Serves 6.*

FINNISH FISH CHOWDER
[Speed-cook; 13 minutes]

⅓ cup finely diced salt pork
1 large celery rib, scraped and chopped
1 medium onion, chopped
Two 10½-ounce cans cream of potato soup
2 cups milk
1 cup sliced cooked carrots
One 8-ounce can whole corn kernels drained
1 small bay leaf
¼ teaspoon pepper
Pinch of dried tarragon
1 pound ocean perch fillets, cut into 1-inch squares
Salt to taste

In a glass casserole, place the salt pork, cover with waxed paper and cook in the center of the oven 3 minutes, stirring after 1½ minutes. Add the celery and onion. Cook 3 minutes, or until soft, stirring after 1½ minutes. Stir in remaining ingredients. Cook 4 minutes. Stir. Cook 3 minutes. Stir. Let set, covered, 5 minutes. Remove bay leaf. The chowder is ready when the fish flakes easily with a fork. Taste for seasoning. *Serves 6 to 8.*

QUICK CLAM BISQUE
[Speed-cook; 8 minutes]

4 tablespoons butter
1 medium onion, minced
1 cup heavy cream
1 cup milk
¼ teaspoon hickory-smoked salt
¼ teaspoon celery salt
Two 8-ounce cans minced clams (undrained)

In a glass casserole, in the center of the oven, melt 2 tablespoons of the butter and cook the onion 3 minutes, or until soft, stirring after 1½ minutes. Stir in the cream, milk, smoked salt and celery salt. Cook 3 minutes, stirring after 1½ minutes. Stir in the clams and their liquid and cook 2 minutes. Taste for seasoning. Stir in the remaining butter and serve piping hot. *Serves 4.*

FAST GREEN CRAB SOUP
[Speed-cook; 6 minutes]

One 10½-ounce can condensed green pea soup
2 cups chicken broth
One 7-ounce can crabmeat, well picked over and flaked
2 tablespoons light rum
Salt and pepper to taste
1 cup heavy cream, whipped
1 tablespoon chopped fresh chives

In a glass casserole, combine the pea soup and chicken broth. Cook in the center of the oven 4 minutes, or until boiling, stirring after 2 minutes. Stir in the crabmeat, rum, salt and pepper. Cook 2 minutes, stirring after one minute. Stir in the whipped cream. Taste for seasoning. Pour into hot bowls and garnish with chopped chives. *Serves 4.*

SHRIMP AND CORN SOUP
[Speed-cook; 9 minutes]

2 tablespoons cornstarch
1 tablespoon soy sauce
1 tablespoon water
5 cups chicken broth
2 cups cooked fresh or frozen corn
½ teaspoon salt
2 eggs, beaten
½ cup coarsely chopped cooked shrimp

Blend the cornstarch, soy sauce and water and set aside. In a glass casserole, heat the chicken broth in the center of the oven 7 minutes, or until simmering. Stir in the corn; cook 30 seconds. Stir in the cornstarch mixture and salt and cook 30 seconds. Stir until the soup thickens. Quickly stir in the eggs. Cook one minute. Serve in hot soup bowls, garnished with the chopped shrimp. *Serves 6.*

BOULA
[Speed-cook; 8 minutes]

Two 10½-ounce cans condensed green pea soup
Two 6½-ounce cans green turtle soup
Salt and pepper to taste
2 tablespoons butter
1 cup dry sherry
½ cup heavy cream, whipped
2 tablespoons grated Parmesan cheese

In a glass casserole, combine the soups. Stir until smooth. Season with salt and pepper. Cook in the center of the oven 3 minutes. Stir. Cook 3 minutes. Stir in the butter and sherry. Cook 2 minutes. Stir. Pour into heated ovenproof soup bowls. Top each serving with a dollop of whipped cream. Sprinkle with the cheese and brown lightly under the broiler of a conventional stove. *Serves 4 to 5.*

CREAMED ASPARAGUS SOUP

[Speed-cook; 25 minutes]

1½ pounds fresh asparagus
4 cups chicken broth
4 tablespoons butter
1 medium onion, chopped
1 large celery rib, chopped
1 cup heavy cream
Salt and pepper to taste

Break off and discard the tough ends of the asparagus stems. With a vegetable peeler, peel the stems. Cut off the tips, then cut the stems into 1-inch pieces. Put the asparagus tips and ¼ cup of the chicken broth in a glass bowl. Cook in the center of the oven 5 minutes, or until the tips are barely tender. Drain, reserving the liquid, and set aside. In a glass casserole, in the center of the oven, melt the butter. Stir in the asparagus stems, onion and celery; cook 3 minutes, stirring after 1½ minutes. Pour in ¼ cup of the chicken broth and cook 7 minutes, or until the vegetables are soft, stirring every 2 minutes. Pour in the reserved chicken broth in which the asparagus tips cooked. Add the remaining 3½ cups chicken broth. Cook 5 minutes, stirring after 2½ minutes. Let cool slightly, then pour contents of the casserole into a blender and puree. Return to the casserole and cook in the center of the oven 4 minutes, or until simmering. Stir in the heavy cream. Cook one minute. Season with salt and pepper. Let set, covered, 5 minutes. Serve garnished with the asparagus tips. *Serves 4 to 6.*

PO VALLEY POTATO SOUP
[Speed-cook; 11 minutes]

3 tablespoons butter
1 tablespoon olive oil
1 medium-size white onion, chopped
2 small carrots, scraped and coarsely chopped
2 celery ribs, scraped and coarsely chopped
1 garlic clove, crushed
Salt and pepper to taste
1 cup tomato sauce
4 cups hot beef broth
1 large boiled potato, skinned and put through a ricer
2 tablespoons chopped fresh parsley
Grated Parmesan cheese

In a glass casserole, heat the butter and oil. Stir in the onion, carrots, celery and garlic. Cook in the center of the oven 4 minutes or until the vegetables are soft, stirring after 2 minutes. Remove the garlic. Stir in the salt, pepper, tomato sauce, beef broth and potato. Cook 7 minutes, or until simmering, stirring after 3 and 5 minutes. Let set, covered, 5 minutes. Serve with the parsley and Parmesan cheese sprinkled atop. *Serves 6.*

HEARTY ZUCCHINI SOUP
[Speed-cook; 15 minutes]

4 tablespoons butter
2 small white onions, thinly sliced
1 large celery rib, scraped and thinly sliced
1 large carrot, scraped and thinly sliced
3 cups chicken broth
3 medium zucchini (unpeeled), cut into quarters lengthwise, then thinly sliced
Salt and pepper to taste
Grated Parmesan cheese
Heavy cream (optional)
Sour cream (optional)

In a glass casserole, melt the butter. Stir in the onions, celery and carrot and cook in the center of the oven 3 minutes or until soft, stirring after 1½ minutes. Stir in ¼ cup of the chicken broth, and the zucchini. Cook 8 minutes or until the zucchini are tender, stirring every 2 minutes. Stir in the remaining chicken broth, and salt and pepper. Cook, covered, 4 minutes, or until simmering, stirring after 2 minutes. Taste for seasoning. Let set, covered, 10 minutes. Serve hot as is, with the cheese sprinkled atop, a lusty soup that demands buttered crusty bread as an accompaniment.

The soup also can be served cold omitting the cheese. Let cool and puree in a blender. Just before serving, stir in one tablespoon of heavy cream for each individual bowl and top with a dollop of sour cream. *Serves 4 to 6.*

OLD-TIME VEGETABLE SOUP
[Speed-cook; 45 minutes]

On a conventional stove, this soup would take about 3 hours. Microwaves not only cook it in a fourth of the time, but the old-fashioned version never had the fresh flavor of this one.

    1 pound lean beef brisket, cut into ½-inch cubes
    1 pound beef shinbone with meat
    8 cups boiling beef broth
    2 small white onions, coarsely chopped
    2 small carrots, scraped and coarsely chopped
    2 small celery ribs, scraped and coarsely chopped
  One 1-pound can plum tomatoes, broken up
    1 tablespoon chopped fresh parsley
    ¼ teaspoon dried basil
    ¼ teaspoon dried marjoram
    1 teaspoon salt
    ½ teaspoon pepper
    ½ cup fresh or defrosted frozen peas
    ½ cup fresh or defrosted frozen baby lima beans

In a large casserole, place the beef cubes, shinbone and boiling beef broth. Stir in remaining ingredients except peas and lima beans. Cover and cook in the center of the oven 10 minutes. Stir. Rotate the casserole half a turn. Cook 10 minutes. Stir. Rotate half a turn. Cook 10 minutes. Stir in the peas and lima beans. Cover and cook 5 minutes. Stir; cook 5 minutes, then stir again and cook 5 minutes longer. Let set, covered, 15 minutes. Before serving, skim any fat. Remove the shinbone, dice the meat, and stir it back into the soup. *Serves 8 to 10.*

4
Eggs

In 1945, when scientist Percy L. Spencer discovered microwave cookery, partly by accident, one of the experimental food items that he placed before a radar horn antenna was a raw egg—in its shell. It exploded.

Thirty-two years later, raw eggs in their shells still explode in microwave ovens. That lightning-fast heat of the microwaves expands the air inside the shell of the egg, forcing it to burst. Therefore, cook hardboiled eggs on your conventional stove; it will be much less messy! We also suggest that you use a conventional stove for fried eggs and omelettes. You can cook them under microwaves in the browning skillet, but we think that the conventional stove prepares them just as well, perhaps better. But for scrambled eggs, poached eggs, even baked eggs, microwaves are nothing short of marvelous.

Egg cookery under microwaves, however, is a delicate operation that requires attention to detail—and precise timing.

As all cholesterol watchers know, the egg yolk has more fat than the white, thus it cooks faster. Especially under microwaves. If you have a choice, scramble the eggs. This produces the most even results. Use butter. In microwave cookery it gives more flavor and less is needed. The reason: Conventional heat breaks down fats. Microwaves are so speedy this does not happen, so scrambled eggs cooked in butter are more buttery, softer and tastier.

When scrambling eggs, stir them often, fluffing them with a fork. This will result in a lighter texture.

For any method other than scrambling make certain that you carefully puncture the surface of the yolk twice with the tines of a fork, the sharp point of a knife, or even a toothpick. This will break the membrane encasing the yolk and prevent the egg from popping or exploding. Do it *carefully*. It is only the thin outer skin surrounding the yolk that you want to break.

Always make sure that eggs to be poached are completely covered with water, or whatever liquid they are to be cooked in. The liquid slows down the cooking and evens the heat.

Cooking time will vary from half a minute to 2 or more minutes, depending upon the size of the egg, its temperature (do not cook eggs right out of the refrigerator) and the number of eggs to be cooked.

All food cooked under microwaves continues to cook after being removed from the oven. Teach yourself to take egg dishes from the microwaves *before* they are completely cooked, even if only by seconds. Then you can let them set, covered, depending upon how well done you like them, to complete the cooking. This is an important technique and can be impressed upon you only through trial and error. Overpoach an egg and it's a bullet; bake an egg too long and you can use it to play Ping-Pong; cook scrambled eggs too long and you've got rubber. The microwaves are so fast that a minute, sometimes only 30 seconds, can make all the difference. Those particular people who like three-minute eggs, sunny-side up and "lightly poached," take care. We repeat: This is sensitive cookery!

POACHED EGG

[Speed-cook; 2 minutes, 45 seconds, including boiling the water]

Start your microwave egg cookery simply. Poach a single egg. It will be a graphic lesson in the importance of timing. If you like your poached egg softer than we do, perhaps only 30 seconds will be enough time. Invest in a dozen eggs and run a series of tests. It will be time and money well spent.

1 cup water
½ teaspoon white vinegar
1 large egg at room temperature
Salt and pepper to taste

In a measuring cup, in the center of the oven, combine the water and vinegar (it helps set the egg white) and bring to a boil, about 2 minutes. A 10-ounce custard cup or a small pyrex skillet make perfect egg poachers. Break the egg into either one. With a fork or a toothpick carefully pierce the surface of the yolk twice, puncturing the membrane. Pour the boiling water around the egg. Cover with plastic wrap and cook in the center of the oven 45 seconds. Place the egg in its cooker on a plate on the table and let it set, covered, 30 seconds, so you can educate yourself by watching the carry-over cooking at work. Season with salt and pepper. *Serves 1.*

SCRAMBLED EGGS
[Speed-cook; 2 minutes]

Scrambled eggs cooked under microwaves are superb: soft, creamy, done to perfection—providing your timing is right. We again remind you that, as with all food subjected to this sensitive style of cooking, you must be careful not to overcook. A minute too long and your scrambled eggs will be hard and dry. Start off with this simple recipe for two, then experiment and expand your repertoire as you go along.

4 eggs
¼ cup light cream
¼ teaspoon salt
2 tablespoons butter

In a bowl, beat the eggs, cream and salt. In a glass pie plate, in the center of the oven, melt the butter. Pour in the beaten eggs. Cover with waxed paper and cook one minute. Stir. Cook 30 seconds. Stir. Cook 30 seconds. Stop cooking the eggs while they still look underdone. *Serves 2.*

EGGS WITH CHICKEN LIVERS
[Speed-cook; 7 minutes]

4 tablespoons butter
2 small white onions, chopped
½ pound chicken livers, each cut into 4 pieces
8 small eggs
1 teaspoon salt
½ teaspoon pepper
1 tablespoon chopped fresh parsley

In a glass casserole, in the center of the oven, melt 2 tablespoons of the butter. Add the onions and cook for 2 minutes, or until soft. Stir in the chicken livers. Cook one minute. Turn the livers and cook one minute. In a bowl, beat the eggs with the salt and pepper until frothy. Melt the remaining butter in the dish with the onions and livers. Pour in the beaten eggs and cook one minute. Stir. Cook one minute. Stir. Cook one minute. Let set, covered, 2 minutes. Sprinkle with the parsley. *Serves 4.*

HAM AND CHEESE SCRAMBLE
[Speed-cook; 6 minutes]

2 tablespoons butter
1 tablespoon olive oil
1 small sweet red pepper, cored, seeded and chopped
1 medium-size white onion, chopped
½ cup chopped cooked ham
One 11-ounce can condensed cheddar cheese soup
8 small eggs, beaten

In a glass casserole, in the center of the oven, heat the butter and oil. Add the pepper and onion and cook 3 minutes, or until they are soft, stirring after 1½ minutes. Stir in the ham. In a bowl, stir the soup until smooth. Blend in the beaten eggs. Pour the soup-egg mixture into the casserole with the ham and vegetables. Cover with waxed paper and cook one minute. Stir. Cook one minute. Stir. Cook one minute. Let set, covered, for 2 minutes. *Serves 4.*

BAKED HAM AND EGGS

[Speed-cook; 3 minutes]

2 cups soft ¼-inch bread cubes
1½ cups ground cooked ham
One 10½-ounce can condensed cream of celery soup
4 large eggs

In a bowl, mix the bread cubes, ham and soup. Divide the mixture among four 1½-cup glass baking dishes. Break one egg into the center of each. With a fork, carefully pierce the surface of the egg yolk twice, puncturing the membrane. Place the small dishes in one large baking dish in the center of the oven. Cover with waxed paper and cook 2 minutes. Rotate the dish half a turn. Cook one minute. Let set, covered, 2 minutes. *Serves 4.*

MEXICAN EGGS

[Speed-cook; 8½ minutes]

2 tablespoons butter
2 small white onions, minced
2 medium-size ripe tomatoes, peeled, seeded, chopped and drained in a strainer
1 tablespoon minced fresh parsley
1½ teaspoons chili powder
8 small eggs and 1 teaspoon salt, beaten well with a fork

In a glass casserole, melt the butter. Add the onions and cook in the center of the oven for 2 minutes, or until soft. Stir in the tomatoes, parsley and chili powder. Cover with waxed paper and cook 4 minutes. Stir. Stir in the beaten eggs. Cook 1½ minutes. Stir. Cook one minute. Stir. Stop cooking while the eggs still look slightly underdone. Let set, covered, 2 minutes. Eggs should be soft and creamy. *Serves 4.*

EGGS POACHED IN MUSHROOM SAUCE
[Speed-cook; 5 minutes]

2 tablespoons butter
One 10½-ounce can condensed cream of mushroom soup
½ cup milk
4 large eggs
Salt and pepper to taste
2 English muffins, split, toasted and buttered

In a shallow glass casserole, in the center of the oven, melt the butter. Stir in the soup and milk. Cover with waxed paper and cook 2 minutes, or until simmering. Stir. Break the eggs, one at a time, into a small dish. With a fork, pierce the surface of each egg yolk twice, puncturing the membrane. Slide the eggs into the sauce, making sure the eggs are covered with the sauce. Season with salt and pepper. Cover with plastic wrap and cook 2 minutes. Rotate the dish half a turn. Cook one minute. Baste the eggs. Let set 2 minutes. Serve the eggs on the English muffins, with the mushroom sauce spooned atop. *Serves 4.*

EGGS WITH SCALLIONS
[Speed-cook; 7 minutes]

4 tablespoons butter
1 tablespoon olive oil
10 whole scallions, chopped
1 tablespoon flour
8 small eggs
½ cup heavy cream
1 teaspoon salt

In a glass casserole, in the center of the oven, heat the butter and oil. Add the scallions and cook 3 minutes, or until soft, stirring after 1½ minutes. Sprinkle with the flour. Cook one minute. Stir. Cook one minute. Stir. In a bowl, beat the eggs, cream and salt until frothy. Pour into the casserole with the scallions. Cook 1 minute. Stir. Cook one minute. Stir. Let set, covered, 2 minutes. *Serves 4.*

SCRAMBLED EGGS WITH SHRIMP

[Speed-cook; 4 minutes 20 seconds]

4 tablespoons peanut oil
½ pound medium shrimp, shelled, deveined and each cut into 4 equal-size pieces
8 small eggs, beaten
4 whole scallions, chopped
1 teaspoon salt

In a glass pie plate or shallow casserole, in the center of the oven, heat 2 tablespoons of the oil 30 seconds. Stir in the shrimp and cook 20 seconds, or until the shrimp begin to turn pink. Remove the shrimp and drain the liquid from the cooking dish. In a bowl, blend the eggs, scallions and salt. In the cooking dish heat the remaining oil 30 seconds. Add the egg mixture. Cook one minute. Stir. Cook one minute. Stir in the shrimp. Cook one minute. Let set, covered, 2 minutes. *Serves 4.*

EGGS BAKED ON SPINACH BED

[Speed-cook; 10 minutes)

One 10-ounce package frozen chopped spinach
½ teaspoon salt
4 large poached eggs (see Poached Egg, page 57, but cook eggs only 30 seconds)
One 10¾-ounce can condensed cream of mushroom soup
½ cup grated cheddar cheese

Place the spinach in a glass dish. Sprinkle with the salt, cover and cook in the center of the oven 3 minutes. Separate unthawed portions. Rotate the dish half a turn. Cook 3 minutes. Drain well. Arrange the spinach in a baking dish. Make 4 depressions for the eggs and place the poached eggs in the "nests" you have prepared. Pour the soup into a glass measuring cup. Cover with waxed paper and cook 2 minutes. Stir. Cook one minute, or until very hot. Spoon the soup over the eggs and spinach and sprinkle with the cheese. Cover with plastic wrap and cook 30 seconds. Rotate the dish half a turn. Cook 30 seconds. Let set, covered, one minute. *Serves 4.*

MARIA LIMONCELLI'S EGGS POACHED
IN TOMATOES
[Speed-cook; 14 minutes]

3 tablespoons olive oil
2 small white onions, chopped
1 garlic clove, minced
One 1-pound can plum tomatoes, pushed through a food
  mill
1 tablespoon chopped fresh parsley
½ teaspoon salt
¼ teaspoon pepper
Pinch of dried marjoram
4 large eggs

In a glass casserole, in the center of the oven, heat the
olive oil and cook the onions and garlic 2 minutes, or
until soft. Stir in the tomatoes, parsley, salt, pepper
and marjoram. Cover with waxed paper and cook 10
minutes, stirring every 2 minutes. Break the eggs, one at
a time, into a small dish; with a fork, carefully pierce
the surface of each yolk twice to break the membrane,
then slip the eggs into the sauce. Spoon the sauce over
them. Cover the casserole with waxed paper and cook
one minute. Baste the eggs with the sauce. Rotate half
a turn. Cook one minute. Let set, covered, 2 minutes.
Serves 4.

EGGS WITH VEGETABLES, YUGOSLAVIAN STYLE
[Speed-cook; 10½ minutes]

2 tablespoons butter
1 tablespoon olive oil
1 medium green pepper, cored, seeded and chopped
1 small white onion, chopped
1 small hot chili pepper, cored, seeded and finely
  chopped
1 medium-size ripe tomato, peeled and cut into eighths
8 small eggs
½ cup large curd cottage cheese, well drained
1 teaspoon salt

In a glass casserole, in the center of the oven, heat the
butter and olive oil. Stir in the green pepper, onion and

chili pepper and cook 3 minutes, stirring after 1½ minutes. Stir in the tomato. Cook 5 minutes, carefully stirring after 1½ minutes. In a large bowl, beat together the eggs, cottage cheese and salt. Stir in the vegetable mixture. Pour the mixture into the casserole. Cook one minute. Stir. Cook 30 seconds. Stir. Cook 30 seconds. Stir. Cook 30 seconds. When you stop cooking, the eggs should be slightly softer than desired for serving. *Serves 4.*

5

Fish and Shellfish

Fish lead the list of foods overcooked by new owners of microwave ovens. Overcooked fish are dry, without flavor. The temptation, regardless of instructions received with the new microwave oven, is to play it on the safe side and "give it just one more minute." That minute equals four, maybe five on your conventional stove. Few of us would gamble that much extra time in ordinary cookery to make certain that the fish is ready—at least, those of us who like fish and respect the rules used in cooking it.

Fish have very fragile connective tissue and can easily be overcooked, using any medium. We remind you again that in microwave cookery there is carry-over cooking time. Whatever comes out of the microwave oven will continue cooking for a short period while it is out of the oven. Nothing can stop that action. But you can foresee, plan ahead and undercook, allowing for that carry-over cooking.

Don't let these warning tips discourage you. The reward is great. Fish properly cooked in a microwave oven is unexcelled—moist, flaky, tender, with an unusually delicate flavor that other cookery somehow seems to diminish. And it is easier to cook than baiting a fish hook!

It is advised to cook fish about 4 minutes per pound. We cook it 3 minutes per pound, sometimes even less. Many claim that because of its irregular shape and uneven weight, you cannot successfully cook a whole fish. We have cooked whole bluefish, red snapper and bass. The head and tail aren't eaten anyway—at least not by us—and the remainder is deliciously moist and tender.

But to play it safe (if you aren't an experimenter), cook just the fillets and steaks. They are uniform in size and are the best parts of the fish, anyway.

No fat is needed with microwave fish cookery, thus cholesterol-minded cooks get a double benefit, for the fish itself has little fat. You can use butter or oil if you wish, but it isn't necessary. We happen to like butter and sauces.

Remember to keep the thicker parts of the fish toward the outside of the cooking dish.

Covering the fish with plastic wrap or waxed paper while cooking will contain the steam, thus accelerating the cooking time.

Test! When the fish is easily flaked with a fork it is cooked. We remove our fish before it flakes easily, when it still has some resistance. Then we let it set, covered, for one or 2 minutes. The carry-over time produces a fish that does flake easily, and isn't over-cooked.

When defrosting frozen fish fillets or steaks, place them in their package on a paper towel. (Note: *Not* those wrapped in aluminum foil.) Only partially defrost fish. Overlong heating of frozen fish will cook the outer areas; when you cook the fish they will certainly be overdone. Defrost one pound of fillets only 2 minutes on the regular cycle (4 minutes on automatic defrost), turning the package every 30 seconds. Separate the partially thawed pieces under cold running water. And always cook defrosted fish *soon*. Depending upon the size of the fish, a glass pie plate is excellent for cooking fillets and steaks.

BLUEFISH FILLETS WITH TOMATOES AND VERMOUTH

[Speed-cook; 13 minutes, including sauce]

1 teaspoon salt
½ teaspoon pepper
Juice of 2 lemons
6 tablespoons olive oil
2 bluefish fillets (about 1½ pounds), cut into 4 equal-size pieces

In a bowl, blend the salt, pepper, lemon juice and olive oil. Place the fillets in one layer in the bottom of a glass dish. Pour the marinade over the fillets, cover and let marinate 3 hours, turning several times. Remove the fish from the marinade and pat dry.

2 tablespoons butter
1 tablespoon cooking oil
2 medium white onions, minced
One 1-pound can plum tomatoes, broken up
2 garlic cloves, cut into slivers
½ teaspoon dried oregano
½ teaspoon salt
¼ teaspoon pepper
½ cup dry white vermouth

In a skillet on a conventional stove, or in a preheated browning skillet, heat the butter and oil and brown the bluefish fillets, evenly. Transfer to a shallow glass baking dish just large enough to hold them. In a glass bowl, blend the onions, tomatoes, garlic, oregano, salt, pepper and vermouth. Cover with waxed paper and cook in the center of the oven 2½ minutes. Stir. Cook 2½ minutes. Stir. Spoon the tomato mixture evenly over the bluefish fillets. Cover the dish and cook in the center of the oven 4 minutes, rotating the dish half a turn at 2 minutes. Cook 4 minutes, rotating half a turn at 2 minutes. Let set, covered, 3 minutes. The fish is ready when it flakes easily with a fork. *Serves 4.*

WHOLE BLUEFISH IN WAXED PAPER

[Speed-cook; 7 minutes]

Here's the perfect recipe for that bluefish that a friend drops off, and you're doubtful about how to handle. Scale and clean it, but leave it whole; it makes a dramatic presentation.

One 3- to 3½-pound whole bluefish, scaled and cleaned
Lowry's seasoned salt
4 tablespoons Herb Butter, softened (page 137)

Sprinkle the inside of the fish with seasoned salt. Place it on a large sheet of waxed paper on an inverted plate or two saucers (to hold it above any liquid that may collect in the bottom of the dish) in a shallow glass baking dish. Spread the Herb Butter evenly over the fish. Fold the edges of the waxed paper together, making the seam above the top of the fish (for easier testing). Cook in the center of the oven 4 minutes. Rotate the dish half a turn. Cook 3 minutes. Let set, still wrapped in the paper, 5 minutes. Test. The fish is ready when it flakes easily with a fork. *Serves 4 to 6.*

CODDLED COD

[Speed-cook; 10 minutes, including the poaching liquid]

½ cup bottled clam juice
½ cup water
3 tablespoons lemon juice
2 tablespoons white wine vinegar
2 small white onions, thinly sliced
1 celery rib, chopped
2 garlic cloves, coarsely chopped
1 small bay leaf
4 whole cloves
1 teaspoon salt
¼ teaspoon dried thyme
4 cod steaks (6 to 8 ounces each)
Melted parsley butter, Hollandaise sauce, or Green Mayonnaise (page 47)

Blend all the ingredients except the cod steaks in a glass dish or bowl. Cover with waxed paper. Cook in the center of the oven 6 minutes, stirring after each 3 minutes. Strain. Place the cod steaks in one layer in a shallow glass baking dish. Pour the strained liquid over them. Cover with waxed paper and cook in the center of the oven 2 minutes. Carefully turn the cod steaks over. Cook 2 minutes. Let set, covered, 2 minutes. Fish is ready when it flakes easily with a fork.

This dish can be served hot or cold. If served hot, remove from the liquid and serve with melted parsley butter. If served cold, let it cool in its liquid, then drain and serve with Hollandaise sauce, or Green Mayonnaise. *Serves 4.*

MACKEREL FILLETS À LA FRANÇAISE

[Speed-cook; 9 minutes, including sauce]

This is a French classic that converts a mackerel into a morsel that trout fishermen would resent and envy. Caution: Make certain that the mackerel are fresh; otherwise, they will taste too "fishy." Clear, unclouded eyes mark fresh fish.

    4 mackerel fillets (about 1½ pounds)
    Salt and pepper to taste
    2 tablespoons fresh lemon juice
    ¼ cup dry white wine
    4 tablespoons butter
    1 medium-size white onion, minced
    4 small fresh mushrooms, sliced
    2 tablespoons tomato sauce
    ½ cup bread crumbs

Season the fillets with salt and pepper. Arrange them in a buttered shallow glass baking dish just large enough to hold them in one layer. Pour the lemon juice and wine over the fish. Cover with plastic wrap, puncturing the center to permit the steam to escape. Cook in the center of the oven 4 minutes. Rotate the dish half a turn at 2 minutes. Let set, covered, 3 minutes. In a glass bowl, melt 2 tablespoons of the butter and cook the onion 2 minutes. Stir in the mushrooms; cook one minute. Stir in the tomato sauce. Drain or siphon off the cooking liquid from the fillets into a glass measuring cup. Cook 2 minutes. Stir it into the bowl with the onions and mushrooms. Pour this sauce over the fillets in their dish. Sprinkle with the bread crumbs, dot with the remaining butter and place under the broiler of a conventional stove until the butter melts and the crumbs brown. *Serves 4.*

OCEAN PERCH FILLETS IN CELERY SAUCE
[Speed-cook; 5 minutes]

1½ pounds ocean perch fillets
Salt and pepper to taste
One 10½-ounce can condensed cream of celery soup
⅓ cup shredded sharp cheddar cheese
1 tablespoon chopped fresh parsley
½ cup bread crumbs

Place the fillets side by side in a shallow glass baking dish just large enough to hold them in one layer. Lightly season with salt and pepper. Stir the soup well and spoon it over the fish. Cook in the center of the oven 3 minutes. Rotate half a turn. Cook 2 minutes. Sprinkle the cheese, parsley and bread crumbs over the fillets and place under the broiler of a conventional stove until the cheese melts and bread crumbs are brown. *Serves 4.*

CREAMED SALMON WITH PEAS
[Speed-cook; 6 minutes]

2 tablespoons butter
1 medium onion, chopped
4 medium mushrooms, thinly sliced
One 10½-ounce can condensed cream of mushroom soup
⅓ cup medium cream
2 cups canned red salmon, drained, picked over and flaked
1 cup cooked fresh or frozen peas
2 tablespoons lemon juice
Salt and pepper to taste

In a glass bowl or casserole, melt the butter and cook the onion in the center of the oven for 2 minutes, or until soft. Stir in the mushrooms and cook one minute. Add the remaining ingredients, stirring well. Cover with waxed paper and cook 3 minutes, stirring after each 1½ minutes. Let set, covered, 3 minutes. Taste for seasoning. This is excellent over creamy mashed potatoes, *Serves 4.*

JAMBALAYA

[Speed-cook; 26 minutes]

Here's a party-dish surprise from the Deep South that will please the palates of your guests.

- ½ pound pork loin, shredded
- ½ pound smoked ham, shredded
- 2 tablespoons cooking oil
- ½ pound bulk pork sausage
- 1 medium-size white onion, chopped
- 2 garlic cloves, chopped
- 1 cup canned plum tomatoes, broken up
- 1 teaspoon chili powder
- 1 cup chicken broth
- 1 tablespoon chopped fresh parsley
- 1 tablespoon mixed pickling spices
- 1½ pounds medium shrimp, shelled and deveined
- Salt and pepper to taste
- Hot cooked rice

In a large glass casserole, in the center of the oven, cook the pork and ham in the oil 4 minutes, stirring after 2 minutes. Add the sausage and cook 4 minutes, stirring after 2 minutes. Stir in the onion, garlic and tomatoes. Cook 2 minutes, stirring after one minute. Stir in the chili powder, chicken broth, parsley and pickling spices. Cook 15 minutes, stirring after each 5 minutes. Stir in the shrimp. Cook one minute, or until the shrimp are pink but firm. Stir. Let set, covered, 5 minutes. Test for seasoning. Serve over rice. *Serves 6 to 8.*

SCROD STEAKS LOUISIANA
[Speed-cook; 14 minutes]

Scrod, tender young codfish, is too often overlooked in our fish cookery.

  4 scrod steaks, (6 to 8 ounces each)
  2 tablespoons butter
  1 medium-size white onion, chopped
  1 small sweet red pepper, cored, seeded and chopped
  1 large celery rib, scraped and chopped
  2 garlic cloves, minced
  One 1-pound can stewed tomatoes
  Salt and pepper to taste
  One tablespoon red wine vinegar

Arrange the scrod steaks side by side in a buttered shallow glass baking dish. In a glass bowl or casserole, heat the butter. Add the onion, sweet red pepper, celery, and garlic and cook 4 minutes, stirring after 2 minutes. Stir in the tomatoes, salt, pepper and vinegar. Cook 2 minutes. Stir. Cook 2 minutes. Stir. Pour this sauce over the fish. Cover with waxed paper and cook, in the center of the oven, for 3 minutes. Rotate the dish half a turn. Cook 3 minutes. Let set, covered, 3 minutes. Fish is ready when it flakes easily with a fork. *Serves 4.*

RED SNAPPER FILLETS WITH HERB BUTTER
[Speed-cook; 4 minutes]

This is a fine-textured fish with a delicate flavor that needs little except its own personality in the preparation.

  2 red snapper fillets (each about 1 pound)
  1 teaspoon salt
  ½ teaspoon pepper
  ½ teaspoon paprika
  4 tablespoons butter
  4 cubes Herb Butter (page 137)

No need to use a casserole for this; you can cook the fish on its serving platter. Place the fillets on the platter.

Sprinkle with the salt, pepper and paprika. Dot with butter. Cook, uncovered, 2 minutes. Rotate platter half a turn. Cook 2 minutes. Let set, covered with aluminum foil, 5 minutes. If it flakes easily with a fork it is cooked. Serve with a cube of the Herb Butter melting atop each offering. *Serves 4.*

MEXICAN SNAPPER

[Speed-cook; 11 minutes]

Here, from Yucatan, is a red snapper dish with a fascinating character.

4 red snapper fillets (6 to 8 ounces each)
Salt and pepper to taste
2 tablespoons olive oil
1 medium-size white onion, chopped
¼ cup coarsely chopped green olives
¼ cup coarsely chopped pimiento
2 tablespoons chopped fresh parsley
⅛ cup orange juice
Juice of 1 lemon
1 hard-cooked egg, coarsely chopped

Place the fillets side by side in a shallow glass baking dish. Season lightly with salt and pepper. In another glass dish or casserole, cook the onion in the oil in the center of the oven for 2 minutes, or until soft. Stir in the olives, pimiento, parsley, orange juice and lemon juice. Cook 3 minutes, stirring after 1½ minutes. Spoon over the fillets. Cover with waxed paper and cook in the center of the oven 3 minutes. Rotate dish half a turn. Cook 3 minutes. Let set, covered, 3 minutes. Fish is ready when it flakes easily with a fork. Serve in the sauce, sprinkled with the chopped egg. *Serves 4.*

FILLETS OF SOLE WITH CRABMEAT
[Speed-cook; 12 minutes]

Microwaves give you the extra time to get fancy, once in a while, with a company dish. Don't let this list of ingredients deter you. The recipe isn't complicated.

⅓ cup dry white wine
⅓ cup bottled clam juice
1 small celery rib with leaves, coarsely chopped
1 small bay leaf
¼ teaspoon dried thyme

In a glass bowl, combine all of the above ingredients. Cook in the center of the oven 4 minutes. Strain and reserve the liquid.

3 tablespoons butter
4 medium mushrooms, thinly sliced
2 tablespoons flour
Reserved strained wine-clam juice mixture (above)
½ cup grated Parmesan cheese
¼ cup dry sherry
¼ cup heavy cream
One 8-ounce can crabmeat, picked over and flaked
Salt and pepper to taste
4 sole fillets (about 1½ pounds)

In a glass bowl, melt the butter and cook the mushrooms in the center of the oven one minute. Remove with a slotted spoon and reserve. Stir the flour into the liquid in the bowl. Cook one minute, or until you have a smooth paste, stirring every 30 seconds. Gradually add the wine-clam juice mixture, stirring into a smooth sauce. Stir in the mushrooms, half the cheese, the sherry, cream and crabmeat. Cook 2 minutes, stirring after one minute. Season with salt and pepper; blend well. Cover the bottom of a large, shallow baking dish with half the sauce. Arrange the fillets side by side in the dish and cover with the remaining sauce. Sprinkle the remaining cheese over the sauce. Cover with waxed paper and cook in the center of the oven 4 minutes, rotating the dish half a turn after 2 minutes. Let set, covered, 3 minutes. The fish is ready when it flakes easily with a fork. Place under the broiler of a conventional stove until a golden-brown crust has formed. *Serves 4.*

FILLET OF SOLE DUGLÈRE
[Speed-cook; 10 minutes)

4 sole fillets (about 1½ pounds)
Salt and pepper to taste
3 tablespoons butter
1 medium-size white onion, chopped
2 tablespoons flour
¼ cup Chablis
¼ cup chicken broth
¼ cup heavy cream
2 medium tomatoes, peeled, seeded, coarsely chopped, and drained in a strainer
½ cup bread crumbs, lightly browned in butter
¼ cup grated Swiss cheese

Arrange the fillets side by side in a buttered shallow glass baking dish. Season with salt and pepper. In a glass casserole, in the center of the oven, melt the butter and cook the onion 2 minutes, or until soft. Stir in the flour. Gradually add the wine and chicken broth, stirring into a smooth sauce. Cook one minute, stirring after 30 seconds. Slowly stir in the cream. Cook one minute, stirring after 30 seconds. Stir in the tomatoes. Cook 2 minutes, stirring at one minute. Spoon the sauce over the fillets. Cover with waxed paper. Cook in the center of the oven 4 minutes, rotating the dish half a turn at 2 minutes. Let set, covered, 3 minutes. The fish is ready when it flakes easily with a fork. Sprinkle the bread crumbs and cheese atop and brown quickly in a conventional oven broiler. *Serves 4.*

SOLE WITH YOGURT
[Speed-cook; 4 minutes]

4 sole fillets (about 1½ pounds)
1 tablespoon prepared horseradish
1 tablespoon Dijon mustard
2 tablespoons fresh lemon juice
2 tablespoons grated Gruyère cheese
⅓ cup plain yogurt
2 tablespoons butter, softened

Place the fillets side by side in a shallow glass baking dish. In a bowl, blend the remaining ingredients and spread evenly over the fillets. Cover with waxed paper and cook in the center of the oven 2 minutes. Rotate the dish half a turn. Cook 2 minutes. Let set, covered, 3 minutes. Fish is ready when it flakes easily with a fork. *Serves 4.*

FILLETS OF SOLE ONE STEP AHEAD
[Speed-cook; 3 minutes]

Microwaves are unequalled for getting the host or hostess out there with the guests. One step of the cooking (of just about every kind of food) can be done early in the day, the rest quickly finished under the microwaves minutes before you are ready to have dinner. In Copenhagen, a Danish fisherman taught us this simple way of cooking sole. The fillets are liberally dipped in beaten egg, then in bread crumbs, then sautéed in butter until both sides are crusty. The fisherman's secret was not to eat the bread-crumb crust, but to slide this off, and eat the moist, delicate fish underneath.

4 sole fillets (about 1½ pounds)
Salt and pepper to taste
2 eggs, beaten
About 2 cups of bread crumbs
3 tablespoons butter
1 tablespoon cooking oil

Lightly sprinkle the fillets with salt and pepper. Dip them in the beaten egg, then dredge with bread crumbs.

On a conventional stove or in a preheated browning skillet, heat the butter and oil and brown the fillets until crusty. (If you use a browning skillet, use half the butter and oil and cook only 2 fillets at a time; pour off any liquid left in the pan after browning, then add the remaining butter and oil.) Arrange the fillets on a serving platter and wrap with waxed paper. Let cool; they should be at room temperature when placed under the microwaves hours later. Cook on the serving platter in the center of the oven 3 minutes. Rotate the platter half a turn at 1½ minutes. Let set, covered, 2 minutes. Fish is ready when it flakes easily with a fork. *Serves 4.*

STRIPED BASS STUFFED WITH SHRIMP
[Speed-cook; 14 minutes]

One 3- to 3½-pound whole striped bass, scaled and cleaned
Juice of 2 lemons
1 tablespoon butter
1 medium-size white onion, chopped
1 garlic clove, minced
1 tablespoon flour
½ cup hot beef broth
½ teaspoon salt
½ teaspoon black pepper
Dash of cayenne pepper
½ teaspoon dry mustard
½ pound shrimp, shelled, deveined and chopped
4 medium mushrooms, chopped
1 tablespoon chopped fresh parsley
2 egg yolks, beaten
4 thin slices larding pork

Marinate the bass in the lemon juice one hour, turning 2 or 3 times. Melt the butter in a glass bowl. Add the onion and garlic and cook in the center of the oven 2 minutes, or until soft. Stir in the flour. Cook one minute. Stir in the beef broth and cook, stirring, one minute, or until the sauce is smooth and thickened. Let cool, then mix in the salt, pepper, cayenne pepper, mustard, shrimp, mushrooms, parsley and egg yolks.

Stuff the bass with this mixture and close the cavity with toothpicks. Place the bass on 2 inverted saucers in a glass baking dish. Arrange the larding pork atop the bass. Cover loosely with waxed paper and cook in the center of the oven 5 minutes. Baste with the juices. Rotate the dish half a turn. Baste. Cook 5 minutes. Let set, covered, 5 minutes. Do not overcook. The fish is ready when it flakes easily with a fork. *Serves 4 to 6.*

SWORDFISH STEAKS WITH MAÎTRE D'HÔTEL BUTTER

[Speed-cook; 4 minutes]

Four ¾-inch-thick swordfish steaks (each about 6 ounces)
2 tablespoons cooking oil
Salt and pepper to taste
Maître d'Hôtel Butter (below)

Brush both sides of the steaks with the oil; sprinkle lightly with salt and pepper. We like a 9½-inch browning skillet for this dish, but you can use a shallow baking dish. To use a browning skillet: Preheat the pan 4½ minutes. Cook the fish 2 minutes on each side. Let set, covered, 2 minutes. The fish is ready when it flakes easily with a fork. If you use a shallow glass baking dish, place the oiled steaks in the dish and cook in the center of the oven 3 minutes on each side. Let set, covered, 3 minutes. Serve with a dollop of soft Maître d'Hôtel Butter melting atop each steak.

Salmon steaks can be substituted for the swordfish. *Serves 4.*

Maître D'Hôtel Butter

½ cup unsalted butter, softened
½ cup minced fresh parsley
1½ tablespoons fresh lemon juice
¼ teaspoon pepper

In a bowl, blend all of the above ingredients.

STUFFED BROOK TROUT
[Speed-cook; 12½ minutes]

  4 slices bacon
  2 tablespoons butter
  2 shallots or 1 small white onion, minced
  2 tablespoons tomato sauce
  1 tablespoon chopped fresh parsley
  1 cup bread crumbs
 12 raisins, chopped
  ½ teaspoon salt
  ½ teaspoon pepper
  2 teaspoons Madeira
Dash of Tabasco sauce
Dash of Maggi liquid seasoning
  4 whole brook trout (each 6 to 8 ounces), cleaned
Paprika
  1 lemon, quartered and seeded

Place 2 or 3 paper towels on a plate and arrange the bacon on them in one layer. Cover with a paper towel and cook in the center of the oven 3½ minutes. Pat off the fat. Let cool, then finely crumble. In a glass bowl, melt the butter and cook the shallots or onion 2 minutes, or until soft. To this bowl add the bacon and remaining ingredients except the trout, paprika and lemon. Blend well. Divide the mixture into 4 parts and stuff the trout; close the cavities with toothpicks. Place the trout on a serving platter or in a shallow glass baking dish. Sprinkle with paprika and cover loosely with waxed paper. Cook 4 minutes. Rotate the dish half a turn and cook 3 minutes. Let set, covered, 2 minutes. The trout are ready when they flake easily with a fork. Serve garnished with the lemon wedges. *Serves 4.*

SPEEDY SHRIMP CURRY
[Speed-cook; 8 minutes]

1 pound medium shrimp, shelled and deveined
¼ cup hot water
1 small celery rib, sliced
1 small white onion, quartered
2 tablespoons lemon juice
1 teaspoon salt
½ teaspoon pepper

In a glass casserole, place all of the above ingredients.
Cook in the center of the oven 2 minutes, stirring after
each minute. Drain shrimp and set aside.

2 tablespoons butter
1 medium-size white onion, minced
1 tablespoon curry powder
One 10-ounce can frozen condensed cream of shrimp
    soup, thawed
One 10½-ounce can condensed cream of mushroom soup
Salt and pepper to taste
Hot cooked rice

In a glass casserole, melt the butter and cook the onion
in the center of the oven 2 minutes, or until soft. Stir in
the curry powder and the soups, blending well. Cook 2
minutes, or until simmering. Stir. Taste for seasoning,
adding salt and pepper, if necessary. Stir in the shrimp
and cook 2 minutes. Stir. Shrimp should be firm but
not hard. Serve spooned over rice, and pass the chutney.
Serves 4.

TUNA OR SALMON LOAF
[Speed-cook; 6 minutes]

6 ounces potato chips, broken up
Two 7-ounce cans chunk tuna, or salmon, drained and
    flaked
One 10½-ounce can condensed cream of mushroom soup
1 tablespoon chopped pimiento

In a bowl, mix thoroughly all the ingredients. Butter a
glass loaf dish and spoon the mixture evenly into it.

Cook in the center of the oven 4 minutes. Rotate the dish half a turn and cook 2 minutes. Let set, covered, 5 minutes. *Serves 4.*

TUNA SCALLOP
[Speed-cook; 9 minutes]

2 tablespoons butter
1 medium-size white onion, chopped
1 celery rib, scraped and chopped
1 garlic clove, minced
1 small sweet red pepper, cored, seeded and chopped
Two 7-ounce cans fancy white chunk tuna, drained and flaked
2 tablespoons chopped fresh parsley
½ teaspoon salt
¼ teaspoon pepper
1 cup coarse unsalted cracker crumbs
¼ cup medium cream
2 eggs, beaten

Melt the butter in a bowl. Add the onion, celery, garlic and sweet red pepper and cook in the center of the oven 3 minutes, or until soft, stirring after 1½ minutes. Let cool slightly, then add all the remaining ingredients. Mix well. Spoon the mixture into a buttered glass casserole, dot the top with butter and cook in the center of the oven 4 minutes. Rotate the dish half a turn. Cook 2 minutes. Let set, covered, 5 minutes. *Serves 4 to 6.*

WHITING WITH CLAMS
[Speed-cook; 8 minutes]

4 whiting (each about ½ pound after cleaning)
3 tablespoons olive oil
Salt and pepper to taste
2 garlic cloves, minced
2 tablespoons minced fresh parsley
¼ cup fresh lemon juice
1½ cups dry white wine
12 clams, scrubbed

Roll the whiting in the oil, coating them well. Place them side by side in a large glass casserole. Sprinkle lightly with salt and pepper. Sprinkle on the garlic, parsley and lemon juice. Pour the wine around the fish to a depth of ½ inch. Cook, covered, in the center of the oven, 2½ minutes. Turn the fish. Cook 2½ minutes. Arrange the clams around and between the fish. Cook, covered, 3 minutes, or until the clams open and fish flakes easily with a fork. Discard unopened clams. Serve in warm deep plates with the broth. Pass warm buttered crusty bread for dunking. *Serves 4.*

COQUILLES ST. JACQUES

[Speed-cook; 6 minutes]

2 tablespoons butter
1 medium-size white onion, minced
1 garlic clove, minced
1 tablespoon chopped fresh parsley
1 pound whole bay scallops or cut-up ocean scallops
⅓ cup dry white wine
One 10½-ounce can condensed cream of mushroom soup
½ cup grated Gruyère cheese
2 tablespoons flour blended with ¼ cup water
Salt and pepper to taste
½ cup bread crumbs
Paprika

In a glass casserole, in the center of the oven, melt the butter. Add the onion, garlic and parsley. Cook 2 minutes, or until the onion is soft. Stir in the scallops and wine. Cook 2 minutes. Stir. Blend in the soup and cheese. Stir in the flour-water mixture, blending well. Cook 2 minutes. Stir. Season with salt and pepper. Test scallops. They should be just firm, but not hard. Place mixture in individual scallop shells or ramekins. Sprinkle with bread crumbs and paprika. Place under the broiler of a conventional stove until the bread crumbs are brown. *Serves 4.*

6

Poultry

Although most foods do well under microwaves, we believe that poultry does best. Whereas other methods of cooking tend to remove moisture, microwaves seem to moisten and tenderize everything from a Cornish game hen to a turkey.

There are moot points, however, to keep in mind when preparing poultry. We will be repeating ourselves at the beginnings of some chapters, for we think that it is pertinent to state the facts where they will be helpful and not refer the reader back to other pages, except where it is necessary.

Even if you have a defrost setting on your microwave oven, your roast poultry will be more satisfactory if you let them defrost slowly in their wrappings in the refrigerator, for 24 hours; turkeys, depending upon their size, probably will take twice that long. The defrosting capabilities of the microwave oven, as stated elsewhere, are unequalled for emergencies. If you must defrost fast, by all means do so, following the outlined routine carefully. There is a proper defrosting time, followed by a resting time, which insures that the meat will not be overcooked on the outside and undercooked on the inside, where defrosting wasn't complete. There's no trick to it. It's a great help. But why use microwaves to defrost if you don't have to?

Most microwave experts state that poultry should be cooked 7 minutes to the pound. We disagree. We cook ours perfectly at 6 minutes to the pound. Why? Heat equalization in microwave cookery always must be taken into consideration. The cooking will continue while you cover the bird and let it set. We also give another reason for "resting" or "setting" the bird in our roast turkey recipe (page 107).

Not one reference is made in any other microwave cookbook about the importance of proper trussing. We stress this. Protruding legs, thighs, wings, anything "akimbo" will be dried out quickly by the superfast microwaves. A well-trussed bird should be as tight and compact as a clenched fist. This skillful trussing will keep it moist and tender, permitting more even cooking.

The French needle system is the best by far. We offer a diagram to help you learn the technique which, at first glance, may appear a bit complicated, but which proves to be simple, once you put your mind to it.

A long trussing needle, similar to a mattress needle, draws the cord "through," not around, the bird. They are available in most shops that sell sophisticated cooking equipment.

There are only two tie positions: near the tail, to truss the legs and drumsticks; and through the thighs, which also ties in the wings and neck skin.

The needle passes through the lower carcass, comes back over (not through) one leg, *through* the tip of the breast bone and *over* the second leg. The cord is then tied tightly. In the second tie, using a new piece of cord, the needle is pushed through the apex of the second joint and the drumstick, emerging at that same point on the opposite side. The bird is then turned over, the wings are folded back and the needle is pushed through one wing. The needle's emerging point catches the loose neck skin, and passes through the other wing. The cord is again drawn as tightly as possible and tied. The diagram will take you through these simple steps to a better bird.

After the bird is trussed (your way or our way) we like to brush it with Herb Butter (page 137). Melt enough to yield one tablespoon and brush the bird well with it.

Next, place pieces of aluminum foil on protruding wing tips and legs, and on the part of the breast adjacent to the cavity. These should not be large pieces of foil. They should cover only those "akimbo" portions that will dry out quickly unless they are shielded from the microwaves. Make certain that this foil does not touch the sides of the oven as it may pit them. Some authorities suggest that you remove this foil after half the

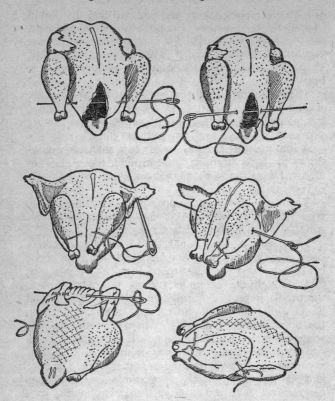

cooking time has elapsed. We leave it on, however, throughout the cooking period.

Do not salt any large piece of poultry or meat. The salt will draw moisture to the surface, forming a crust that will slow microwave penetration. You will note that our Herb Butter contains unsalted butter.

The bird to be cooked also must be placed on an inverted saucer, plate, or nonmetal trivet, to keep it above the juices. But that is not enough. You also should siphon off (with a bulb baster) or spoon off any liquid that accumulates. Baste the bird each time that you do this; save some for gravy, if you wish and discard the rest. This is moist cookery and you will find that liquid continually accumulates. Liquid absorbs microwaves, and if you do not get rid of it, it will throw off your timing; even with carry-over cooking when the bird sets, covered, you may end up with undercooked poultry.

The bird also must cook evenly. The one sure way to do this is to *turn* the bird. Start it off on one side, then breast down, then the other side, then breast up. Recipes will give you the timing for these steps.

If you are cooking poultry pieces, make sure the thicker portions are near the outside of the casserole or dish, the slender or thinner portions nearer the center.

You'll find that the microwave oven can be a great help if you are going to have a barbecue feast for a number of people, and plan to cook the chicken pieces outside over a charcoal grill. You can precook the chicken in minutes under microwaves, then bring them to crisp perfection over charcoal. The chicken will be evenly cooked; charcoal-barbecued chicken too often is very crisp and brown on the outside and underdone inside.

To prevent splatters, cover the poultry loosely with waxed paper. It will not prevent browning.

We also remind you that each chicken or turkey or duck probably will vary in cooking time according to its age, diet, and the length of time it was frozen or stored. A tender, coddled chicken will cook fast (so will one that has been held overlong in cold storage); a tough one will take longer. Primer rules, true, but timely tips. For example, we use frying chickens for any stew-type dish. A stewing chicken is an old bird and tough. It cannot tenderize in the short time it takes to cook a bird under microwaves. By using the slo-cook timer we have successfully poached a stewing chicken, but if you attempt it in the speed-cook, or fast, setting, it will be chewy.

Cooking times in this book are predicated on the fact that the food is at room temperature. If you take it right out of the refrigerator and pop it into the microwave oven naturally it will take longer.

Microwaves will turn poultry and meat golden brown. Anything that cooks less than 18 minutes will not brown. We like the color of microwave poultry, but if you want yours browner and crisper it is a simple matter to slide it under the broiler of your conventional stove.

Last words:

Watch it. Don't overcook. You can always microwave for a few more seconds or even minutes. But you cannot uncook anything.

Let food set, covered, to permit the heat and juices to equalize. Internal temperature can rise as much as 40 degrees in 20 minutes. This is why we cook 6 minutes to the pound, not 7, or 8 as others recommend.

BIRD IN A BAG

If you are addicted to cooking poultry in bags, microwaves will do the job nicely. Place the stuffed, seasoned, trussed bird in the special poultry bag and tie the neck of the bag. Punch 5 small holes all the way around near the neck of the bag to allow steam to escape. Place the bird in a shallow glass baking dish. Allow 6 minutes cooking time per pound, and to make sure it cooks evenly, turn the bird at intervals, first on one side, then the other, then breast down, then breast up. Let set 10 minutes.

CREAMED CHICKEN BREAST CASSEROLE
[Speed-cook; 16 minutes]

5 tablespoons butter
6 large mushrooms, thinly sliced
3 tablespoons flour
1 cup chicken broth
½ cup dry white wine
½ cup heavy cream
Salt and pepper to taste
2 large whole chicken breasts, cut into halves

In a skillet on a conventional stove, or in a preheated browning skillet, melt 2 tablespoons of the butter and lightly brown the mushrooms. Remove and reserve them. Heat the remaining butter in the skillet and stir in the flour, blending into a smooth paste. Add the chicken broth, a small amount at a time, stirring until you have a thickened smooth sauce. Stir in the wine and cream, simmering and stirring until well blended. Season with salt and pepper. Stir in the mushrooms. Place the chicken breasts in a glass casserole, skin side down, in one layer, thicker parts near the edge of the casserole. Pour the sauce over them. Cover with waxed paper and cook in the center of the oven 8 minutes, rotating the casserole half a turn at 4 minutes. Turn the breasts over, spoon the sauce over them, and cook 8 minutes, rotating half a turn at 4 minutes. Let set, covered, 10 minutes. Test for tenderness and seasoning. *Serves 4.*

CHICKEN WITH ARTICHOKE HEARTS
[Speed-cook; 18 minutes]

Here is a fancy one that is easier than fried chicken.

One 3½-pound chicken, cut up
Salt and pepper to taste
⅛ teaspoon dried thyme
3 tablespoons butter
1 tablespoon cooking oil
8 small mushrooms, cut into halves
2 tablespoons flour
1 cup chicken broth
2 tablespoons Madeira
One 15-ounce can artichoke hearts packed in water, drained

Sprinkle the chicken pieces with salt, pepper and the thyme. In a skillet on a conventional stove, or in a preheated browning skillet, heat the butter and oil and brown the chicken. Place in a glass casserole, skin side down, in one layer, thicker parts near edge of the dish. Stir the flour into the skillet; pour in the broth and wine, simmering and stirring into a smooth sauce. Arrange the mushrooms and artichoke hearts between the chicken pieces. Pour the sauce over the ingredients in the casserole. Cover and cook in the center of the oven 9 minutes. Turn the chicken over and rotate the dish half a turn. Cook, uncovered, 9 minutes. Let set, covered, 10 minutes. Test for tenderness. *Serves 4.*

CHICKEN BOMBAY
[Speed-cook; 10 minutes)

This is a fine spicy chicken we enjoyed in Bombay. We had it hot, nestled in rice, and also cold, served with a salad heavy with mangoes.

⅓ cup chicken broth
Juice of 3 limes
Juice of 2 lemons
1 teaspoon tomato paste
2 teaspoons ground cardamom
1 teaspoon sugar
½ teaspoon salt
⅛ teaspoon hot chili powder
2 large whole chicken breasts, cut into halves and skinned (make several slashes in each breast with a sharp knife to allow the chicken to absorb more of the marinade)

In a glass casserole large enough to hold the chicken breasts in one layer, blend well all of the ingredients except the chicken. Add the chicken breasts and turning them several times, marinate at room temperature 2 hours. Remove the chicken breasts and place the casserole with the marinade in the center of the oven. Bring to a simmer. Add the breasts in one layer, the thicker parts near the edge of the casserole. Cook, covered, 5 minutes. Rotate the dish half a turn. Cook 5 minutes. Let set, covered, 5 minutes. Test for tenderness and seasoning. This dish is very easy to overcook. The breasts will still be cooking in the hot marinade after the casserole is removed from the oven. *Serves 4.*

BREAST OF CHICKEN IN LEEK SAUCE
[Speed-cook; 14 minutes]

2 large whole chicken breasts, cut into halves
2 tablespoons butter
½ tablespoon cooking oil
Salt and pepper to taste
One 2¾-ounce envelope dry leek soup mix (Knorr is
    excellent)
⅔ cup chicken broth
⅓ cup medium cream
¼ cup dry sherry
2 tablespoons brandy
4 large pitted black olives, sliced

In a skillet on a conventional stove, or in a preheated
browning skillet, heat the butter and oil and brown the
chicken breasts. Season with salt and pepper and place
in a glass casserole, skin side down, in one layer,
thicker parts near the edge of the casserole. In the
skillet in which the breasts browned, stir in the leek
soup mix, chicken broth, cream, sherry and brandy.
Simmer, stirring until well blended into a smooth sauce.
Pour the sauce over the chicken breasts. Cook in the
center of the oven, covered, 5 minutes. Turn the
breasts over. Cook 5 minutes. Rotate the casserole half
a turn. Cook 4 minutes. Let set, covered, 10 minutes.
Test for tenderness and seasoning. Serve with the leek
sauce spooned over each breast, topped with sliced
black olives. (They should be black truffles. But who
can afford them?) *Serves 4.*

ROAST BUTTERY CHICKEN
[Speed-cook; 18 minutes]

One 3½-pound chicken
Lawry's seasoned salt
1 large white onion, cut into quarters
½ cup (¼ pound) *unsalted* butter, softened
½ teaspoon pepper

Liberally sprinkle the cavity of the bird with seasoned
salt. Add the onion and truss the chicken. Coat it well

with the butter and sprinkle with the pepper. Cover the ends of the legs and wings with small strips of aluminum foil, also the breast tip at the cavity, so that small portion will not overcook. Place the chicken on its side on an inverted saucer in a glass baking dish. Cover loosely with waxed paper to prevent splatter. Cook in the center of the oven 6 minutes. Baste. Siphon or spoon off any liquid. Turn the chicken on its other side; each time you turn the bird, do it carefully so you do not dislodge the foil strips. Cook 6 minutes. Baste. Siphon or spoon off any liquid. Turn the bird breast up. Baste. Cook 6 minutes. Turn breast side down and let set, covered with foil, for 15 minutes. Test for tenderness. Prick the thick part of the thigh with a fork. If the juices run clear, the chicken is done; if yellowish-pink, it will need about another 3 minutes. The bird will be golden brown. Season to taste with salt. If you want it browner or crisper, place it under the broiler of your conventional oven. *Serves 4.*

CHICKEN CACCIATORE
[Speed-cook; 21 minutes]

Most chicken cacciatore recipes are heavy on tomatoes and red wine. Here is a white one with a delicious taste difference.

One 3½-pound chicken, cut up
Salt and pepper to taste
5 tablespoons olive oil
2 medium-size white onions, chopped
2 celery ribs, scraped and chopped
2 garlic cloves, minced
1 small bay leaf
¼ teaspoon dried oregano
1 cup dry white wine

Season the chicken with salt and pepper. In a skillet on a conventional stove, or in a preheated browning skillet, heat 3 tablespoons of the olive oil and brown the chicken. Place it in a glass casserole, skin side down, in one layer, the thicker parts near the edge of the dish. In a glass bowl heat the remaining olive oil. Add the onions, celery and garlic and cook in the center of the oven 3 minutes, or until soft. Add the bay leaf, oregano and wine. Mix well; bring to a simmer and pour over the chicken in the casserole. Cook in the center of the oven, covered, 10 minutes, turning the chicken over at 5 minutes. Cook 8 minutes, rotating the casserole half a turn at 4 minutes. Let set, covered, 10 minutes. Test for tenderness and seasoning. *Serves 4.*

COUNTRY CHICKEN WITH CORN

[Speed-cook; 16 minutes]

This quick Brunswick stew is so simple and speedy that it seems to take mere seconds, yet its succulence will surprise you.

  2 small whole chicken breasts, cut into halves
  4 chicken thighs
One 10¾-ounce can condensed chicken gumbo soup
One 10-ounce package frozen whole kernel corn, defrosted
1½ teaspoons Worcestershire sauce
Salt and pepper to taste

In a skillet on a conventional stove, or in a preheated browning skillet, brown the chicken pieces. Place them in one layer in a glass casserole, skin side down, with thicker parts near edge of dish. In a bowl, blend the soup, corn, Worcestershire sauce, salt and pepper. Pour the mixture over the chicken. Cover and cook in the center of the oven 8 minutes. Turn the chicken parts over, spooning the sauce over them, and rotate the dish half a turn. Cook 8 minutes. Let set, covered, 10 minutes. Test for tenderness and seasoning. *Serves 4.*

CHICKEN CURRY WITH ALMONDS
[Speed-cook; 14 minutes]

4 chicken legs
4 chicken thighs
One 10½-ounce can condensed cream of chicken soup
½ cup dry sherry
1 teaspoon curry powder
1½ tablespoons chopped pimiento
⅓ cup slivered almonds, toasted

In a skillet on a conventional stove, or in a preheated browning skillet, brown the chicken pieces. Place them in a glass casserole, skin side down, in one layer, thicker parts near the edge of the dish. In a bowl, blend the soup, sherry, curry powder and chopped pimiento. Pour over the browned chicken. Cook, covered loosely with waxed paper, 5 minutes. Rotate the dish half a turn. Cook 4 minutes. Turn the chicken pieces over and spoon the sauce over them. Cook 4 minutes, rotating the dish half a turn at 2 minutes. Sprinkle with the almonds. Cook one minute. Let set, covered, 10 minutes. Test for tenderness and seasoning. *Serves 4.*

CHICKEN OR RABBIT FRANÇAISE
[Speed-cook; 16 minutes]

This is a favorite recipe, one usually made with domestic rabbit, available in many supermarkets.

1 cup flour
1½ teaspoons salt
½ teaspoon pepper
½ teaspoon dried thyme
One 3½-pound chicken or rabbit, cut up
2 tablespoons butter
1 tablespoon cooking oil
4 garlic cloves
⅓ cup dry white wine

Blend the flour, salt, pepper and thyme. Dredge the chicken pieces with the seasoned flour. In a skillet on a conventional stove, or in a browning skillet, heat the butter and oil; add the garlic and chicken pieces and brown them. Place the chicken in a glass casserole, skin side down, in one layer, thicker parts near the edge of the dish. Pour off the oil and liquid from the skillet, leaving the garlic and the browned specks. Stir in the chicken broth and wine, scraping the bottom of the skillet. Bring to a boil. Pour this and the garlic over the chicken. Cook, covered, in the center of the oven 10 minutes. Rotate the casserole half a turn. Turn the chicken over, spooning some liquid over it, and cook, uncovered, 6 minutes. Let set, covered, 10 minutes. Remove the garlic. Test for tenderness and seasoning. *Serves 4.*

FAST COQ AU VIN
[Speed-cook; 20 minutes]

This is a French classic. We've skipped a few steps without any loss of flavor.

¼ pound lean salt pork, cut into ½-inch cubes
One 3½-pound chicken, cut up
Salt and pepper to taste
12 small white onions, root ends scored
8 medium mushrooms, sliced
2 garlic cloves, crushed
2 ounces brandy
½ cup dry red wine
½ cup beef broth
⅛ teaspoon dried thyme
1 small bay leaf
2 tablespoons butter blended with 2 tablespoons flour

In a skillet on a conventional stove, or in a preheated browning skillet, lightly brown the salt pork. Season the chicken pieces with salt and pepper; add to the skillet with the salt pork and brown. Place the chicken in a glass casserole, skin side down, in one layer, thicker parts near the edge of the dish. Add the salt pork cubes, onions, mushrooms and garlic. In a glass bowl, blend the brandy, wine, beef broth, thyme and bay leaf. Bring to a simmer, stir and pour over the chicken and vegetables. Cook, covered, in the center of the oven

10 minutes, rotating the casserole half a turn at 5 minutes. Turn the chicken over and cook 10 minutes, rotating half a turn at 5 minutes. Add the blended butter and flour to the liquid in the casserole, stirring until it has thickened. Let set, covered, 10 minutes. Remove garlic and bay leaf. Test for tenderness and seasoning. *Serves 4.*

GARLIC CHICKEN SURPRISE
[Speed-cook, 16 minutes; slo-cook, 32 minutes]

This unique dish will come as a surprise to guests. Garlic cooked this way is sweet, not overwhelming, imparting a singularly delicious flavor. Even if you are cautious with garlic, give this a try.

    ⅓ cup olive oil
    24 large garlic cloves
     1 celery rib, thinly sliced
     2 tablespoons chopped fresh parsley
    ½ teaspoon dried tarragon
    1½ teaspoons salt
    ½ teaspoon pepper
    Pinch of ground nutmeg
     4 large chicken legs
     4 large chicken thighs

The marinating stage can be done early in the day, but marinate the chicken parts at least 3 hours. In a glass casserole that will hold the chicken in one layer, combine the oil, garlic, celery, parsley, tarragon, salt, pepper and nutmeg. Stir well. Add the legs and thighs and mix well with your hands, coating all the chicken pieces. Turn several times during the marinating period. When you are ready to cook the chicken, place waxed paper snugly over the casserole. Place the casserole lid over the waxed paper. To speed-cook: Cook in the center of the oven 4 minutes. Rotate the casserole half a turn. Cook 4 minutes. Rotate half a turn. Cook 4 minutes. Rotate half a turn. Cook 4 minutes. Let set, covered, 15 minutes. To slo-cook, rotate the dish half a turn every 8 minutes. Serve the chicken with slices of good bread and "butter" them with the soft garlic. *Serves 4.*

FRIED CHICKEN
[Speed-cook; 4 to 6 minutes for each skilletful]

With the invention of the browning skillet, this all-American favorite now can be cooked speedily and succulently in the microwave oven. For the best fried chicken, select birds no larger than 2½ pounds; two-pounders are even better. Inasmuch as the chicken will be cooked with simple seasonings, quality and freshness are important. It also is important not to crowd the pieces in the browning skillet. If necessary, fry them in batches, and keep them warm in a 200° conventional oven. Remember to fry the legs and thighs first. Wings and breast pieces won't take as much time. You can use either flour or bread crumbs as a coating to keep the chicken moist and tender inside and crisp outside. We like both but use flour more often.

This may seem to be an overconcentration on such a simple dish as fried chicken. But it is everyone's favorite, and, until the recent advent of the browning skillet, chicken was not successfully fried under microwaves. One more point: Arrange the thicker parts of the chicken pieces toward the outside of the skillet, the thinner parts nearer the center.

```
  1  clean brown paper bag
 1½  cups flour
 1½  teaspoons salt
  ½  teaspoon pepper
  ¼  teaspoon dry mustard
Juice of 1 lemon
Two 2-pound fryers, cut up (do not use the backs or
     wing tips)
  4  tablespoons butter (or more, if needed)
  4  tablespoons cooking oil (or more, if needed)
Paprika
```

Combine the flour, the salt, pepper and mustard in the paper bag and mix well. Sprinkle the chicken pieces with the lemon juice. Place the chicken, a few pieces at a time, in the paper bag and shake until they are lightly coated. Remove the chicken from the bag and lightly shake the pieces free of excess flour. They should be coated, but not too thickly. Heat the browning skillet in the center of the oven 4½ minutes. Remove from the oven, add 2 tablespoons of the butter and 2 of the oil, then add the thighs and legs (do not crowd), skin side down, thicker parts near the edge of the skillet. Loosely cover with waxed paper to prevent splattering. Cook in the center of the oven 3 minutes. Turn the chicken pieces over and lightly sprinkle with paprika. Cook 3 minutes. Test for tenderness. Place the cooked chicken on a platter, covered with foil, in a conventional 200° oven to keep warm while you cook the other pieces. If you are cooking only one batch, let the chicken set, outside the oven, covered with foil, 5 minutes. Pour all liquid from the browning skillet and reheat it 2½ minutes. Add 2 tablespoons butter and 2 of oil and repeat the frying procedure, reheating the skillet 2½ minutes each time and adding more butter and oil, if necessary. Cook the wings and breasts 4 minutes, turning the pieces at 2 minutes. *Serves 4.*

NOTE: You can approximate "fried" chicken in the microwave oven even without a browning skillet. Cook cut-up chicken in a casserole in butter (6 minutes per pound), turning the chicken pieces over midway through cooking. The chicken then can be crisped and browned under the broiler of a conventional stove.

CHICKEN WITH ONIONS, GREEK STYLE
[Speed-cook; 26 minutes]

    1 clean brown paper bag
    ½ cup flour
    1½ teaspoons salt
    ½ teaspoon pepper
    One 3½-pound chicken, cut up
    3 tablespoons cooking oil
    6 medium-size white onions, chopped
    3 garlic cloves, minced
    1 cup chicken broth

In the paper bag, combine the flour, salt and pepper. Shake, then add the chicken pieces. Shake them until

they are evenly coated with flour. Remove the chicken
and shake off any excess flour. In a skillet on a conventional stove, or in a preheated browning skillet,
brown the chicken. Place in a glass casserole, skin side
down, in one layer, thicker parts near the edge of the
dish. In a glass dish, in the center of the oven, cook
the onions and garlic in the oil 4 minutes, or until soft.
Pour in the chicken broth. Blend well. Bring to a simmer; this should take about 4 minutes. Pour the onion
sauce over the chicken. Cook in the center of the oven,
covered, 18 minutes, rotating the dish half a turn at 4
minutes and turning the chicken at 9 minutes. Spoon
the sauce over the chicken after turning. Let set,
covered, 10 minutes. Test for tenderness and seasoning.
Serves 4.

HUNGARIAN CHICKEN MAGYAR
[Speed-cook; 19 minutes]

- 4 chicken legs
- 4 chicken thighs
- 3 medium-size white onions, minced
- 2 garlic cloves, pushed through a garlic press
- Salt and pepper to taste
- 3 tablespoons chopped fresh dill or 1 tablespoon dried
  dill weed
- ½ cup chicken broth
- ⅓ cup dry white vermouth
- 2 tablespoons good paprika, preferably Hungarian
- 3 tablespoons tomato sauce
- ¼ cup sour cream

Place the chicken pieces in a glass casserole, skin side
down, in one layer, with thicker parts near the edge of
the dish. Sprinkle the onions, garlic, salt, pepper and
half the dill over the chicken. Add the chicken broth
and vermouth. Cook in the center of the oven, covered,
4 minutes. Rotate dish half a turn. Cook 4 minutes.
Turn the chicken pieces over, spooning the sauce over
them. Cook 4 minutes. Rotate dish half a turn. Cook
4 minutes. Let set, covered, 10 minutes. Test for tenderness. Transfer the chicken to a deep, warm serving

platter, cover with foil and keep warm. Simmer the liquid in the casserole 2 minutes, stirring. Blend in the paprika and tomato sauce. Cook one minute, or until just simmering. Stir in the sour cream. Spoon the hot sauce over the warm chicken on its serving platter. Sprinkle with the remaining dill. *Serves 4.*

CHICKEN ROMANO
[Speed-cook; 12 minutes]

This longtime favorite was discovered in a little trattoria *in Rome.*

  4 large chicken thighs
  3 tablespoons olive oil
  1 teaspoon salt
  ⅛ teaspoon pepper
  ¼ teaspoon dried basil
  ¼ teaspoon dried oregano
  1 cup bread crumbs
  2 medium potatoes, peeled and quartered lengthwise, with the ends squared for evenness in shape and size
  Paprika

In a bowl, place the chicken thighs, olive oil, salt, pepper, basil and oregano. Mix well, coating the chicken. Let set 2 hours. Remove the chicken and dredge with bread crumbs. Place in a glass baking dish, skin side down, in one layer, thicker parts near the edge of the dish. Dry the potatoes and roll them in the liquid remaining in the bowl the chicken marinated in, adding more oil, if necessary, to coat them lightly. Space the potatoes in a circle around the chicken. Cook, loosely covered with waxed paper, in the center of the oven 5 minutes. Turn the chicken and potatoes over. Sprinkle the chicken lightly with paprika. Cook 2½ minutes. Rotate the dish half a turn. Cook 2½ minutes. Rotate the dish half a turn. Cook 2 minutes. Let set, covered with aluminum foil, 5 minutes. Test for tenderness. You can place the dish under the broiler of a conventional stove until the chicken and potatoes brown, but it will not improve the flavor. *Serves 4.*

CHICKEN CÔTELETTES POJARSKI
[Speed-cook; 15 minutes]

You'll probably be sorry if you don't double this recipe. Guests always ask for more, and these delicate côtelettes *are delicious served cold the next day. They are also fine picnic fare.*

  4 slices white bread, crusts removed
  1 cup chicken broth
  ¼ cup butter, melted
  1½ pounds skinned, boned chicken breasts, ground
  1½ pounds skinned, boned chicken thighs, ground
  2 small eggs, beaten
Salt and pepper to taste
  4 tablespoons dill weed
Flour for dredging
  5 tablespoons butter
  2 tablespoons olive oil
  2 cups heavy cream

Break up the bread in a bowl and stir in the chicken broth and melted butter. Using a fork so you won't pack down the meat and bread, stir in the ground chicken, eggs, a heavy sprinkling of salt and pepper and 2 tablespoons of the dill weed. Mix well. This will be a soft mixture. Refrigerate 3 hours so it can be handled more easily. Form plump, oblong patties, 2 by 3 inches. Dredge them with flour. In a skillet on a conventional stove, or in a browning skillet, heat 2 tablespoons of the butter and one of the oil. Brown the *côtelettes* evenly on both sides, several at a time, adding more butter and oil as you need it. If you can, place them in one layer in a large shallow glass casserole or, if necessary, overlap them. Cover with the heavy cream and sprinkle with the remaining dill weed. Cook in the center of the oven, uncovered, for 10 minutes. Rotate the casserole half a turn. Cook 5 minutes. Let set, covered, 10 minutes. *Serves 6.*

ROSEMARY CHICKEN OR RABBIT
[Speed-cook; 12 minutes]

If you want a new taste treat, substitute rabbit for chicken in this recipe. Delicate, white-fleshed rabbits are sold in supermarkets, have less fat than chicken and, many people (including us) believe, more flavor.

    3 garlic cloves
    5 sprigs fresh rosemary or 1 teaspoon dried rosemary
    Pinch of hot chili powder
    ¼ cup dry white wine
    ¼ cup olive oil
    3 tablespoons lemon juice
    1 teaspoon salt
    ½ teaspoon pepper
    One 3½-pound chicken, cut up, or 3 pounds rabbit

In a glass casserole, blend the garlic, rosemary, chili-powder, wine, olive oil, lemon juice, salt and pepper. Add the chicken or rabbit, turning to coat with the mixture. Marinate at least 3 hours, turning the pieces several times. Remove the chicken or rabbit. In the center of the oven, bring the marinade to a simmer. Add the chicken or rabbit pieces, skin side down, in one layer, with the thicker parts near the edge of the dish. Cook, covered, 4 minutes. Turn the chicken or rabbit over. Cook 4 minutes. Rotate dish half a turn. Cook 4 minutes. Let set, covered, 15 minutes. Test for tenderness. *Serves 4.*

CHICKEN OR PHEASANT WITH SHALLOTS AND CHABLIS
[Speed cook; 20 minutes]

You can get as fancy as you want with microwaves. If you can afford it, make this dish with pheasant rather than chicken. This is a delicately flavored dish.

    One 3½-pound chicken or pheasant, cut up
    24 medium shallots, peeled
    1 cup Chablis
    ½ teaspoon dried savory
    Salt and pepper to taste

In a skillet on a conventional stove, or in a preheated browning skillet, brown the chicken or pheasant pieces. Place them in a glass casserole, skin side down, in one layer, thicker parts near the edge of the dish. Arrange the shallots between the chicken or pheasant pieces. Pour in the wine. Sprinkle with the savory, salt and pepper. Cook in the center of the oven, uncovered, 8 minutes. Turn the chicken or pheasant over. Cook 8 minutes. Rotate dish half a turn. Cover. Cook 4 minutes. Let set, covered, 10 minutes. Test for tenderness. Serve the shallots with the chicken or pheasant. *Serves 4.*

PO VALLEY FARMER'S CHICKEN
[Speed-cook; 27 minutes]

3 tablespoons butter
1 tablespoon olive oil
4 small chicken thighs
2 small whole chicken breasts, cut into halves
Salt and pepper to taste
4 anchovy fillets, cut into pieces
2 garlic cloves, minced
One 16-ounce can plum tomatoes, put through a food mill
4 black olives, sliced
4 green olives, sliced
1 teaspoon dried basil
¼ teaspoon hot red pepper flakes
1 teaspoon capers, rinsed and drained

In a glass casserole, in the center of the oven, heat the butter and the oil. Add the chicken and cook 3 minutes. Turn the chicken and cook 3 minutes. Sprinkle lightly with salt and pepper, then remove from the casserole. In the same dish, cook the anchovies one minute or until they can be stirred into a paste. Stir in the garlic, tomatoes, olives, basil, red pepper flakes and capers, blending well. Cook 5 minutes. Stir. Add the chicken pieces, skin side down, in one layer, thicker parts near the edge of the dish. Spoon the sauce over the chicken. Cook in the center of the oven, covered with waxed paper, 7 minutes. Rotate casserole half a turn. Cook 5 minutes. Turn the chicken pieces over. Spoon the sauce over them. Cook 3 minutes. Let set, covered, 10 minutes. Test for tenderness. Serve the chicken with the spicy sauce spooned atop. *Serves 6.*

CHICKEN WITH SWEET AND HOT SAUSAGES
[Speed-cook; 40 minutes]

One 16-ounce can Italian plum tomatoes, broken up
Salt and pepper to taste
One 3½-pound chicken, cut up
2 small sweet Italian sausages, cut into halves
2 small hot Italian sausages, cut into halves
2 tablespoons olive oil
2 small white onions, chopped
2 garlic cloves, minced
1 medium green pepper, cored, seeded and cut into 1-inch cubes
½ teaspoon dried oregano
¼ cup chicken broth
¼ cup dry white wine

In a glass bowl, in the center of the oven, cook the tomatoes for 10 minutes, stirring once or twice; set aside. Lightly sprinkle the chicken pieces with salt and pepper. Prick the sausages in several places with the point of a knife. In a large glass casserole, in the center of the oven, heat the olive oil. Arrange the chicken (skin side down, thicker parts near the edge of the dish) and the sausages in the casserole in one layer. Cover the dish with waxed paper to prevent splattering. Cook 5 minutes. Turn the chicken and sausages over; cook 5 minutes. Remove from the casserole. Pour off all but one tablespoon of the liquid. Stir in the onions, garlic and green pepper. Cook 5 minutes, or until soft. Stir in the tomatoes, chicken and sausages, and sprinkle with the oregano; pour in the broth and wine and stir well. Cover and cook 10 minutes. Rotate dish half a turn. Cook 5 minutes. Let set, covered, 15 minutes. Test for tenderness. *Serves 4.*

PERUVIAN CHICKEN
[Speed-cook; 27 minutes]

2 slices bacon, diced
One 3½-pound chicken, cut up
Salt and pepper to taste
1 medium-size white onion, chopped
2 medium-size ripe tomatoes, peeled, seeded and coarsely chopped
4 pork link sausages, cut into ¼-inch-thick slices
1 cup rice
2 cups chicken broth
2 tablespoons chopped chives
⅛ teaspoon hot red pepper flakes

In a skillet on a conventional stove, or in a preheated browning skillet, cook bacon two minutes. Sprinkle the chicken pieces with salt and pepper and brown in the bacon fat. Remove the chicken. Stir into the skillet the onion, tomatoes, sausage, rice, broth, chives and red pepper flakes. Cook 5 minutes. Transfer this mixture to a glass casserole and add the chicken, skin side down, in one layer, thicker parts near the edge of the dish. Cover with waxed paper. Cook in the center of the oven 10 minutes. Rotate the dish half a turn at 5 minutes, and turn the chicken pieces over at 10 minutes. Cook another 10 minutes, rotating the dish half a turn at 5 minutes. Almost all of the broth should be absorbed, and the rice should be moist, not dry. Let set, covered, 5 minutes. Test for tenderness and seasoning. *Serves 4.*

VIRGINIA CHICKEN STEW
[Speed-cook; 20 minutes]

One 10½-ounce can condensed chicken gumbo soup
2 ounces brandy
2 tablespoons lemon juice
1 celery rib, scraped and sliced
1 small bay leaf
1 teaspoon salt
¼ teaspoon pepper
¼ teaspoon poultry seasoning
2 small whole chicken breasts, cut in halves
4 small chicken thighs
8 small white onions, root ends scored
2 medium potatoes, peeled and cut into 1-inch cubes

In a glass casserole, in the center of the oven, stir in the soup, brandy, lemon juice, celery, bay leaf, salt, pepper and poultry seasoning. Cook 5 minutes. Stir well into a smooth sauce. Add the chicken pieces, skin side down, in one layer, thicker parts near the edge of the dish. Cook, covered, 4 minutes. Turn the chicken. Cook 4 minutes. Arrange the onions around the outer edge, and the cubed potatoes around the chicken pieces, near the center. Cover. Cook 7 minutes. Let set, covered, 10 minutes. Test chicken and vegetables for tenderness. *Serves 4.*

THYME CHICKEN IN TOMATO SAUCE
[Speed-cook; 14 minutes]

2 large whole chicken breasts, cut in halves and boned
1 small green pepper, cored, seeded and cut into thin strips
1 medium-size white onion, thinly sliced
Salt and pepper to taste
¼ teaspoon dried thyme
One 10½-ounce can condensed tomato soup
2 tablespoons red wine vinegar

Place the chicken breasts in a glass casserole, skin side down, in one layer, thicker parts near the edge of the dish. Arrange the pepper strips and onion slices around the chicken. Sprinkle lightly with salt and pepper and the thyme. Blend the tomato soup and vinegar and pour over the chicken. Cover with waxed paper. Cook in the center of the oven 7 minutes, rotating the dish half a turn at 4 minutes. Turn the chicken over. Cook 7 minutes, rotating the dish half a turn at 4 minutes. Let set, covered, 5 minutes. Test for tenderness and seasoning. *Serves 4.*

YUCATAN CHICKEN IN PAPER
[Speed-cook; 20 minutes]

In Yucatan this tasty boned chicken would be cooked, wrapped in banana leaves. But parchment paper works well.

```
  1  cup olive oil
  ½  cup lemon juice
1½  teaspoons salt
  ½  teaspoon black pepper
  ⅛  teaspoon hot red pepper flakes
  ¼  teaspoon dried oregano
  ¼  teaspoon ground cumin
  4  garlic cloves, crushed
  2  whole chicken breasts, cut in halves and boned
  4  chicken thighs, boned
  8  sheets parchment cooking paper, each large enough
     to completely encase a chicken piece
```

In a large bowl, blend the olive oil, lemon juice, salt, black pepper, red pepper flakes, oregano, cumin and garlic. Marinate the chicken pieces in this mixture 8 hours, turning several times. Do not drain the chicken, but remove from the dish well coated with the marinade. Wrap each piece in a sheet of the cooking paper, envelope fashion, completely encasing it. Arrange the wrapped chicken pieces in a glass casserole in one layer. Cover and cook 10 minutes. Turn the chicken over. Cook 10 minutes. Let set, covered, 10 minutes. Serve in the paper for guests to unwrap. *Serves 4.*

CORNISH GAME HENS IN SAUERKRAUT AND WHITE WINE
[Speed-cook; 35 minutes]

This is a famous Alsatian recipe. Partridge or pheasant is usually used, but Cornish game hens are excellent for a fraction of the cost.

Four ¾-pound Cornish game hens, trussed
Salt and pepper to taste
  3 tablespoons butter
  1 tablespoon cooking oil
  5 small shallots or 2 small white onions, chopped
  2 garlic cloves, chopped
  1 quart well-drained sauerkraut
1½ teaspoons caraway seeds
  1 cup Chablis

Sprinkle the game hens lightly with salt and pepper. On a conventional stove, or in a preheated browning skillet, brown the game hens in the butter and oil, being careful not to tear the skins. Remove. Add the shallots or onions and garlic and cook until soft. Transfer the contents of the skillet into a glass casserole. Stir in the sauerkraut, caraway seeds and wine, mixing them well with the shallots and garlic. Cook in the center of the oven 10 minutes, stirring well after 5 minutes. Stir well and bury the birds on their sides in the sauerkraut. Cover the casserole. Cook 10 minutes. Rotate casserole half a turn. Cook 5 minutes. Stir the sauerkraut well and turn the birds on their other side. Bury them again in the sauerkraut. Cook 10 minutes. Let set, covered, 15 minutes. Test for tenderness and seasoning. *Serves 4.*

Variations: After you have accomplished this dish, try interesting variations using the same technique (increase the cooking time 5 minutes), substituting pork hocks, pork chops or boned loin of pork.

NOTE: Freeze some of the sauerkraut after the dish has cooked, to serve with hot dogs. See Super Hot Dog I and II, page 173–74.

ROAST TURKEY WITH RICE AND SAUSAGE STUFFING

[Speed-cook, 48 minutes; slo-cook, 96 minutes]

We suggest a stuffing that will be a welcome change from the bread-and-sage type that everybody uses. Do this your own way, using microwaves to save both your own energy and cooking energy, adjusting amounts according to the size of the turkey. We cook poultry 6 minutes to the pound, allowing for carry-over cooking while the bird is setting, covered, after removing it from the microwaves.

Rice and Sausage Stuffing

3 cups cooked rice
½ pound sweet Italian sausage meat, cooked and drained
2 tablespoons each of chopped onion and chopped celery, sautéed until soft in butter
½ cup spinach, cooked, drained and chopped
⅛ teaspoon dried oregano
⅛ teaspoon dried tarragon
Salt and pepper to taste

In a large bowl mix all stuffing ingredients well.

One 8-pound turkey
1 large garlic clove, mashed
2 tablespoons cooking oil
1 teaspoon pepper

Fill the turkey with the stuffing. Truss. If you French-truss with a needle as we suggest (page 83), it won't be necessary to skewer the cavity closed to keep the stuffing inside. If you don't, use a crust of bread, and/or skewers (not metal), or sew the opening closed. Dry the bird, rub it well with the garlic, then the oil and sprinkle with pepper. With small strips of aluminum foil, cover the ends of the legs and wings, and the breast tip adjacent to the cavity, so that small portion of the breast will not dry out and harden. Make certain that no foil touches the sides of the oven; it could cause pitting. Place the turkey on its side on an inverted plate in a large glass baking dish in the center of the oven. Cover the turkey loosely with waxed paper to prevent the sides of the oven from being splattered.

To speed-cook: Cook 12 minutes. Turn the turkey, breast down. Baste the bird, then remove all of the liquid. Cook 12 minutes. Rotate the dish half a turn at 6 minutes. Turn the turkey on the other side. Remove the liquid in the bottom of the dish, reserving some if you are making gravy. Cook 12 minutes, rotating dish half a turn at 6 minutes. Place the turkey on its back. Baste. Remove liquid. Cook 12 minutes, rotating dish half a turn at 6 minutes.

If you are using a meat thermometer (only when the bird is out of the oven!), the turkey should be removed when it reads 180°. It is properly cooked at 190°, but letting it set, covered with aluminum foil, for 20 minutes will finish the cooking. The proper time to test for tenderness is after the setting period. We prefer the old sharp-fork test rather than the meat-thermometer test. Pierce the thickest part of the thigh. If the juices run clear, it is done. If yellowish-pink, it isn't ready and probably will need another 5 minutes under microwaves. Besides finishing the cooking, it is also advantageous to let the bird set, covered, to give the juices time to settle, making it more moist and easier to carve. This turkey will be golden brown from the microwaves. If you like it darker, place it under a conventional broiler, or under the browning unit on your microwave oven, if you are lucky enough to have one.

To slo-cook, or simmer: Start off as with speed-cook, with the bird on its side, but make the position change after cooking 24 minutes, and the other position-of-the-bird changes after each 24 minutes. Rotate the dish half a turn after each 12 minutes. *Serves 8 to 10.*

BONELESS TURKEY BREAST
[Speed-cook; 22 minutes]

Popular today are offerings of boned turkey in varying sizes: breasts, white and dark meat rolls, also whole legs and thighs. It is no longer necessary to buy an entire turkey. You can have the parts of the bird that you like best. The breast leads in popularity.

One 4-pound boned turkey breast
3 tablespoons *unsalted* butter
1 tablespoon cooking oil
½ teaspoon pepper
1 tablespoon lemon juice
¼ teaspoon dried tarragon
Salt to taste

Place the breast on an inverted saucer in a glass casserole. Heat the butter and oil in a measuring cup under microwaves until the butter melts. Remove. Blend in the pepper, lemon juice and tarragon. Brush the breast lightly with this sauce. Cover with waxed paper. In the center of the oven, cook the breast 6 minutes. Rotate the dish half a turn. Baste with the butter sauce. Cook 6 minutes. Turn the breast over. Baste with the butter sauce. Cook 5 minutes. Baste. Turn breast over. Cook 5 minutes. Baste. Let set, covered, 10 minutes. Test for tenderness. Add salt to your taste. *Serves 4 to 6.*

ROAST DUCKLING TARRAGON
[Speed-cook; 28 minutes]

It is surprising how few of us eat duckling. It could be that the cooking mystifies. These delicious dark-fleshed birds do well under the microwaves.

One 4½- to 5-pound Long Island duckling
Salt and pepper to taste
1 tablespoon chopped fresh tarragon or ½ teaspoon dried tarragon
2 small garlic cloves
Grated rind of 1 small lemon
1 small apple, sliced
2 small carrots, sliced
3 small white onions, sliced

Cut off the tips of the wings. Sprinkle the cavity of the bird with salt, pepper and the tarragon. Place the garlic, lemon rind and apple inside the cavity. Truss the bird. Prick the thighs, back and breast. With small strips of aluminum foil, cover the ends of the legs and wings, and the breast tip adjacent to the cavity. Place an inverted saucer in a glass casserole. Lay the duckling on its side on the saucer. Arrange the carrots and onions around it. Cook in the center of the oven, covered, 10 minutes. Turn the duckling on the other side. Baste the bird, then siphon off all liquid. Cook 10 minutes. Rotate the dish half a turn. Turn the duckling breast up. Baste. Cook 8 minutes. Let set, covered, 15 minutes. Test for tenderness. If the bird is more duck than duckling, it may need another 5 minutes under microwaves. Duckling is medium rare (at its best) if the juices that run from the thick part of the thigh are pink (not red!) when pricked; well done if the juice is yellow. If you want the duckling dark brown and crusty, place it under the broiler of a conventional stove for a few minutes. *Serves 4.*

ROAST DUCKLING WITH PARSNIPS
[Speed-cook; 25 minutes]

The French often pair parsnips with duckling. It seems an odd couple, but is a winning combination.

One 4½- to 5-pound Long Island duckling
Salt and pepper to taste
⅛ teaspoon dried thyme
2 tablespoons butter
1 tablespoon cooking oil
1 herb bouquet (2 sprigs of parsley and of thyme, 1 sprig of tarragon, 1 bay leaf tied in a cheesecloth bag. You can use dried herbs, but not ground ones)
1 pound scraped firm parsnips
½ cup hot chicken broth

Cut off the tips of the wings. Season the cavity with salt, pepper and the dried thyme. Truss the bird. Prick the thighs, back and breast. With small strips of aluminum foil, cover the ends of the legs and wings, and the breast tip adjacent to the cavity. In a skillet on a conventional stove, or in a preheated browning skillet, heat the butter and oil. Using a wooden spoon and fork, being careful not to break the skin, brown the duckling evenly. Place the bird on its side on an inverted saucer in a glass casserole. Add the herb bouquet. Cook in the center of the oven, covered, 10 minutes. Siphon off the liquid. Turn the duckling on the other side. Cook 5 minutes. Siphon off all liquid. Rotate the dish half a turn. Place the bird breast side down. Arrange the parsnips around the duckling and pour in the hot chicken broth. Cook 5 minutes. Place the bird on its back. Cook 5 minutes. Baste the duckling and parsnips. Let set, covered, 15 minutes. Test parsnips and bird for tenderness. If the bird is more duck than duckling, it may need another 5 minutes under microwaves. Duckling is medium rare (at its best) if juices that run from the thick part of the thigh are pink (not red!) when pierced with a knife or fork; well done, if yellow. If you want the duckling dark brown and crusty, place it under the broiler of a conventional stove for a few minutes. *Serves 4.*

7

Meats

Now we come to the heart of the matter: meat and microwaves. Microwaves do magical things, cooking a meat loaf in 10 to 15 minutes, a hamburger in a minute or two, a hot dog in 25 seconds. As stated elsewhere, they will cook all meats in a quarter of the time of conventional cooking, some in less time.

Finicky guests, who threaten to take the bloom off that beautiful rare roast of beef by wanting it well done, can be pleased in seconds. Simply slice off their portions and cook them to their preference under microwaves. Fifteen seconds will make a juicy piece of rare beef medium; in 25 seconds it will be well done.

There are other benefits of cooking meat under microwaves, many of which you will discover for yourself by trial. For example, you will discover that while cooking, meat shrinks only 10 to 12 percent, not the 25 to 35 percent of conventional cooking. The speed is responsible for this saving.

Microwaves, however, do not have the magic to tenderize the less tender cuts of meat such as chuck and stewing beef. Thus, as in conventional cookery, it pays dividends in the long run to use the better cuts. If you use stewing meats or bargain cuts, they should be tenderized first according to the directions on the tenderizer package. A meat hammer for steaks, and marinating in tomato juice and wine, etc., also help.

If you have a slo-cook, or simmer, setting on your microwave oven (and most late models do), it is possible to cook a savory, reasonably tender stew, using ordinary stew meat. Even so, stews may end up on the chewy side. Much depends upon the condition of the meat, the cut, its age, what you cook it in, and other factors in this mysterious chemistry of cooking. We use good aged sirloin in our stews, and always cut up a nice small leg of lamb for stews, skipping the tougher cuts. Usually our stews are tender. However, not always. If you overcook for even 2 minutes, the meat can become chewy.

It is simple common sense to reason that larger pieces of meat in a stew will take longer to cook than the smaller pieces. Thus, it is important to try to cube them all the same size, so that some are not overdone and chewy and others undercooked.

Be advised that rib or sirloin cook quickly, and that round and chuck do not.

Smaller cuts, 3 to 3½ pounds, do better than larger cuts.

Any piece of meat that cooks in less than 15 minutes will not brown under microwaves. But steaks, chops and hamburgers can be beautifully cooked and browned in minutes, using the effective microwave browning skillet. We will use the skillet often in this chapter. It is a marvel for the small, tender cuts.

Ground meat does better than any other meat under microwaves. Grinding, of course, tenderizes it and the extremely fast cooking results with it seem almost magical.

Do not salt large pieces of meat before cooking, even with seasoned salt. Salt will toughen the outer layer of meat. Pepper, spices, herbs and soy sauce are fine to use. Season to taste with salt after the cooking is completed.

Microwave cookery is similar to the Chinese method, which also is fast, requires that pieces of meat be small and of uniform size, and is stirred often to change the cooking position of the meat and/or vegetables.

It is more effective to cook a dinner for eight in two batches. Also, when doubling a recipe, add two-thirds of the original cooking time.

Begin cooking roasts with the fat side down. Place the roast on a baking or roasting dish on a special microwave trivet, or on an inverted saucer to keep it out of its juices. Cover loosely with waxed paper or a paper towel to prevent splattering. Baste the meat with the juices and, using a large spoon or a bulb baster, remove all liquid periodically, saving some for gravy, if you wish, discarding the rest. This is important.

Liquid absorbs microwave energy, stealing it from the meat, slowing and altering the cooking period, throwing your timing off.

Halfway through the cooking time, turn the roast over. In order to ensure even cooking, it is also a good idea to rotate the dish half a turn each fourth of the cooking time.

After the meat is removed from the oven it will continue to cook, heat flowing to the center. Allow for this in your timing. If you want it rare at 6 minutes per pound, cook it only 5 per pound. Then let it set, covered, 20 minutes before testing for tenderness or using the meat thermometer.

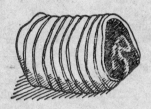

Try to select uniformly shaped roasts. If they taper, the slender end will cook faster, drying out. This can be averted by covering the end with a small piece of aluminum foil. Do not use large pieces of foil. And do not let them touch the sides of the oven. They can pit them.

Cooking times that follow are based on meat at room temperature. *Do not* take meat from the refrigerator and immediately cook it. Let it stand at least one hour or longer, depending upon the size of the meat.

Because they are more uniform, rolled roasts do better than bone-in roasts. Bones also prevent microwaves from penetrating properly. Cover any protruding bones with small strips of aluminum foil. Do the same with a leg of lamb or veal.

Pot roasts, and all roasts from less tender cuts, need a setting period of at least 20 minutes, covered, after the cooking time has been completed.

If you are going to cook meat that you have defrosted, let large pieces set at room temperature for at least 1½ hours after defrosting, smaller pieces 45 minutes to an hour.

Some tips about roasts: If cooking a standing rib roast, turn it over 3 times during the cooking period, side to side and then fat side up. If the boned, rolled roast is thicker than 5 inches, turn it over 4 times during cooking period, top to bottom, then end to end. This balances the cooking, assisting the waves in cooking the meat evenly.

And undercook! Even though we are cautious and undercook, do not even trust our directions. Take a minute from our cooking time, or even more, until you are certain that the meat is cooked to your taste. You can always let it set for 10 minutes or so and test a piece to see if it is cooked as you like it.

The danger and confusion in all meat cookery is the astounding speed of the microwaves. Even after you have used a microwave oven for months, you'll find that you are tempted, because of the years at the conventional stove, to "put it back for just a few more minutes." Don't. That's the way to disaster.

Beef

Hamburgers and the Browning Skillet: A Discussion

Why open this chapter with hamburger recipes? Two reasons: They are everybody's favorite, and ground meat cooks very easily and well under microwaves. The browning skillet is not needed to cook hamburgers—or anything. As noted, you can even place a hamburger on a paper plate and cook it. But do *not* ever cook a hamburger on a bun, as some books suggest. The juices from the meat will make the bun a soggy mess.

Back to the browning skillet. Follow the simple directions that come with it and it will not only produce a superior hamburger (without the use of cooking fat or oil) but also will brown, sear, grill, fry and sauté everything from steak, chicken and lamb chops to mushrooms in butter.

You will have to experiment with the skillet, using

your own taste as the test, whether you want your hamburgers (or steaks or chops) rare, medium or well done, taking into consideration the thickness of the hamburger. We like rare hamburgers; we cook our half-pound patties in the browning skillet 45 seconds on one side and 30 seconds on the other, and let them set on hot, toasted, buttered buns for 30 seconds before we add mustard, relish, catsup or chili sauce.

If you do not want to use the browning skillet, you can time one quarter-pound hamburger at one minute on one side and ½ minute on the other for medium rare. Cook two quarter-pounders 2½ minutes for medium rare, and four for 4 minutes, 2 minutes on one side, 2 on the other. If you are not using the browning skillet, brush the hamburgers when you turn them with whatever drippings have collected. If you want the hamburgers to look brown, dilute Kitchen Bouquet liquid seasoning with a little water and brush it over them.

We point out that no one knows the color of a hamburger once it has been doused with catsup, or covered with melted cheese.

But we also point out that the browning skillet is a unique utensil that does more than brown. It sears, and cooks very hot and very fast, thus retaining the juices in hamburgers, steaks and chops. We recommend using the browning skillet on some of our favorite recipes that follow. A tip for better browning: If liquid has collected in the skillet after you have browned one side of the meat, the other side will brown better if you pour off that liquid and cook with a dry pan.

BLUE CHEESE BURGERS
[Speed-cook; 3 minutes]

All ground meats need the addition of some liquid to keep them moist throughout cooking, helping prevent the "dry" flavor of too many so-called "hamburgers."

1½ pounds ground top or bottom round
1 teaspoon Lawry's seasoned salt
¼ cup beef broth
Four ½-inch cubes blue cheese, chilled

In a bowl, blend well the beef, seasoned salt and broth. Form into four 1½-inch-thick patties. Bury a cube of the blue cheese in the center of each, molding the beef around it. Preheat the 9½-inch browning skillet 4½ minutes. Add the patties and cook 1½ minutes on each side. These will be on the rare side. Let them set, covered, 35 seconds to continue to melt the cheese. *Serves 4.*

BURGUNDY BURGERS
[Speed-cook; 3 minutes]

As we've said, one of the many advantages of micro-wave cooking is that it can do away with cooking oils and fats—if you will let it. Thus it will help keep your weight down. Steaks, chops and hamburgers can all be grilled to perfection on the browning skillet without cooking oils or fats. This also gives the meat a much better flavor, as it is prepared, so to speak, with its own personality. Here is a recipe that will surprise you with its flavor.

1½ pounds good ground chuck
2 ounces dry red wine
1 teaspoon Lawry's seasoned salt

In a bowl blend well all ingredients. Shape into four 1½-inch-thick patties. Preheat the 9½-inch browning skillet 4½ minutes. Add the beef patties. Cook 1½ minutes on each side. These will be on the rare side. If you like yours cooked a bit more, add another 25 seconds to each side. Careful, though! Almost before you can say "medium rare," the microwaves will have prepared a well-done patty. *Serves 4.*

ITALIAN CHEESEBURGERS
[Speed-cook; 3 minutes]

"Hamburger" is a catchall word for chopped meat that isn't always of the highest grade. We call ours "ground meat" and always grind our own. We suggest that you do, too, thereby being certain of what you are getting. In Italy, beef isn't of the quality it is here. Often the Italians grind it and couple it with imagination to produce a simple but exceptional dish.

1½ pounds ground beef, preferably sirloin
½ small white onion, minced
1 teaspoon Dijon mustard
Salt and pepper to taste
¼ pound Gorgonzola cheese, crumbled into small pieces

In a bowl, place the ground beef, onion, mustard, salt and pepper, blending well. Shape into 1½-inch-thick patties, oblong rather than the usual round form. Preheat the 9½-inch browning skillet 4½ minutes. Add the meat patties. Cook 1½ minutes on each side. Sprinkle the cheese evenly over each patty. Cook just until melted. These will be rare. If you like yours cooked a bit more, add another 25 seconds to each side before sprinkling with the cheese. *Serves 4.*

HAMBURGER SHELL PIE
[Speed-cook; 11 minutes]

1½ pounds ground chuck
1 egg, beaten
1 teaspoon salt
½ teaspoon pepper
One 10½-ounce can condensed vegetable soup
1 garlic clove, minced
¼ teaspoon dried oregano
½ cup grated sharp cheese

Mix together the ground chuck, egg, salt and pepper. Line the sides and bottom of a 9-inch glass pie plate with the meat mixture, making a shell. In a glass measuring cup, blend the soup, garlic and oregano and cook in the center of the oven 3 minutes. Pour the warm soup mixture into the meat pie shell. Cook in the center of the oven 4 minutes. Rotate the plate half a turn. Cook 4 minutes. Sprinkle with the cheese; place under the broiler of a conventional stove until the cheese is melted. *Serves 4.*

MILANO MEAT LOAF
[Speed-cook; 15 minutes]

Meat loaf may seem mundane to many, but not this one, which will have your guests asking for the recipe.

½ pound bulk pork sausage
½ pound ground beef chuck
½ pound ground pork
½ pound ground veal
One 8-ounce can tomato sauce with spices and green pepper
2 eggs, beaten
¾ cup bread crumbs
2 white onions, finely chopped and sautéed in butter until soft
½ cup grated Parmesan cheese
2 tablespoons minced white raisins
2 tablespoons minced fresh Italian parsley
2 teaspoons salt
1 teaspoon pepper

Place all the ingredients in a large bowl and blend well. Lightly butter a 2-quart glass loaf dish. Spoon the meat mixture evenly into the dish but do not pack it down. Do not let the ends taper down as they will dry out. Place, uncovered, in the center of the oven. Cook 15 minutes, rotating half a turn every 5 minutes. Let set, covered, 10 minutes. *Serves 6.*

LOW-COST MINUTE MEAT LOAF
[Speed-cook; 10 minutes]

2 pounds ground chuck
One 10-ounce can condensed chicken gumbo soup
1 egg, beaten
½ cup bread crumbs
1 medium onion, chopped
2 tablespoons chopped fresh parsley
1 tablespoon Worcestershire sauce
1 teaspoon salt
½ teaspoon pepper
Pinch of nutmeg

In a bowl, combine all the ingredients and mix well. Butter a glass loaf pan and spoon the mixture evenly into it. Do not pack it. Cook in the center of the oven 5 minutes. Rotate the pan half a turn. Cook 5 minutes. Let set, covered, 5 minutes. *Serves 6.*

FAST-MIX MICROWAVE MEATBALLS
[Speed-cook; 14 minutes]

This is excellent with rice, barley or couscous (page 185).

1 pound ground chuck
½ cup bread crumbs
1 medium onion, chopped
1 egg, beaten
½ teaspoon Lawry's seasoned salt
¼ teaspoon pepper
2 tablespoons butter
One 10½-ounce can condensed cheddar cheese soup
⅓ cup milk
2 tablespoons chopped fresh parsley

In a bowl, blend the ground meat, bread crumbs, onion, egg, seasoned salt and pepper. Shape into small meatballs. In a glass casserole, in the center of the oven, melt the butter, add the meatballs and cook 4 minutes, turning them at 2 minutes to cook evenly. Blend the soup, milk and parsley and pour over the meatballs. Cover with waxed paper. Cook 5 minutes. Stir. Cook 5 minutes. Stir. Let set, covered, 5 minutes. *Serves 4.*

MEATBALLS STROGANOFF
[Speed-cook; 8½ minutes]

1 pound ground sirloin or other cut of beef
1 egg, beaten
⅔ cup bread crumbs
¼ cup light cream
1 teaspoon salt
½ teaspoon pepper
⅛ teaspoon ground mace
2 tablespoons Hungarian paprika
3 tablespoons butter
1 tablespoon olive oil
4 medium mushrooms, thinly sliced
4 shallots, chopped
2 tablespoons Madeira
¼ cup canned beef gravy
¼ cup heavy cream
½ cup sour cream

In a bowl, blend well the ground beef, egg, breadcrumbs, light cream, salt, pepper and mace. Shape into balls about 1 to 1½ inches in diameter. Sprinkle the paprika on a sheet of waxed paper. Roll the meatballs in it, covering them evenly. Heat the butter and oil in a glass casserole and cook the meatballs in the center of the oven 2 minutes. Turn them; cook one minute. Add the mushrooms and shallots. Cook one minute. Stir in the wine, beef gravy and heavy cream. Cover with waxed paper and cook 2 minutes. Stir. Cook 2 minutes. Stir in the sour cream. Cook 30 seconds. Stir. This should be hot but not boiling. Excellent with rice, couscous (page 185), or fine noodles. *Serves 4.*

HUNGARIAN BEEF GOULASH WITH MEATBALLS
[Speed-cook; 19 minutes]

A real goulash is mainly meat, usually served with noodles. This is an authentic goulash, modified for the microwaves, using ground beef instead of the usual cubes, which often end up chewy. The flavor secret is in using Hungarian paprika. Try to get it, for it can make all the taste difference. We like this with green noodles that have been tossed with butter and cheese.

2 pounds ground chuck
2 large eggs, beaten
2 tablespoons beef broth
1 medium onion, minced
⅛ cup bread crumbs
1 teaspoon salt
½ teaspoon pepper
½ cup flour
2 tablespoons butter
1 tablespoon cooking oil
5 medium onions, chopped
2 small green peppers, cored, seeded and chopped
One 16-ounce can heavy tomato puree
⅛ cup dry red wine
½ teaspoon salt
2 tablespoons Hungarian paprika

In a bowl, blend the ground beef, egg, beef broth, minced onion, bread crumbs, the teaspoon of salt and the pepper. Form into meatballs the size you prefer and roll them in the flour. In a glass casserole, in the center of the oven, heat the butter and oil. Cook the meatballs 3 minutes. Turn them. Cook for 3 minutes. Remove the meatballs. To the same casserole, add the chopped onions and green peppers. Cook 3 minutes, or until soft. Stir in the tomato puree, wine, ½ teaspoon salt and the paprika. Cook 5 minutes. Stir. Add the meatballs. Cover with waxed paper. Cook 2½ minutes. Stir. Cook 2½ minutes. Stir. Let set, covered, 10 minutes. *Serves 4 to 6.*

CORNY BEEF
[Speed-cook; 14 minutes]

1 pound ground round steak
2 tablespoons butter
1 small sweet red pepper, cored, seeded and chopped
1 small green pepper, cored, seeded and chopped
2 medium-size white onions, finely chopped
Salt and pepper to taste
One 16-ounce can cream-style corn
2 medium-size ripe tomatoes, sliced
½ cup buttered bread crumbs

In a glass casserole, in the center of the oven, cook the beef in the butter for 5 minutes, stirring after 2½ minutes. Pour off the liquid. Stir in the peppers and onions. Season with salt and pepper. Cook 5 minutes, stirring after each 2½ minutes. In another glass casserole, alternate layers of the meat mixture with the corn. Place the sliced tomatoes atop. Sprinkle lightly with salt and pepper. Sprinkle with the bread crumbs. Cook 4 minutes, rotating the dish half a turn at 2 minutes. Place the casserole under the broiler of a conventional oven until the breadcrumbs are browned. *Serves 4.*

"HOT" CHINESE BEEF SHREDS
[Speed-cook; 3 minutes 10 seconds]

1 pound flank steak, shredded (see note)
1½ tablespoons dry sherry
¼ cup soy sauce
½ cup peanut oil
¾ cup shredded carrots
1½ tablespoons finely shredded ginger root
½ teaspoon hot red pepper flakes
1½ cups shredded celery ribs
Salt to taste

Place the beef in a bowl and mix well with the sherry and soy sauce. Preheat a 9½-inch browning skillet 4½ minutes. Remove from the microwave oven. Add half the oil, and carefully, as it may splatter. Add the beef to the skillet, also carefully. Place in the center of the oven and cook 2 minutes, stirring every 30 seconds. The edges of the beef should be brown. Remove the beef with a slotted spoon and place in a strainer over a bowl. Pour off the liquid and preheat the skillet 2½ minutes. Add the remaining oil. Stir in the carrot shreds. Cook 30 seconds, stirring after 15 seconds. Stir in the ginger root, red pepper flakes and celery. Cook 20 seconds, stirring at 10 seconds. Return the beef to the skillet, mixing it well with the other ingredients. Cook 20 seconds. Test for seasoning, adding salt if necessary. If vegetables are too crunchy for your taste, put the skillet under the microwaves until they are soft enough, remembering that both beef and vegetables can be overcooked in seconds. *Serves 4.*

NOTE: Modern Chinese cooks make shredding an easy operation by putting the meat in the freezer until it is firm enough to shred quickly, but is not solidly frozen. Hold at room temperature one hour before cooking.

TEXAS CHILI CON CARNE
[Speed-cook; 29 minutes]

2 small white onions, chopped
½ green pepper, cored, seeded and chopped
1 garlic clove, minced
1 tablespoon olive oil
1½ pounds ground beef chuck
1 small dried red chili pepper, minced
1 tablespoon chili powder
½ teaspoon ground cumin
½ teaspoon salt
1 small bay leaf, crumbled
One 16-ounce can plum tomatoes, broken up
3 tablespoons tomato paste
Two 16-ounce cans dark red kidney beans (undrained)

In a deep glass casserole, in the center of the oven, cook the onions, green pepper and garlic in the olive oil 3 minutes, or until soft, stirring after 1½ minutes. Stir in the ground beef. Cook 5 minutes, stirring at 2½ minutes. Stir in the chili pepper, chili powder, cumin, salt, bay leaf, tomatoes and tomato paste. Mix well. Cover and cook in the center of the oven 7 minutes. Stir. Rotate casserole half a turn. Cook 7 minutes. Stir in the beans and their liquid. Cover. Cook 4 minutes. Stir. Cook 3 minutes. Let set, covered, 10 minutes. This is delicious served with nothing but a spoon, but it can become a fast and savory supper spooned over buttered noodles. *Serves 6 to 8.*

BEAUMONT BEEF AND RICE
[Speed-cook; 20 minutes]

Here's a tasty one-dish meal that is simple and savory.

　1½ pounds ground chuck
　2 medium onions, chopped
　1 garlic clove, chopped
　1 celery rib, scraped and chopped
　1 small sweet red pepper, cored, seeded and chopped
One 10-ounce package frozen okra, defrosted
　½ cup rice
One 16-ounce can plum tomatoes, broken up
　½ cup dry red wine
Salt and black pepper to taste
　3 teaspoons chili powder
　¼ teaspoon cayenne pepper

In a glass casserole, in the center of the oven, cook the beef 3 minutes. Stir in the onions, garlic, celery, red pepper, okra and rice. Cook 2 minutes. Stir in the tomatoes, wine, salt, black pepper, chili powder and cayenne pepper. Blend well. Cover. Cook 10 minutes, rotating the dish half a turn after 5 minutes. Uncover. Cook 5 minutes. Stir well. Let set, covered, 10 minutes. *Serves 4 to 6.*

CHINESE CURRIED BEEF TENDERLOIN
[Speed-cook; 4½ minutes]

   2 tablespoons peanut oil
   5 whole scallions, thinly sliced
   3 thin slices fresh ginger root, shredded
   1 tablespoon curry powder
1½ pounds beef tenderloin, cut into ¼-inch slices, then
     into strips
Salt to taste
   2 tablespoons dry sherry
   ½ cup beef broth mixed with 1 teaspoon sugar
   1 tablespoon cornstarch dissolved in 2 tablespoons
     water

In a glass casserole, in the center of the oven, heat the peanut oil. Add the scallions and cook one minute. Stir in the ginger root and curry powder. Cook one minute. Stir. Lightly salt the beef and stir it into the casserole with the other ingredients. Cook one minute, stirring well after 30 seconds. Stir in the sherry and the sweetened beef broth. Cover the casserole. Cook 45 seconds. Stir in the cornstarch, blending well with the beef and onions. Cook 45 seconds. Stir. Let set, covered, 5 minutes. Test for tenderness and seasoning. *Serves 4.*

SIMPLE STROGANOFF
[Speed-cook; 12½ minutes]

   2 tablespoons butter
   1 medium onion, chopped
   1 garlic clove, minced
   1 pound round steak, cut in narrow, 1-inch-thick strips
     and tenderized (if you feel wealthy, use fillet of beef)
Salt and pepper to taste
One 10½-ounce can condensed mushroom soup
Pinch of nutmeg
One 4-ounce can sliced mushrooms, drained
   1 cup sour cream

In a glass casserole, in the center of the oven, heat the butter and cook the onions and garlic 2 minutes, or until soft. Stir in the beef, seasoning lightly with salt and pepper. Cook 4 minutes. Turn the beef. Stir in the mushroom soup and nutmeg. Cook 4 minutes, stirring after 2 minutes. Stir in the mushrooms. Cook 2 minutes. Let set, covered, 5 minutes. Test for tenderness. Stir in the sour cream. Cook 30 seconds, or until just hot but not boiling. Serve with buttered noodles. *Serves 4.*

FLEMISH BEEF STEW
[Slo-cook; 48 minutes]

    2 tablespoons butter
    2 garlic cloves, cut into halves
    2 pounds top sirloin, cut into 1½-inch cubes or pieces
    ⅜ teaspoon dried thyme
    1 teaspoon pepper
    2 tablespoons flour
   12 ounces beer at room temperature
    1 teaspoon salt
    8 small white onions, root ends scored
    4 medium carrots, scraped and halved

In a glass casserole, in the center of the oven, melt the butter, add the garlic and cook one minute. Add the beef, sprinkle with thyme and pepper, and cook one minute. Sprinkle with the flour. Stir. Cook one minute. Pour in the beer and sprinkle with the salt. Stir. Cover and slo-cook in the center of the oven 10 minutes. Rotate the casserole half a turn. Cook 10 minutes. Stir. Cook 10 minutes. Let set, covered, 10 minutes. Arrange the onions and carrots in a circle around the side of the casserole, surrounding the beef. Cover. Cook 10 minutes. Rotate casserole half a turn. Cook 5 minutes. Let set, covered, 10 minutes. Test the meat and vegetables for tenderness. Serve with lavishly buttered warm bread and, of course, beer. *Serves 4 to 6.*

QUICK TOMATO BEEF STEW
[Speed-cook; 28 minutes]

2 tablespoons butter
1 pound stewing beef, cut into cubes and tenderized
Salt and pepper to taste
One 10½-ounce can condensed tomato soup
½ cup beef broth
¼ teaspoon dried thyme
4 medium-size white onions, root ends scored
4 medium carrots, cut into halves
3 potatoes, peeled and cut into quarters

In a glass casserole, in the center of the oven, melt the butter, and cook the beef 4 minutes, stirring, seasoning lightly with salt and pepper. Blend the soup and beef broth; pour into the casserole. Sprinkle in the thyme. Cover and cook 8 minutes. Stir. Rotate the casserole half a turn. Cook 8 minutes. Stir. Rotate the casserole half a turn. Arrange the vegetables in an outside circle around the beef. Cook 8 minutes. Let set, covered, 15 minutes. Test meat and vegetables for tenderness. *Serves 4.*

BOEUF À LA MODE (POT ROAST)
[Speed-cook, 38 minutes; slo-cook, 1 hour 16 minutes]

Select a piece of beef that is evenly shaped. If one end is narrower it will cook more quickly and be dryer than the rest of the roast. Remember, too, that the meat will cook while it is setting, so work that into your cooking computations. For example, with this recipe, in a

conventional stove, we cook the beef 3 hours at 300°. Thus, a quarter of that time at speed-cooking would be 45 minutes. Slo-cooking would be half that time, or 1½ hours. But allowing for the carry-over cooking while the meat is setting, we have adjusted the times to 38 minutes for speed-cook, and 1 hour 16 minutes for slo-cooking. We prefer to slo-cook pot roasts and stews. The meat is more tender.

Cut against the grain when you are slicing pot roasts and braised meats. The meat will not break up and shred.

½ cup flour
1 teaspoon salt
½ teaspoon pepper
One 3½-pound bottom round roast
2 tablespoons butter
1 tablespoon cooking oil
One 8-ounce can Hunts seasoned tomato sauce
¼ cup red wine
¼ cup water
3 medium-size white onions, quartered
2 garlic cloves, cut into quarters

Blend the flour, salt and pepper and dredge the beef. On a conventional stove, or in a preheated browning skillet, heat the butter and oil and brown the beef evenly. Transfer the beef to a glass casserole with a tight-fitting lid. Blend the tomato sauce, wine and water and, in a 2-cup glass measuring cup, bring to a boil in the microwave oven. Pour it over the meat and surround the meat with the onions and garlic. Place the casserole, covered, in the center of the oven.

To speed-cook: Cook 9 minutes. Rotate the dish half a turn. Cook 9 minutes. Rotate the dish half a turn. Cook 9 minutes. Turn the roast over. Cook 9 minutes. Rotate the dish half a turn. Cook 2 minutes. Baste. Let set, covered, 15 minutes. Test for tenderness.

To slo-cook: Cook 15 minutes. Rotate the dish half a turn. Cook 15 minutes; rotate half a turn. Cook 15 minutes. Turn the roast over. Cook 15 minutes. Rotate dish half a turn. Turn the roast over. Cook 16 minutes. Let set, covered, 15 minutes. Test for tenderness.

Strain the sauce. Heat to simmering and pass it *au natural* in a gravy boat at the table, for guests to spoon over their sliced beef. *Serves 6.*

SAUERBRATEN
[Speed-cook; 45 minutes]

We've proven to ourselves often that microwaves can master many classic dishes. Here is a German offering that will have family and friends purring. Don't let the list of ingredients put you off. It's easy. Insasmuch as this dish marinates two days in your refrigerator, we'll balance the time by speed-cooking it. In the regular oven, this dish ordinarily cooks about three hours; it can be slo-cooked under microwaves in half that time. Please yourself!

1 cup dry red wine
1 cup red wine vinegar
1 cup water
1 large onion, sliced
2 medium carrots, sliced
2 celery ribs, sliced
3 small bay leaves
8 whole black peppercorns, crushed
1 teaspoon salt
One 3- to 3½-pound rolled, tied beef rump, bottom or top round (select a uniformly solid, fat-free chunk)
½ cup gingersnap cookie crumbs

Two days before you wish to cook this dish, place all the ingredients except the beef and the gingersnaps in a large glass casserole. Mix them thoroughly, then add the beef; cover the casserole and marinate the beef in the refrigerator for two days, turning the beef several times. Remove the beef and strain the marinade. Bring the strained marinade to a boil on the conventional stove. Return the beef to the glass casserole and pour the hot marinade over it. Cook in the center of the oven 20 minutes. Turn the beef over. Cook 20 minutes. Let set, covered, 20 minutes. Test for tenderness. Set the meat aside on a warm serving platter and make the sauce: In a glass bowl, mix the gingersnap cookie crumbs with 2 cups of the marinade in which the beef cooked. Cook 5 minutes, stirring, until the cookie crumbs are dissolved and sauce is simmering, and has been sufficiently thickened with the gingersnaps. If not thick enough, add more gingersnap crumbs. Cut the warm beef into ⅛-inch-thick slices, against the grain, and arrange overlapping slices on the platter. Mask each slice with a thin film of the hot sauce. Pass the remaining sauce at the table. *Serves 4 to 6.*

CLASSIC SWISS STEAK
[Speed-cook; 33 minutes]

½ cup flour
1 teaspoon salt
½ teaspoon pepper
½ teaspoon allspice
Four ½-inch-thick bottom round steaks (each about 4 ounces)
2 tablespoons butter
4 small white onions, thinly sliced
2 garlic cloves, minced
6 medium mushrooms, sliced
1 cup canned tomatoes, put through a food mill
3 tablespoons tomato paste
½ cup beef broth

Blend the flour, salt, pepper, and allspice. Dredge the steaks well with the seasoned flour. With the edge of a heavy saucer, pound the flour into the steaks. This will tenderize and somewhat flatten them. In a skillet on a conventional stove, or in a 9½-inch browning skillet, brown the steaks one minute on each side, two at a time. If using a browning skillet, wipe the skillet with a paper towel before browning the last two steaks. Transfer the steaks to a glass casserole just large enough to hold them in one layer. In a small glass casserole, heat the butter and cook the onions and garlic 2 minutes, or until soft. Stir in the mushrooms, tomatoes, tomato paste and beef broth and cook 3 minutes, or until simmering, stirring after 2 minutes. Pour this vegetable sauce over the steaks. Cover the casserole and cook in the center of the oven 8 minutes. Rotate the casserole half a turn. Cook 8 minutes. Turn the steaks over, spooning the sauce over them, and cook 8 minutes. Let set, covered, 10 minutes. Test for tenderness and seasoning. *Serves 4.*

PALMINA THOMPSON'S BAKED STEAK
[Speed-cook; 18 minutes]

We have three points to make before we describe this simple but delicious dish: (1) You can cook the steaks without prebrowning, adding about 6 minutes to the cooking time, but the dish won't be as tasty. (2) You can use the conventional stove for browning. But we use the 9½-inch browning skillet, as we do with most steaks, chops and hamburgers, and this recipe follows that technique. (3) It isn't necessary to partially precook the potatoes, but we found that doing this made them more mealy and flavorful.

    2 medium potatoes of equal size (unpeeled)
    3 medium onions, thinly sliced
  Salt and pepper to taste
    4 top or bottom round steaks (each about 4 ounces)
    ⅜ cup flour
    3 tablespoons butter
    1½ cups beef broth

Pierce the potatoes in several places with the sharp point of a knife. Cook in the center of the oven 2 minutes, turning them at one minute. Let cool, then peel and cut into ¼-inch-thick slices. In a glass baking dish, arrange the onions in one layer, seasoning lightly with salt and pepper. Arrange the potatoes in one layer on the onions. Lightly season the steaks with salt and pepper and dredge with the flour. With the edge of a heavy saucer, pound the flour well into both sides of the steaks. Preheat a 9½-inch browning skillet 4½ minutes. Remove from the oven and add half the butter. When melted add two steaks and cook in the center of the oven 2 minutes on each side. Repeat pro-

cess with remaining steaks, first wiping the skillet with
a paper towel and preheating 2½ minutes. Arrange the
steaks on top of the potatoes in the baking dish. Pour
the beef broth into the browning skillet. Cook 2
minutes, stirring after each minute. Pour the broth
over the steak. Cover the dish. Cook in the center of
the oven 3 minutes. Turn the steaks. Cook 3 minutes.
Let set, covered, 10 minutes. Test for tenderness.
Serves 4.

GREEN PEPPER STEAK
[Speed-cook; 31 minutes]

½ cup flour
1 teaspoon salt
¼ teaspoon pepper
¼ teaspoon dried marjoram
Four ½-inch-thick slices round steak (each about 4
    ounces)
One 10½-ounce can condensed tomato soup
¼ cup water
2 medium green peppers, cored, seeded and cut into
    8 strips
2 small white onions, sliced
1 garlic clove, minced
2 tablespoons lemon juice

Blend the flour, salt, pepper and marjoram and pound
into both sides of the steaks with the edge of a heavy
saucer. This will also tenderize and somewhat flatten
them. On a conventional stove, or in a preheated browning skillet, brown the steaks evenly on both sides two at
a time. In a large glass casserole, blend well the soup,
water, peppers, onions, garlic and lemon juice. Cook 4
minutes, stirring at 2. Add the steaks. Cover them well
with the sauce. Cover the casserole and cook in the center of the oven 8 minutes. Rotate the dish half a turn.
Cook 7 minutes. Turn the steaks over, spooning the
sauce over them. Cook 7 minutes, uncovered; rotate
dish half a turn. Cook 5 minutes. Let set, covered, 10
minutes. Test for tenderness and seasoning. *Serves 4.*

EASY SWISS STEAK WITH VEGETABLES
[Speed-cook; 21 minutes]

One 1-pound round steak ½ inch thick
Salt and pepper to taste
4 medium carrots, scraped and cut into 2-inch pieces
2 medium potatoes, each cut into equal-size quarters
One 10½-ounce can condensed onion soup
¼ cup beef broth

With a meat mallet, or the edge of a heavy saucer, pound the steak well to tenderize it. Season lightly with salt and pepper and cut into 4 serving pieces. Place the steaks in a glass casserole and arrange the vegetables in a circle around them. Blend the soup and beef broth. Pour over the steaks and the vegetables. Cook, covered, in the center of the oven 7 minutes. Rotate the dish half a turn. Cook 7 minutes. Turn the steak and vegetables over. Cook 7 minutes. Let set, covered, 10 minutes. Test for tenderness. *Serves 4.*

SIRLOIN STEAK AU POIVRE
[Speed-cook; 6½ minutes]

For this dish you must use the 9½-inch browning skillet. This delicious steak with its unique flavor is famed in Europe, but seldom served here. Oddly enough, we discovered it in Hong Kong.

2½ tablespoons whole black peppercorns (preferably Tellicherry)
4 strip sirloin or shell steaks (each about 7 ounces)
2 tablespoons butter
2 teaspoons olive oil
2 tablespoons brandy
¼ cup beef gravy (canned or your own)
½ teaspoon Dijon mustard
¼ teaspoon Worcestershire sauce
Salt to taste

Place the peppercorns between sheets of waxed paper and crush them, using a rolling pin. Spread the crushed peppercorns on a large piece of waxed paper. Press both sides of the steaks firmly into the peppercorns until they are almost completely coated. Using your fingers and the heel of your hand, press the peppercorns into the steaks. For steaks on the rare side, follow our cooking time; or cook to your preference, adjusting the time accordingly. Preheat a 9½-inch browning skillet 4½ minutes. Remove from microwaves. Add half the butter and oil. Place two steaks in the skillet and cook in the center of the oven 75 seconds on each side. Transfer the steaks to a hot serving platter and keep warm. Wipe the skillet with a paper towel and preheat 2½ minutes. Add the remaining butter and oil and cook the other two steaks 75 seconds on each side. Transfer to the serving platter. To the juices in the browning skillet add the brandy, beef gravy, mustard, Worcestershire sauce and salt, stirring until well blended. Place under microwaves for 1½ minutes, or until the sauce is simmering. Stir well, then spoon the hot sauce over the steaks. *Serves 4.*

CHINESE-STYLE SIRLOIN STEAK
[Speed-cook; 10 minutes]

Yes, the Chinese cook steak. Their problem is getting it, for in China it is very expensive. We had it this way in Hong Kong. If you are tired of serving steak the same old way, here's a tasty change of pace.

One 2-pound sirloin steak, about 1 inch thick
  3 whole scallions, chopped
  1 garlic clove, minced
  2 thin slices fresh ginger
  ¼ cup dry sherry
  ¼ cup soy sauce
  ¼ teaspoon salt
  1½ teaspoons monosodium glutamate
  2 tablespoons peanut oil

Trim half the fat from the steak, then cut in half to make two small steaks. In a bowl, blend the scallions, garlic, ginger, sherry, soy sauce, salt and monosodium glutamate. Place the steaks in a flat-bottomed dish. Pour the marinade over them and let set ½ hour at room temperature. Turn the steaks, spooning the marinade over them, and let set ½ hour. Drain and reserve the marinade. Dry the steaks; brush on both sides with the oil. Preheat a 9½-inch browning skillet for 4½ minutes. Cook one of the steaks in the skillet for 2 minutes, covered with waxed paper. Turn and cook one minute. Brush the steak with marinade. Cook the steak one minute. Turn. Brush with the marinade. Cook one minute. Transfer to a warm platter and cook the other steak after wiping the skillet with a paper towel and preheating it 2½ minutes. Test the steaks. They should be tender and pink. *Serves 4.*

GARLIC STEAK ROMANO
[Speed-cook; 6 minutes]

Here is a Roman specialty combining beef and cheese, giving steaks a new personality for a main course. The recipe is also excellent for hamburgers.

- 3 garlic cloves, minced
- ⅓ cup grated Romano cheese
- 3 tablespoons butter, softened
- 1 tablespoon Marsala
- 1 tablespoon brandy
- 1 teaspoon tomato sauce
- ¼ teaspoon salt
- ½ teaspoon pepper
- 4 strip sirloin or shell steaks (each about 7 ounces)

In a bowl combine all ingredients except the steaks and blend into a paste. Preheat a 9½-inch browning skillet 4½ minutes. Cook two steaks in the center of the oven 75 seconds on each side. Remove steaks and keep warm. Wipe the skillet with a paper towel, preheat it 2½ minutes and cook the remaining two steaks 75 seconds on each side. Test the steaks to see if they are done to your taste. Spread the seasoning paste over the steaks. Place all four steaks under microwaves for one minute or until the mixture bubbles. *Serves 4.*

FILLET OF BEEF WITH HERB BUTTER

[Speed-cook; 5½ minutes, cooking 2 fillets at a time]

This is the tenderest of all beef. If some say that it is tasteless, then they do not know how to cook it. Most people overcook these nuggets. A browning skillet plus microwaves handle them beautifully, leaving them moist, pink and full of flavor—if you time correctly. Herb Butter also enhances their flavor.

Four ½-inch-thick slices beef fillets (each 6 to 8 ounces)
Pepper to taste
4 tablespoons Herb Butter (below)
2 teaspoons olive oil
Salt to taste

Sprinkle the fillets with pepper. Preheat the 9½-inch browning skillet 4½ minutes. Add one tablespoon of the Herb Butter and half the oil, distributing it evenly in the hot skillet. Add two fillets. Cook in the center of the oven 1½ minutes on each side. Remove the fillets and keep warm. Pour off any liquid in the skillet and heat it 2½ minutes. Add one tablespoon of the Herb Butter and the remaining oil. Cook the remaining fillets 1½ minutes on each side. Sprinkle the fillets lightly with salt. Serve with the remaining Herb Butter spread over them. The fillets will be rare. Increase the cooking time according to your preference. *Serves 4.*

Herb Butter

1 cup (½ pound) chilled unsalted butter
1 teaspoon lemon juice
½ teaspoon soy sauce
½ teaspoon Worcestershire sauce
1 teaspoon Dijon mustard
1 tablespoon chopped fresh parsley
½ teaspoon pepper
¼ teaspoon dried tarragon
¼ teaspoon dried thyme

Take the butter from the refrigerator and place in a glass measuring cup. Heat under microwaves in the center of the oven 10 seconds. It should be just slightly softened. Blend in remaining ingredients, working into a smooth mixture. Shape into two sticks. Wrap in plastic wrap, then in aluminum foil and freeze. To use, take right from the freezer and slice off pieces as you need them. Let come to room temperature before you place a slice or two atop steak. Herb Butter is also excellent on fish.

Makes 1 cup (½ pound), enough for 16 steaks.

FILLET MIGNON ROSSINI
[Speed-cook; 8 minutes, including the sauce]

This is a special recipe for those times when you want to celebrate. It's expensive. It's memorable. It's perfect for the browning skillet and microwaves.

    Four 1½-inch-thick slices beef fillets (each 6 to 8 ounces)
    3 tablespoons butter
    2 tablespoons flour
    1 cup beef broth
    ½ cup dry red wine
    Salt and pepper to taste
    Four ¼-inch-thick slices *pâté de foie gras*

Preheat the 9½-inch browning skillet 4½ minutes. Do not add any butter or fat. Grill the four fillets for 1½ minutes. Turn them. Grill 1½ minutes. These will be rare. Increase the cooking time according to your preference. Transfer the fillets to a warm platter and cover with aluminum foil to keep warm. Pour off liquid from the skillet. Add the butter and flour to the skillet, stirring into a smooth paste. Gradually stir in the beef broth. Place in the center of the oven 2 minutes, stirring every 30 seconds. Remove. Stir into a smooth sauce. Heat one minute, stirring after 30 seconds. Gradually stir in the wine. Heat one minute, stirring after 30 seconds. Stir in salt and pepper. Cook one minute, or until the sauce is smooth and thickened, stirring every 30 seconds. Place one slice of *pâté* atop each warm fillet. Make sure that the sauce is piping hot, and spoon some over the *pâté*. Serve immediately. You also may serve the fillet on a half-inch-thick slice of bread fried in butter; top with the *pâté* and sauce, as above. *Serves 4.*

ROAST BEEF SIRLOIN WITH QUICK SAUCE BORDELAISE
[Speed-cook; 15 minutes]

Save this one for guests who truly appreciate elegant beef accompanied by your best burgundy. Talk to your butcher; get his best. You need a fine piece of boneless sirloin strip, the meat from which superb steaks are cut.

One 3-pound piece boneless sirloin strip
Pepper to taste
Quick Sauce Bordelaise (below)

Sprinkle the beef lightly with pepper. On a conventional stove, or in a preheated browning skillet, brown the beef evenly. Transfer it to a glass casserole, on an inverted saucer. Cover with waxed paper. Cook in the center of the oven 4 minutes. Rotate the casserole half a turn. Cook 4 minutes. Pour or siphon off any liquid in the casserole, reserving one tablespoon for the sauce. Turn the meat over. Cook 4 minutes. Rotate half a turn. Cook 3 minutes. Transfer the roast to a warm platter. Let set, covered with aluminum foil, 10 minutes while you prepare Quick Sauce Bordelaise. When ready to serve, slice the beef and pass the sauce at the table. *Serves 4 to 6.*

Quick Sauce Bordelaise
[Speed-cook; 3 minutes]

1 tablespoon reserved liquid from Roast Beef Sirloin casserole (above)
3 medium-size white onions, minced
½ cup dry red wine
½ cup beef gravy (canned or your own)
½ teaspoon salt
1 teaspoon cornstarch blended with 2 tablespoons water
2 tablespoons butter, softened

In the casserole you cooked the sirloin roast in, combine reserved liquid, the onions, wine, gravy and salt.

Cook 2 minutes, or until the onions are soft, stirring after one minute. Stir in the cornstarch. Cook for one minute, stirring each 30 seconds. Remove from the oven and stir in the softened butter.

Veal

VEAL-RICE LOAF
[Speed-cook; 14 minutes]

The less expensive cuts of veal can be used for this. The loaf is also excellent cold for a summer supper.

  1 small sweet red pepper, cored, seeded and chopped
  1 medium-size white onion, chopped
  1 garlic clove, minced
  2 tablespoons butter
  1½ pounds ground veal
  3 slices bacon, cooked until crisp, drained and finely chopped
  1½ cups cooked rice
  2 eggs, beaten
  ¼ teaspoon Maggi liquid seasoning
  ½ cup heavy cream
  2 tablespoons dry vermouth
  2½ tablespoons chopped fresh parsley
  1½ teaspoons salt
  ½ teaspoon pepper
  ½ teaspoon dried tarragon

Cook the first three ingredients together in the butter until soft. In a bowl, combine with the remaining ingredients, blending well. Butter a glass loaf dish. Spoon the meat mixture into it evenly, but do not pack it down. Do not let the ends taper down or they will dry out. Cook, uncovered, in the center of the oven 14 minutes, rotating the pan half a turn at 7 minutes. Let set, covered, 10 minutes before slicing. *Serves 4 to 6.*

VEAL CHOPS MILANESE
[Speed-cook; 15 minutes]

This is a classic dish, its name derived from its sauce.

- ½ cup flour
- 1 teaspoon salt
- ½ teaspoon pepper
- 4 boned loin veal chops (each about 8 ounces), pounded until ¼ inch thick
- 2 eggs
- 2 teaspoons water
- 1 tablespoon olive oil
- 1 cup bread crumbs (approximately)
- 6 tablespoons butter
- 1 tablespoon butter
- 1 tablespoon flour
- 4 medium mushrooms, thinly sliced
- 2 ounces boiled calf tongue (not pickled), cut into very thin strips (optional)
- 1 cup tomato sauce
- Salt and pepper to taste

Blend the first three ingredients and dredge the chops with the seasoned flour. Beat together the eggs, water and olive oil and dip the chops into the mixture, then dredge with the bread crumbs, pressing the crumbs into the meat with your fingers until they are well coated. In a skillet on a conventional stove, or in a pre-heated browning skillet, melt 2 tablespoons of butter. Cook two chops, one minute on each side, or until brown. Place them in a glass baking dish just large enough to hold four chops in one layer. If using the browning skillet, dry with paper towels, preheat, then add 2 tablespoons of butter. Cook the remaining two chops as you did the others and add them to the baking dish. Place the dish in the center of the oven and cook 3 minutes. Turn the chops over. Cook 3 minutes. Let set, covered, 10 minutes. Test for tenderness and seasoning. Meanwhile, blend one tablespoon each of butter and flour and reserve.

While the chops are setting, heat 2 tablespoons of

butter in a glass casserole and cook the mushrooms one minute. Stir in the tongue and tomato sauce. Cook 3 minutes, stirring every minute. Stir in the blended butter and flour. Cook one minute. Stir well. Add salt and pepper to taste. Spoon the sauce over the chops and serve. *Serves 4.*

VEAL SCALLOPS PARMESAN
[Speed-cook; 12 minutes]

This is an Italian classic, adapted a bit for the micro-waves.

½ cup flour
1 teaspoon salt
½ teaspoon pepper
2 eggs beaten with 2 tablespoons heavy cream
Four ½-inch-thick veal slices from the leg (each about 6 ounces), flattened slightly
1 cup bread crumbs (approximately)
⅓ cup grated Parmesan cheese
1 tablespoon butter
2 medium-size white onions, chopped
2 small garlic cloves, chopped
One 6-ounce can tomato paste
3 tablespoons dry white wine
⅛ cup water
¼ teaspoon dried basil
¼ teaspoon dried oregano
4 thin slices mozzarella cheese

Blend the first three ingredients and dredge the veal slices with the mixture. Dip them into the eggs, then dredge with bread crumbs. In a skillet on a conventional stove, or in a preheated browning skillet, brown the veal in oil or butter lightly on both sides. Arrange the veal in a glass casserole in one layer and sprinkle with the Parmesan cheese. In a small glass casserole, melt the butter and cook the onions and garlic about 2 minutes, or until soft, stirring after one minute. Stir in the tomato paste, wine, water, basil and oregano. Cook, uncovered, 3 minutes, stirring after each minute. Spoon the sauce over the veal. Cover. Cook the veal 6 minutes, rotating the dish half a turn at 3 minutes. Let set, covered, 5 minutes. Test for tenderness. Top each piece of veal with a slice of mozzarella cheese. Cook one minute, or until the cheese melts. *Serves 4.*

STUFFED VEAL ROLLS
[Speed cook; 5 minutes]

12 slices veal, each 3 inches by 1 inch and ½ inch thick, flattened very thinly between sheets of waxed paper
12 very thin slices prosciutto or ham, each 3 inches by 1 inch
12 very thin slices mozzarella cheese, each 2 inches by 1 inch, chilled
½ cup flour
1 teaspoon salt
½ teaspoon pepper
2 tablespoons butter
1 tablespoon olive oil
2 garlic cloves, cut into halves
¼ cup Marsala

On each slice of veal place a slice of ham, then top with a slice of mozzarella. Roll up, like a miniature jelly roll. Pinion with toothpicks to keep the ham and cheese firmly encased. Blend the flour, salt and pepper and dredge the veal rolls in the mixture; shake off any excess flour. In a glass casserole, in the center of the oven, heat the butter and oil, and cook the garlic one minute. Add the veal rolls, arranging them in a circular pattern. Cook 2 minutes, turning the veal over at one minute. Pour in the wine. Cover. Cook 2 minutes, turning the rolls at one minute. Let set, covered, 5 minutes. Test for tenderness. These are delicate little morsels that should not be overcooked. *Serves 4.*

SWISS VEAL
[Speed-cook; 7 minutes]

This delicious offering may well be the national dish of Switzerland. It's a great party dish that few of your guests will ever have eaten.

    4 tablespoons butter
    2 tablespoons cooking oil
    2½ pounds veal from the leg, cut into strips 2 inches by
       1 inch and ¼ inch thick
    2 small white onions, finely chopped
    ⅓ cup dry white wine
    1 cup heavy cream
    1 tablespoon cornstarch dissolved in 2 tablespoons
       water
    Juice of ½ lemon
    Salt and pepper to taste

In a skillet on a conventional stove, or in a preheated browning skillet, heat half the butter and oil and brown the veal. In a glass casserole, cook the onions in the remaining butter and oil under microwaves 2 minutes, or until soft. Stir in the wine. Cook 2 minutes. Stir in the cream. Cook 2 minutes. Stir in the veal strips, cornstarch, lemon juice, salt and pepper. Cook one minute. Stir. Let set, covered, 10 minutes. Test for tenderness and seasoning. *Serves 4 to 6.*

RAGOUT OF VEAL
[Speed-cook; 14 minutes]

    1½ pounds veal shoulder, cut into 1½-inch cubes
    Salt and pepper to taste
    3 tablespoons butter
    1 tablespoon cooking oil
    8 small white onions, root ends scored
    One 10½-ounce can condensed cream of mushroom soup
    Pinch of rosemary
    8 medium mushrooms, cut into quarters
    1 cup sour cream

Lightly season the veal with salt and pepper. In a glass casserole, in the center of the oven, heat the butter and oil. Add the veal. Cook 3 minutes, turning the meat at 1½ minutes. Add the onions. Cook 2 minutes. Stir in the soup and rosemary. Cover. Cook 3 minutes. Rotate casserole half a turn. Cook 3 minutes. Stir in the mushrooms. Cook, uncovered, 2 minutes. Stir in the sour cream. Cook one minute. Stir. Let set, covered, 10 minutes. Test for tenderness and seasoning. *Serves 4.*

Lamb

LESBOS LAMB MEATBALLS
[Speed-cook; 14 minutes]

We spent two pleasant months on this little-known Greek island of Lesbos, dining on little-known lamb dishes and literally nothing else. This was a favorite and was served over rice.

>   2 pounds lean lamb shoulder, ground
>   ½ cup bread crumbs
>   2 eggs, beaten
>   3 tablespoons coarsely chopped pine nuts
>   3 tablespoons finely chopped fresh parsley
>   2 ounces dry red wine
>   1½ teaspoons salt
>   ½ teaspoon pepper
>   ¼ teaspoon ground cumin
>   2 tablespoons butter
>   1 tablespoon cooking oil
>   3 small white onions, finely chopped
>   1 small cucumber, peeled, seeded and diced
>   3 tablespoons chili sauce
>   ½ cup dry red wine

In a bowl thoroughly mix the lamb, bread crumbs, eggs, pine nuts, parsley, 2 ounces wine, the salt, pepper and cumin. Shape into firm meatballs no more than 1½ inches in diameter. In a skillet on a conventional stove, or in a preheated browning skillet, brown the meatballs. Set aside. In a glass casserole heat the butter and oil and cook the onions 2 minutes, or until soft. Add the meatballs, any liquid in their skillet, the cucumber, chili sauce and ½ cup wine. Stir well. Cook, uncovered, 6 minutes. Turn the meatballs. Cook 6 minutes. Let set, covered, 5 minutes. *Serves 4 to 6.*

MIDDLE-EASTERN MEAT LOAF
[Speed-cook; 15 minutes]

1½ pounds ground lamb
½ cup bread crumbs
1 egg, beaten
4 whole scallions, finely chopped
2 large pimientoes, coarsely chopped
¼ cup minced Italian parsley
1 small naval orange, peeled and seeded; membranes removed; diced
Juice of ½ small lemon
1 teaspoon salt
½ teaspoon pepper
¼ teaspoon ground cumin
Pinch of cinnamon

Place all the ingredients in a large bowl and mix well. Butter a glass loaf dish. Spoon in the lamb mixture evenly; do not pack it down. Do not let ends taper down, or they will cook faster and dry out. Cook, uncovered, in the center of the oven 15 minutes. Rotate half a turn every 5 minutes. Let set, covered, 10 minutes. *Serves 4.*

LAMB CHOPS IN MUSHROOM SAUCE
[Speed-cook; 16 minutes]

Four 1½-inch-thick loin lamb chops
Salt and pepper to taste
1 teaspoon dried oregano
2 tablespoons butter
¾ pound fresh mushrooms, coarsely chopped
1 tablespoon flour
3 tablespoons dry red wine
½ cup beef gravy (canned or your own)
2 tablespoons finely chopped roasted unsalted peanuts

Sprinkle the chops lightly with salt and pepper. Sprinkle the oregano over them. In a glass casserole, in the center of the oven, melt the butter, add the mushrooms, and cook one minute. Sprinkle the mushrooms with the flour and stir. Stir in the wine and gravy. Cook 3 minutes, stirring after each minute. Arrange the chops in one layer, with thicker parts near the edge of the dish, in the casserole. Spoon the mushroom sauce over them. Cook 4 minutes. Rotate the casserole half a turn. Cook 4 minutes. Turn the chops over and spoon the sauce over them. Sprinkle with the chopped peanuts. Cook, covered, 4 minutes. Let set, covered, 5 minutes. Test for tenderness and seasoning. *Serves 4.*

LAMB CAKE WITH CURRANT JELLY SAUCE
[Speed-cook; 15 minutes]

1½ pounds ground lean lamb
 2 tablespoons chopped bacon
 1 cup bread crumbs
 1 large onion, chopped
 2 small eggs, beaten
 2 tablespoons coarsely chopped pine nuts
 1 tablespoon chopped fresh parsley
1½ teaspoon salt
 ½ teaspoon poultry seasoning
 2 tablespoons dry red wine
 ½ cup currant jelly
 2 tablespoons water
 1 teaspoon Dijon mustard

In a bowl mix well the lamb, bacon, bread crumbs, onion, eggs, pine nuts, parsley, salt, poultry seasoning and wine. Butter a glass loaf dish. Spoon the mixture into it evenly. Do not pack it down. Don't let the ends taper down, or they will cook faster and dry out. Cook in the center of the oven 15 minutes, rotating the dish half a turn every 5 minutes. Let set, covered, 15 minutes. Place the currant jelly, water and mustard in a small glass bowl or measuring cup. Bring to a boil. Stir well. Pass the hot sauce at the table with the sliced lamb loaf. *Serves 4 to 6.*

LAMB BLANQUETTE
[Speed-cook; 28 minutes]

This is a simple country dish, usually served once a week in French homes. Don't let the list of ingredients discourage you. It is a simple dish to prepare, and a dazzler. Few Americans know it. It can also be prepared with veal, pork, or breast of chicken. We like the delicate flavor of lamb.

  2 pounds boneless leg of lamb, cut into 1-inch cubes
  2 cups boiling water
  2 small white onions, each stuck with a whole clove
  1 carrot, cut into ⅛-inch slices
  1 celery rib, cut into ½-inch slices
  1 small bay leaf
  ½ teaspoon caraway seeds
  ¼ teaspoon dried thyme
  ¼ teaspoon dried marjoram
  2 cups boiling beef broth
  1 teaspoon salt
 12 small fresh mushroom caps
 12 small white onions, root ends scored
  ¼ cup butter
  ¼ cup flour
  ⅓ cup heavy cream
  2 ounces Madeira
  Juice of ½ lemon
  Salt and pepper to taste

Place the lamb in a deep glass casserole. Pour the boiling water over it and cook in the center of the oven 2 minutes. Drain the lamb and rinse it with warm water, then return it to the casserole along with the 2 onions stuck with cloves, carrots, celery, bay leaf, caraway seeds, thyme, marjoram, beef broth and salt. Cover the casserole and cook 15 minutes, rotating the casserole half a turn every 5 minutes. Remove the lamb and strain the liquid. Return lamb to the casserole. In a glass bowl, in ¼ cup of the liquid the lamb cooked in, cook the mushrooms 2 minutes. Remove them with a slotted spoon and add them to the casserole. Using the liquid that you cooked the mushrooms in, cook the 12 small onions 5 minutes. Remove with a slotted spoon, adding them to the casserole. In a separate glass casserole, melt the butter, stir in the flour and blend into a smooth paste. Using the liquid the vegetables cooked in plus about 2 cups of the remaining liquid, make a medium-thick sauce, cooking about 2 minutes, stirring every 30 seconds. Stir in the cream, wine and lemon juice. Blend well. Season with salt and pepper. Add the lamb cubes, mushrooms and onions. Stir. Cook 2 minutes, or until simmering. Stir gently and serve with rice or noodles. *Serves 4 to 6.*

LAMB SHANKS IN WINE
[Speed-cook, 30 minutes; slo-cook, 60 minutes]

These are meaty, tasty, inexpensive cuts of lamb favored in the Middle Eastern countries, but mainly overlooked here.

    4 lamb shanks, each large enough for 1 serving
    Salt and pepper to taste
    Flour for dredging
    2 tablespoons butter
    2 tablespoons cooking oil
    2 garlic cloves
    4 small carrots, scraped and diced
    3 celery ribs, scraped and diced
    2 medium-size white onions, chopped
    1 cup dry red wine
    1 cup fresh or defrosted frozen peas

Season the lamb shanks with salt and pepper and dredge them with flour. Heat the butter and oil in a glass casserole. Add the lamb shanks and garlic, the thicker parts of the shanks near the edge of the dish. To speed-cook, cook in the center of the oven 3 minutes. Turn the shanks. Cook 3 minutes. Cover the casserole. Cook 5 minutes. Turn the shanks. Stir in the carrots, celery and onions; cook 5 minutes. Turn the shanks. Stir in the wine and cook 5 minutes. Rotate the casserole half a turn. Cook 4 minutes. Stir in the peas. Remove the lid and cook 5 minutes. Let set, covered, 15 minutes. Test for tenderness and seasoning. If these are shanks from a sheep, not a lamb, you may have to finish under microwaves for another 4 minutes. Stir the sauce and spoon it over the lamb when serving. To slo-cook, rotate the dish half a turn every 10 minutes, turning the shanks in the middle of the cooking time. *Serves 4.*

FARIKAL LAMB AND CABBAGE
[Speed-cook, 25 minutes; slo-cook, 50 minutes]

This is a favorite Norwegian dish we first had while sailing along that country's coast on the way to the fjord country. It is heavy on pepper and personality.

1½ pounds lean lamb from the shoulder or leg, cut into ¾-inch cubes
1 large head cabbage (Savoy is best), cut into 1-inch cubes
1½ teaspoons caraway seeds
1 teaspoon salt
1½ teaspoons pepper
¼ cup flour
¾ cup water
¾ cup dry white wine

In a glass casserole, arrange alternating layers of cabbage and lamb cubes, sprinkling the caraway seeds, salt, pepper and flour over each layer, and finishing with a layer of cabbage. Place the water and wine in a glass bowl or cup. Bring to a boil under the microwaves. Pour over the cabbage and lamb. Cover the casserole tightly. Speed-cook in the center of the oven 25 minutes, rotating the casserole a fourth of a turn every 5 minutes. If you slo-cook, rotate a fourth of a turn every 10 minutes. Let set, covered, 20 minutes. Test for tenderness. *Serves 4 to 6.*

QUICK THICK LAMB CHOPS
[Speed-cook; 4 minutes]

Lamb chops such as these are a luxury. The browning skillet plus the microwave oven insure that they will be cooked to perfection. Nearly everyone overcooks these meaty masterpieces. Classically, they should be pink when served.

Four 2-inch-thick loin lamb chops, trimmed of most fat, at room temperature
Pepper to taste
1 tablespoon cooking oil
3 garlic cloves, cut in halves
Salt to taste

Sprinkle the lamb chops with pepper. Preheat the 9½-inch browning skillet 4½ minutes. Add the cooking oil and garlic. Cook the chops 2 minutes. Pour off any liquid in the skillet. Turn the chops. Cook 2 minutes. Let set, covered, 5 minutes. Test for tenderness. Sprinkle lightly with salt. If you want them less pink, give them another 15 seconds on each side. Careful, however, as these chops can be overcooked almost at the blink of an eye. *Serves 4.*

DUBLIN LAMB STEW
[Speed-cook, 30 minutes; slo-cook, 1 hour]

6 medium poatoes, cut into ½-inch-thick slices
6 medium-size white onions, cut into ¼-inch-thick slices
2 pounds lean lamb, preferably from the leg, cut into ¾-inch cubes
Salt and pepper to taste
1½ cups beef broth
2 tablespoons chopped fresh parsley

In a large glass casserole, place alternating layers of potatoes, onions and lamb, seasoning each layer lightly with salt and pepper, and finishing with a layer of potatoes. In a glass bowl, bring the beef broth to a simmer. Pour it over the lamb and vegetables, then sprinkle with parsley. Cover the cassrole tightly. To speed-cook: Cook in the center of the oven 10 minutes. Rotate the dish half a turn. Cook 10 minutes. Rotate half a turn. Cook, uncovered, 10 minutes. Let set, covered, 10 minutes. Test for tenderness and seasoning. To slo-cook: Rotate a fourth of a turn every 15 minutes. *Serves 6.*

SIMPLE CALCUTTA LAMB CURRY
[Speed-cook, 30 minutes; slo-cook, 1 hour]

Most of us don't do enough with curried dishes. Why? Stage fright at the last moment, afraid that they may be too "hot," worried that guests won't like them? Curry is pleasing and isn't difficult. We find that mixing our own curry powder, as we learned in India, gives a much more sparkling flavor. By using microwaves, you'll save at least an hour in cooking time on this dish. Use part of that saved time to make your own curry powder. You'll never go back to the commercial mixtures.

3 pounds boneless leg of lamb, cut into 1-inch cubes
Salt to taste
2 tablespoons butter
2 tablespoons cooking oil
1 cup chopped onions
2 garlic cloves, minced
1 medium apple, peeled, cored and chopped
2 tablespoons flour
2 tablespoons Curry Powder (page 153)
1 cup chicken broth
⅓ cup dry white wine
2 medium tomatoes, peeled, seeded and chopped
2 tablespoons heavy cream

Lightly sprinkle the lamb cubes with salt. In a glass casserole, in the center of the oven, heat the butter and oil. Add the lamb. To speed-cook: Cook 2 minutes, turning the lamb. Add the onions and garlic. Cook 3 minutes, or until onions are soft. Stir in the apple and sprinkle in the flour and Curry Powder, mixing well with the lamb and onions. Cook 5 minutes, stirring in the chicken broth at 2½ minutes. Stir in the wine and tomatoes. Bring to a simmer. Stir well. Cover the casserole and cook 10 minutes. Rotate half a turn. Cook 10 minutes. Stir. Let set, covered, 20 minutes. To slo-cook: Rotate a fourth of a turn every 10 minutes, stir-ring each time. Test for tenderness and seasoning. Stir in the heavy cream just before serving. If not hot enough, place under the microwaves until just simmering. Serve immediately. Rice is a must. *Serves 4 to 6.*

Curry Powder

2 teaspoons ground coriander
2 teaspoons ground cumin
1 teaspoon ground cardamom
1 teaspoon ground turmeric
½ teaspoon ground ginger
¼ teaspoon ground black pepper
Pinch of ground hot red pepper

In a bowl, blend all the ingredients thoroughly.

STUFFED LAMB SHOULDER, ITALIAN STYLE
[Speed-cook; 24 minutes]

2 small white onions, chopped
1 celery rib, scraped and chopped
2 garlic cloves, minced
2 tablespoons butter
One 3½-pound boned shoulder of lean lamb
6 slices dry crustless bread, crumbled
1 tablespoon chopped currants
1 tablespoon chopped fresh parsley
3 tablespoons grated Parmesan cheese
1 large egg, beaten
½ teaspoon salt
½ teaspoon pepper
1 garlic clove put through a garlic press and mixed with 1 tablespoon olive oil

Sauté the first three ingredients in the butter until soft. Spread the boned lamb flat, skin side down. In a bowl, blend the bread, sautéed vegetables, currants, parsley, cheese, egg, salt and pepper. Spoon the stuffing onto the lamb, spreading it evenly. Carefully roll up into a compact package; tie well with string to contain the stuffing. Try to do this evenly, so that the ends are not narrow or tapering; microwaves will dry them out. Rub the stuffed shoulder well with the garlic-and-oil mixture. Sprinkle with more pepper. Place on an inverted saucer in a large glass casserole. Cook in the center of the oven, uncovered, 12 minutes, rotating the casserole a fourth of a turn every 4 minutes. Turn the lamb shoulder over. Baste the lamb and spoon or siphon off all liquid. Cook 12 minutes, rotating a fourth of a turn every 4 minutes. Let set, covered, 15 minutes. Test for tenderness. *Serves 4 to 6.*

ROAST MARINATED LEG OF LAMB
[Speed-cook; 25 minutes]

Tired of the old way of serving leg of lamb? Here's a tastebud treat that will sharpen your respect for that old reliable main course.

　　One 4-pound leg of lamb
　2 garlic cloves, each cut into 4 slivers
　2 cups dry red wine
　½ cup olive oil
　2 small carrots, sliced
　1 celery rib, sliced
　1 large onion, sliced
　2 whole garlic cloves
　1 clove
　1 small bay leaf
　1 tablespoon salt
　½ teaspoon pepper
　1½ teaspoons dried oregano
　⅛ teaspoon ground cumin

About 10 to 11 hours before you wish to serve the lamb, cut 8 small slits in it with a sharp knife and insert the garlic slivers. In a large bowl, blend the remaining ingredients. Add the lamb, turning it several times. Cover the bowl and marinate the lamb in the refrigerator 6 hours, turning it four times. Remove from the refrigerator and continue to marinate, at room temperature, 4 hours. Drain and dry the lamb. Cover the bone end with a small piece of aluminum foil. Place the lamb, fat side down, on an inverted plate or saucer in a glass casserole. Cook, uncovered, in the center of the oven 10 minutes. Turn the lamb over and baste it with the pan juices. Spoon or siphon off with a bulb baster all of the liquid in the casserole. Cook the lamb 10 minutes, turn it over, baste with the juices and spoon or baste off all remaining liquid. Cook 5 minutes. Let set, covered, 15 minutes. Test for tenderness. This lamb should be slightly pink, which is classic. If you like it less rare, adjust the cooking time to your taste. *Serves 6 to 8.*

Pork

BERLIN CARAWAY MEATBALLS
[Speed-cook; 13 minutes]

These meatballs, with a Germanic flavor all their own, could be a family and company main-dish hit.

    1 cup sour cream
    3 tablespoons flour
    2 teaspoons caraway seeds
    2 pounds lean pork, ground
    1 cup bread crumbs
    2 eggs, beaten
    ½ cup milk
    1½ tablespoons chopped fresh parsley
    1½ teaspoons salt
    ½ teaspoon pepper
    ¼ teaspoon Bell's poultry seasoning
    1 medium onion, chopped
    2 tablespoons butter
    6 medium mushrooms, sliced
    ½ cup beef broth

Blend the first three ingredients in a bowl and set aside. In a separate bowl, mix well the pork, bread crumbs, eggs, milk, parsley, salt, pepper and poultry seasoning. Shape into 1½-inch meatballs. In a skillet on a conventional stove, or in a preheated browning skillet, brown the meatballs evenly. In a deep glass casserole, in the center of the oven, cook the onion in the butter one minute, or until soft, stirring after 45 seconds. Stir in the mushrooms, cook one minute, stirring after 30 seconds. Stir in the beef broth and meatballs. Cover the casserole and cook 10 minutes, stirring; rotate the dish half a turn after 5 minutes. Stir in the sour cream mixture and cook one minute, or until simmering. Stir and let set, covered, 10 minutes. Serve the meatballs in their sauce. *Serves 6.*

FRICADELLE FLAMANDE
[Speed-cook; 20 minutes]

Here's a novel pork meatball dish from our cooking mentor, the great French chef Antoine Gilly, proving that chefs are not always complicated.

       3 small white onions, chopped
       2 garlic cloves, minced
         Butter for sautéeing
       2 eggs, separated
       2 pounds lean pork, ground
       1 cup bread crumbs
       ½ teaspoon nutmeg
      1½ teaspoons salt
       ½ teaspoon pepper
       3 tablespoons butter
      24 small white onions, root ends scored
       6 medium potatoes, peeled and trimmed into the size
         and shape of eggs
      1½ cups chicken broth
       ½ cup dry white wine
       ½ cup chopped fresh parsley

Sauté the chopped onions and garlic in butter until soft. Beat the egg yolks; beat the egg whites until stiff. In a large bowl mix well the pork, bread crumbs, egg yolks, sautéed onions and garlic, the nutmeg, salt and pepper. Mix in the beaten egg whites. Form meatballs the size and shape of an egg. On a conventional stove, or in a preheated browning skillet, brown the meatballs in the

3 tablespoons of butter. Transfer to a deep glass casserole and arrange the whole onions and the potatoes around them. Pour in the chicken broth and wine. The liquid should only half cover the meatballs and vegetables. Cover. Cook in the center of the oven 10 minutes, rotating the casserole half a turn after 5 minutes. Turn the meatballs and vegetables over. Cook, uncovered, 5 minutes. Rotate half a turn. Cook 5 minutes, or until the vegetables are tender. Let set, covered, 15 minutes. Drain off the cooking liquid before serving. Sprinkle the meatballs with the parsley and serve with the vegetables. Pass a good, sharp mustard. *Serves 6.*

BRAISED PORK CHOPS
[Speed-cook; 14 minutes]

1 white onion, minced
1 small garlic clove, minced
½ cup chicken broth
3 tablespoons lemon juice
3 tablespoons chili sauce
1 tablespoon Worcestershire sauce
1 teaspoon Dijon mustard
½ teaspoon salt
½ teaspoon pepper
Four ¾-inch-thick pork chops

Eight hours before you plan to cook the pork chops, mix thoroughly all ingredients except the pork chops in a flat-bottomed dish. Add the chops, turning to coat both sides with the marinade. Marinate in the refrigerator 6 hours, then at room temperature 2 hours, turning several times. Remove the chops and drain, scraping off the onion and garlic, and dry. Reserve the marinade. In a skillet on a conventional stove, or in a browning skillet, brown the chops evenly on both sides. Arrange in a glass casserole just large enough to hold them in one layer, the thicker parts of the chops near the edge of the dish. Pour the marinade into a glass bowl. Bring to a simmer in the oven. Pour over the chops. Cook in the center of the oven, tightly covered, 7 minutes.

Turn the chops. Rotate the casserole half a turn. Cook 7 minutes. Turn the chops. Let set, covered, 15 minutes. Test for tenderness. *Serves 4.*

PORK CHOPS À LA BOULANGÈRE
[Speed-cook, 15 minutes; slo-cook, 30 minutes]

This unusually tasty dish, named for the local baker's wife, is served weekly in many French villages. In France, bread is baked twice a day, morning and late afternoon. When the afternoon baking is finished and the wood-burning stove is still hot, the housewives arrive at the bakery with their covered casseroles. For a small fee, the baker's wife slides them into her husband's idle oven on the wooden paddle. Microwaves do the job almost as well.

A trick from the French housewife: Leaving the bone in for flavor, pound the chops lightly around the bone with the edge of a heavy saucer or a meat mallet. This somewhat tenderizes and flattens the chops, which will return to near their original thickness while cooking.

Four 1-inch-thick loin pork chops
4 small potatoes, cut in halves
8 small white onions, root ends scored
2 garlic cloves, cut in halves
1½ cups hot chicken broth
1 teaspoon salt
½ teaspoon pepper
⅛ teaspoon dried thyme

Pound the pork chops lightly. In a skillet on a conventional stove, or in a preheated browning skillet, brown the chops evenly. In a glass casserole, place the browned chops in one layer, the thicker parts near the edge of the dish. Arrange the potatoes, onions and garlic in an outer circle around the chops. Pour in the chicken broth and sprinkle with the salt, pepper and thyme. To speed-cook: Cook in the center of the oven, covered, 5 minutes. Rotate the dish half a turn. Cook 5 minutes. Turn the chops and vegetables over. Cook, uncovered, 5 minutes, rotating half a turn at 2½ minutes. Let set, covered, 10 minutes. To slo-cook: Rotate the dish half a turn every 5 minutes. Turn the chops and vegetables at 15 minutes, and let set, covered, 10 minutes. Test for tenderness. *Serves 4.*

Variations: This dish can be interestingly varied by substituting veal chops, chicken pieces or Italian sausage for the pork chops.

PORK CHOPS IN SOUR CREAM
[Speed-cook; 18 minutes]

    1 cup bread crumbs
    1 teaspoon salt
    ½ teaspoon pepper
    ⅜ teaspoon dried thyme
    Four 1-inch-thick pork chops
    Flour for dredging
    2 eggs beaten with 2 tablespoons cream
    1 cup chicken broth
    2 tablespoons wine vinegar
    ½ tablespoon sugar
    1 small bay leaf
    ½ cup sour cream

Blend the first four ingredients. Coat the chops with flour, dip into the eggs, then dredge with the seasoned bread crumbs. In a skillet on a conventional stove, or in a browning skillet, brown the chops evenly. Place them in a large glass casserole in one layer, thicker parts near the edge of the dish. In a glass bowl, blend the chicken broth, wine vinegar and sugar. Add the bay leaf and bring to a simmer in the oven. Stir and pour over the chops in the casserole. Cover the casserole tightly. Cook in the center of the oven 10 minutes. Turn the chops over and rotate the dish half a turn. Cover and cook 7 minutes. Transfer the chops to a warm serving platter. Cover and let set 10 minutes. Test for tenderness. Remove the bay leaf from the casserole, stir in the sour cream and cook one minute, or until hot. Do not boil. Serve over the chops. *Serves 4.*

CANTON PORK CHOPS
[Speed-cook; 10 minutes]

4 whole scallions, chopped
2 garlic cloves, minced
1½ teaspoons brown sugar
⅓ cup soy sauce
2 tablespoons dry sherry
⅛ teaspoon Tabasco sauce
½ teaspoon monosodium glutamate
Four ¾-inch-thick loin pork chops, trimmed of most fat
2 tablespoons peanut oil

In a flat-bottomed dish, mix the scallions, garlic, brown sugar, Tabasco sauce, soy sauce, sherry and monosodium glutamate. Place the chops in the marinade, turning to coat both sides. Let them stand at room temperature 3 hours, turning several times during that time. Remove the chops from the marinade. Reserve the marinade. Dry the chops. Preheat the 9½-inch browning skillet 4½ minutes. Add the peanut oil. Place the chops in the skillet in one layer, the thicker parts near the edge of the pan, and cook 3 minutes. Pour off any liquid in the pan; turn the chops over and cook 3 minutes. Pour the marinade over the browned chops. Cover the skillet. Cook 4 minutes. Let set, covered, 10 minutes. Test for tenderness. *Serves 4.*

BROCCOLI AND SLICED PORK, CHINESE STYLE
[Speed-cook; 8 minutes]

⅓ cup light brown sugar
⅓ cup dry sherry
⅓ cup soy sauce
1 teaspoon monosodium glutamate
1 bunch (about 1½ pounds) fresh broccoli
⅓ cup peanut oil
½ teaspoon salt
3 thin slices fresh ginger, shredded
2 garlic cloves, minced
1 pound pork loin, cut into strips 2 by ½ by ¼ inch

In a bowl, blend the first four ingredients and set aside. Cut the flowerets off the broccoli and cut in half if large. Peel the stems and cut them into ⅛-inch diagonal slices. In a glass casserole, pour the peanut oil. Sprinkle in the salt. Add the ginger and garlic. Cook one minute, stirring after each 30 seconds. Stir in the pork . Cook 1½ minutes. Turn the pork. Cook 1½ minutes. Stir in the broccoli. Cook 1½ minutes, stirring after each 45 seconds. Add the brown sugar-sherry-soy sauce mixture. Stir well. Cook 2½ minutes to heat the sauce through, stirring at one minute. Let set, covered, 10 minutes. Test for tenderness. The meat should be tender; the broccoli, crunchy. *Serves 4.*

STUFFED PORK CHOPS
[Speed-cook; 10 minutes]

The object here is to get nice loin chops and fill them with an interesting stuffing. You can use prepared stuffings; some of them are good, but your own will be better.

    1 small white onion, minced
    1 celery rib, minced
    1 tablespoon butter
    1 cup bread crumbs
    2 prunes, finely chopped
    1 tablespoon chopped fresh parsley
    ½ teaspoon salt
    ¼ teaspoon pepper
    ¼ teaspoon dried basil
    ½ teaspoon Bell's poultry seasoning
    9 tablespoons chicken broth
    Four 1-inch-thick boned loin pork chops

Sauté the onion and celery in the butter until soft. Combine in a bowl with the remaining ingredients except the chicken broth and pork chops and mix well. Gradually add 5 tablespoons of the broth. Divide the stuffing into four portions. With a sharp knife, cut a deep pocket into the side of each chop and fill with the stuffing. Close the cavity with toothpicks. Lightly sprinkle both sides of the chops with salt and pepper. In a skillet on a conventional stove, or in a preheated browning skillet, brown the chops on both sides. Place them in a large glass casserole in a single layer, thicker parts near the edge of the casserole. Pour in the remaining chicken broth. Cover tightly. Cook in the center of the oven 5 minutes. Turn the chops. Cook, uncovered, 5 minutes. Let set, covered, 10 minutes. Test for tenderness. Baste well with the sauce in the casserole, spooning it over the chops just before serving. *Serves 4.*

PORK FROM HEAVEN
[Speed-cook; 17 minutes]

In Germany's Silesia this is called "heavenly pork" or "pork from heaven," depending upon the translation. You can be sure of one thing: It is a unique dish.

> 1 pound mixed dried fruit (apples, pears, pitted apricots and prunes, etc.)
> Port wine (optional)
> 1½ pounds pork shoulder, cut into 1-inch cubes
> Salt and pepper to taste
> 2 tablespoons butter
> 1 tablespoon cooking oil
> 2 tablespoons cornstarch
> 1 clove
> 1 teaspoon brown sugar

Soak the fruit in water as suggested on the package. (If you want to get fancy and give yourself and your guests a new taste delight, soak the fruit in a mixture of half water and half port wine.) Drain the fruit, reserving one cup of the liquid. Sprinkle the pork lightly with salt and pepper. In a skillet on a conventional stove, or in a preheated browning skillet, brown the pork cubes evenly in the butter and oil. Transfer the pork to a glass casserole. Arrange the drained fruit around the meat. In a glass dish or bowl, blend the cornstarch with the reserved cup of liquid the fruit soaked in and cook in the center of the oven 2 minutes, stirring every 30 seconds. Stir in the clove and brown sugar. Bring to a simmer. Pour the sauce over the pork and fruit. Cover the casserole tightly. Cook in the center of the oven 5 minutes. Stir. Cook 5 minutes. Stir. Cook 5 minutes. Let set, covered, 15 minutes. Test for tenderness and seasoning. *Serves 4.*

DANISH PORK TENDERLOIN
[Speed-cook; 16 minutes]

Beef fillets, or tenderloins, are popular, but few of us experiment with those tender nuggets of pork also called tenderloins. This team prefers them to beef. So do the Scandinavians, who have a masterful hand with them. We cook these tender slices in the browning skillet.

½ cup flour
1 teaspoon salt
½ teaspoon pepper
Pinch of rosemary
1½ pounds pork tenderloin, cut into ½-inch-thick slices (allow at least 2 slices for each serving)
2 tablespoons butter
1 tablespoon cooking oil
1 medium-size white onion, thinly sliced
½ cup dry white wine
8 medium mushrooms, thinly sliced
4 large stuffed green olives, sliced
2 tablespoons lemon juice

Blend the first four ingredients and use to dredge the pork slices. Preheat a 9½-inch browning skillet 4½ minutes. Heat half the butter and oil and cook half the pork slices one minute on each side, or until brown. Pour off any liquid or fat in the skillet, dry with a paper towel and preheat 2½ minutes. Brown the remaining pork slices in the remaining butter and oil. Remove the pork. Add the onion to the skillet and cook one minute, or until soft. Pour in the wine. Cook 3 minutes, or just until it simmers. Add the mushrooms and the browned pork slices. Cover the skillet. Cook 3 minutes. Turn the pork slices. Cook 3 minutes. Stir in the olives and lemon juice. Cook 2 minutes. Let set, covered, 10 minutes. Test for tenderness and seasoning. *Serves 4.*

POACHED PORK LOIN
[Speed-cook; 21 minutes]

We'll bet that few of your guests (or even you!) ever have eaten this. Fried, roasted, stewed, broiled—but rarely do we find poached pork in any home or on any menu. This may well be the tastiest of all.

One 3-pound boned loin of pork, tied
1 white onion, cut into halves
2 garlic cloves, cut into halves
2 small carrots, cut into quarters
2 celery ribs, cut into quarters
2 whole cloves
1 small bay leaf
⅛ teaspoon dried thyme
1½ teaspoons salt
⅛ teaspoon pepper
⅛ cup dry white wine
1 cup boiling chicken broth

In a deep glass casserole, just wide enough to hold the pork loin, place the pork, vegetables, herbs, seasonings and wine. Pour in enough boiling chicken broth, to reach halfway up the loin. Cook, covered, in the center of the oven 7 minutes, rotating the dish half a turn. Cook 7 minutes. Turn the pork over. Cook 7 minutes. Let set, covered, 20 minutes. Test for tenderness. Serve either hot or cold, cut into thin slices. *Serves 4 to 6.*

DEVILED HAM
[Speed-cook; 8 minutes]

⅛ cup light brown sugar
⅛ cup butter, softened
1½ teaspoons Coleman's dry mustard
¼ cup hot water
One 2-pound, 1-inch-thick precooked center-cut ham steak
⅛ cup milk

In a bowl, blend the brown sugar, butter, mustard and water. Place the ham in a glass casserole just large enough to hold it. Spread the brown sugar mixture over the ham. Pour the milk around it. Cook in the center of the oven 4 minutes. Rotate the dish half a turn. Cook 4 minutes. Let set, covered, 10 minutes. Test for tenderness. Yams or sweet potatoes baked in the microwave oven are excellent with this. They can be cooked while the ham is "setting." *Serves 4 to 6.*

HAM LOAF WITH MUSTARD SAUCE
[Speed-cook; 16 minutes]

2 medium onions, minced
1 garlic clove, minced
2 tablespoons butter
2½ pounds lean precooked ham, ground
Pepper to taste
2 eggs, beaten
1 cup bread crumbs
½ cup light cream
Brown sugar
1 teaspoon dry mustard
Mustard Sauce (below)

In a glass dish, in the center of the oven, cook the onions and garlic in the butter 2 minutes, or until they are soft. In that dish, mix the onions and garlic in their butter with the remaining ingredients except the brown sugar and dry mustard. Spoon the mixture evenly into a buttered glass loaf pan, making certain that the ends do not taper down, as they could dry out. Cover the loaf with a light layer of brown sugar and sprinkle with the dry mustard. Cook in the center of the oven 7 minutes. Rotate the dish half a turn. Cook 7 minutes. Let set, covered, 10 minutes. Make the Mustard Sauce while the ham is setting, and pass it at the table with the ham loaf. *Serves 6 to 8.*

Mustard Sauce

1 cup heavy cream, whipped
¼ cup Dijon mustard
Pinch of dry mustard
½ cup mayonnaise

Blend the ingredients into a smooth sauce.

RED HAM LOAF WITH HORSERADISH SAUCE
[Speed-cook; 15 minutes]

1 medium onion, finely chopped
1 celery rib, scraped and finely chopped
2 tablespoons butter
1 pound lean ham, ground
½ pound lean pork, ground
½ cup bread crumbs
½ teaspoon dry mustard
⅛ teaspoon pepper
1 egg, beaten
One 10½-ounce can condensed tomato soup
2 teaspoons prepared horseradish

In a glass dish, in the center of the oven, cook the onion and celery in the butter 2 minutes, or until they are soft. In a bowl, mix thoroughly the onion, celery, ham, pork, bread crumbs, mustard pepper, egg and half the tomato soup. Spoon the mixture evenly into a buttered glass loaf pan, making certain that the ends do not taper down, as they could dry out. Cook in the center of the oven 8 minutes. Rotate the pan half a turn Cook 5 minutes. Let set, covered, 10 minutes. Meanwhile, make a simple horseradish sauce: In a glass measuring cup mix the remaining soup with the horseradish. Cook until hot. Pass with the ham. *Serves 4 to 6.*

HAM MEDALLIONS WITH MADEIRA SAUCE
[Speed-cook; 6 minutes]

8 medallions precooked ham, 3 inches in diameter and ¼ inch thick
5 tablespoons butter
2 tablespoons flour
1 teaspoon Dijon mustard
¼ cup Madeira
¼ cup chicken broth
Pepper to taste
¼ cup heavy cream

In a preheated 9½-inch browning skillet, cook half the ham medallions in one tablespoon of the butter, 30 seconds on each side. Dry the skillet with a paper towel and cook the remaining ham slices in one tablespoon of the butter 30 seconds on each side. Transfer the ham to a serving dish and keep warm. In a glass bowl or large measuring cup, heat 2 tablespoons of the butter one minute, or until melted. Blend in the flour and mustard, stirring until you have a smooth paste. Stir in the wine and chicken broth and cook 2 minutes, stirring every 30 seconds until you have a smooth sauce. Stir in the pepper, cream, and remaining tablespoon of butter. Taste for seasoning. Spoon enough sauce over the ham in its serving dish to mask it well. Heat in the oven one minute, rotating the dish half a turn at 30 seconds. It should be just heated through. It is also effective to place the sauced ham under a conventional broiler until the sauce is golden. *Serves 4.*

SCALLOPED HAM WITH POTATOES
[Speed-cook; 20 minutes]

4 medium potatoes, peeled and sliced
¼ cup water
2 medium onions, finely chopped
3 tablespoons butter
3 tablespoons flour
2 cups milk
½ teaspoon pepper
3 cups diced ham
⅜ cup grated sharp cheddar cheese
1 tablespoon chopped fresh parsley

In a glass casserole, cook the potatoes in the water 8 minutes or until they are tender but crisp. Carefully stir at 4 minutes. Let set 5 minutes, then drain. In a glass bowl, cook the onions in the butter 3 minutes or until soft. Stir in the flour and blend well. Stir in the milk and pepper. Stirring after 2 minutes, cook in the center of the oven 4 minutes, or until you have a smooth sauce. In the casserole you cooked the potatoes in, arrange alternating layers of potatoes and ham, spooning the milk sauce over each layer. Sprinkle the cheese and parsley on top and cook in the oven 5 minutes, or until the cheese has melted and the sauce is bubbling. Let set, covered, 3 minutes. *Serves 4 to 6.*

HAM IN BEER
[Speed-cook; 16 minutes]

One 4-pound canned precooked ham (the Polish hams are excellent)
⅓ cup beer
¼ cup molasses
2 teaspoons Coleman's dry mustard
12 whole cloves

Score the ham on both sides and place it on an inverted saucer in a glass casserole just large enough to hold it. Blend the beer, molasses and mustard and brush the ham with the mixture. Cover loosely with waxed paper and cook in the center of the oven 8 minutes, rotating the casserole half a turn at 4 minutes. Siphon off any liquid in the casserole. Turn the ham over, brush with the sauce and stud with the cloves. Cover with waxed paper and cook 8 minutes, rotating half a turn at 4 minutes. Let set, covered, 20 minutes. *Serves 6 to 8.*

COOKING BACON

When we first saw a microwave oven demonstrated (and bought one) over eight years ago, a friend went along as a spectator. As is usual, and spectacular, the demonstrator cooked a slice of bacon on a piece of paper towel in one minute. Our friend, a bacon devotee of long standing, watched open-mouthed. To shorten the anecdote, he bought a microwave oven for the sole purpose of cooking bacon, and even today uses it for little else. Cooked conventionally, bacon can be a messy business, with the cooked result often disappointing.

Of the special utensils for cooking bacon in the microwave oven, the one we like best is a glass tray with a trivet that keeps the bacon out of its own grease. All you need do is place the bacon on it and cover it with a piece of paper towel. When the cooking is finished, pour the grease from the bottom of the tray. Bacon grease is excellent in many recipes, so this is a good gadget if you want to save it.

A couple of other points about bacon: There are dishes such as quiches that call for quite a lot of bacon. It must be cooked, drained of fat, then broken up. Microwaves do everything except break it up. The bacon is crisp in mere minutes. And there is no splattered stove to clean up.

Because the fat flows off the bacon onto the paper towel while the bacon is cooking, the cooked bacon is virtually fat-free. You merely have to blot it with a piece of paper towel. Thus, from a health standpoint (if you can use this criterion at all where bacon is concerned), the fat is cooked out of the bacon and you consume very little. And let's not forget the cleanup: You simply throw the paper towel away. How often have we cooked bacon, forgotten to discard the grease, then had the dickens of a job getting that cold bacon grease out of the pan.

We've probably overextended a little on bacon. But we thought if a friend would buy a microwave oven just to cook it, we could spare a few words about this American breakfast standby. And while we are at it, let us not forget that tasty summer favorite, the bacon, lettuce and tomato sandwich. With microwaves, you can have it in seconds.

Use a triple layer of paper towels in a glass dish. Place from one to four strips on the towels (we've found it more effective to cook no more than four strips at a time), then cover with a paper towel. If you must cook, perhaps, a half pound of bacon at one time, cut the strips in half and make layers, covering each with a paper towel.

Bacon cooked according to the following timing will be crisp; if you like it less crisp, time it according to your own taste.

   1 strip: 1 minute 15 seconds
   2 strips: 2 minutes 20 seconds
   4 strips: 4 minutes
24 half-slices: 6½ minutes

KIELBASA SAUSAGE WITH RED CABBAGE
[Speed-cook; 15 minutes]

This Polish sausage, three-fourths pork, one-fourth beef and lightly flavored with garlic, has become very popular. (See a tasty cocktail treat, Kielbasa Sausage Canapés, page 45). Called Duszone w Czerwonej Kapuscie, this recipe from Polish friends is a favorite of ours, and a unique party dish, as you can increase amounts (and cooking time) without problems.

1 small head red cabbage, shredded, blanched and drained (see note)
1 tablespoon white vinegar
2 tablespoons butter
2 tablespoons flour
1 cup dry red wine
1½ teaspoons Maggi liquid seasoning
½ teaspoon sugar
1 tablespoon lemon juice
Salt and pepper to taste
One 1-pound ring kielbasa sausage

Sprinkle the blanched cabbage with the vinegar. In a suitable glass casserole, in the center of the oven, melt the butter. Blend in the flour and slowly stir in the wine. Stirring every 30 seconds, cook 2 minutes or until you have a smooth sauce. Stir in the cabbage, Maggi, sugar and lemon juice, blending well. Season with salt and pepper. Cover the casserole and cook 4 minutes. Rotate the casserole half a turn and stir. Cook 4 minutes. Prick the sausage in several places with the sharp point of a knife. Push the cabbage aside, making a well and center the coiled sausage in the casserole. Cover and cook 5 minutes, rotating the dish half a turn at 2½ minutes and turning the sausage over. Let set, covered, 10 minutes. Test for tenderness. *Serves 4.*

NOTE: This main dish can be speeded up by using commercial precooked red cabbage, thereby eliminating the seasoning and cooking of the raw cabbage.

Variation: This recipe can be tastefully varied by substituting potatoes and small white onions for the cabbage and its seasonings, and chicken broth for the red wine. Eliminate the flour. Cook the sausage and vegetables together 10 minutes, rotating the dish half turn at 5 minutes and turning the sausage over at that point. This should also set, covered, 10 minutes.

LENTILS AND SAUSAGE SUPPER
[Speed-cook; 35 minutes 20 seconds]

This one, Lenticchie e Cotechino, *we found in Italy, in the Abruzzi. It could be the tastiest lentil dish ever created. This can be prepared ahead and reheated when ready to serve. Preparation on a conventional stove would take about 2 hours.*

> 2 cups dried lentils
> 1½ pounds cotechino sausage (a fine, garlicky Italian sausage) or a sausage of your choice
> 2 cups chicken broth
> 1 celery rib, scraped and chopped
> 2 small carrots, scraped and chopped
> 2 small white onions, minced
> 2 tablespoons olive oil
> 2 garlic cloves, chopped
> 2 sprigs fresh thyme or ¼ teaspoon dried
> Salt and pepper to taste
> 1 teaspoon sweet Hungarian paprika

Wash lentils well and soak them in cold water 2½ hours. Pierce the sausage in several places and place in a deep glass casserole, just large enough to hold it. Half cover with boiling water. Cover the casserole and cook in the center of the oven 5 minutes. Turn the sausage over and cook 5 minutes. Let the sausage set, covered, 10 minutes. Remove from the water and let cool. When cool enough to handle, peel off the skin and cut the sausage into ½-inch-thick slices.

Drain the lentils and place them in a deep casserole. Add the chicken broth, celery, carrots, half the onions, 1 tablespoon of the olive oil, the garlic, thyme, salt,

pepper and sausage slices. Cover the casserole and cook
in the center of the oven 20 minutes, rotating the dish
half a turn every 5 minutes.

In a glass pie plate, cook the remaining onions in
the remaining oil 2 minutes, or until soft. Stir in the
paprika and cook 20 seconds—no longer. If overcooked, paprika becomes bitter. Stir the onions and
paprika into the lentil casserole, cover, and let set one
hour.

When ready to serve, return the lentil casserole to the
center of the oven and cook 3 minutes, or until it is
simmering. Stir well. This is not a soup, but is thick
and should be eaten with a spoon. Serve it in warm
soup bowls with plenty of warm, buttered, crusty bread.
Serves 4 to 6.

SAUSAGE ALLA PIZZAIOLA
[Speed-cook; 27 minutes]

4 medium-size hot Italian sausages
4 medium-size sweet Italian sausages
3 tablespoons olive oil
3 garlic cloves, cut into halves
One 29-ounce can heavy tomato puree
½ teaspoon sugar
1 teaspoon salt
⅛ teaspoon pepper
½ teaspoon dried oregano
1 tablespoon chopped Italian parsley

With the sharp point of a knife, prick the sausages in
several places. In a glass casserole, in the center of the
oven, cook the garlic in the oil one minute. Add the
sausages. Cook 3 minutes. Turn the sausages. Cook 3
minutes. Pour off all but 1½ tablespoons of the liquid and
oil. Add the tomato puree, sugar, salt, pepper, oregano
and parsley. Stir. Cover the casserole with waxed paper
to prevent splattering. Cook in the center of the oven
10 minutes. Stir. Turn the sausages. Cook 5 minutes.
Rotate casserole half a turn. Cook 5 minutes. Let set,

covered, 15 minutes. Test for tenderness. This is excellent with small boiled potatoes, or a pasta such as rigatoni. *Serves 4.*

Hot Dogs

You will have been told in microwave instructional booklets that all you have to do is place the frankfurter in a bun, wrap it in a paper napkin or paper towel, slip it into the oven and, almost before you can say "mustard and relish," the hot dog is ready. True. But by using part of the leftovers from another dish (Cornish Game Hens in Sauerkraut and White Wine, page 106), you can prepare a hot dog that will be your all-time favorite sandwich—if you like sauerkraut. What you must do is save the leftover sauerkraut from that Cornish hen dinner and freeze it in two-tablespoon portions in plastic wrap. Then you're in business for the super dogs. Here are two ways to serve them.

SUPER HOT DOG #1
[Speed-cook; 25 to 28 seconds for 1 hot dog,
40 seconds for 2 hot dogs]

This will taste much like those hot dogs sold from the carts that steam the franks and the rolls. If those are a favorite, then this recipe won't disappoint you. Also try the next one (our creation) and see what you've been missing.

1 frankfurter
1 hot dog roll
One 2-tablespoon portion wine sauerkraut (page 106)

Place the frankfurter in the roll. Spread sauerkraut (defrosted) on it. Close the roll as tightly as possible. Wrap it in a paper napkin. Tuck in the ends. Cook in the oven 25 to 28 seconds. This sandwich will be quite soft, even though the napkin will absorb part of the moisture. *Serves 1.*

SUPER HOT DOG #2
[Speed-cook; hot dog and sauerkraut, 45 seconds;
toasting bun, about 30 seconds]

Butter
1 hot dog roll
1 frankfurter
One 2-tablespoon portion wine sauerkraut (page 106)

Butter the bun lavishly and toast it. Keep it warm.
If the sauerkraut is frozen, defrost it 20 seconds in the
oven. Remove when hot. Cook the hot dog 25 seconds.
Place it on the toasted bun. Spread on the hot sauerkraut. Super! *Serves 1.*

8

Pasta, Rice and Some Unusual Grains

Pasta

We find it more effective, and the pasta better, if we
limit the servings to four for each cooking period, allowing about 2 ounces of pasta for each serving. Also, it is
best to have the water boiling first, rather than waiting
for it to boil under microwaves. In fact, the conventional stove brings water to a boil faster than the microwaves. We will describe here the pasta microwave cooking technique and, in most cases, the recipes in this
chapter will call for cooked pasta rather than repeat
the cooking procedure.

COOKED PASTA
[Speed-cook; 6 minutes]

8 ounces pasta
½ tablespoon salt
6 cups boiling water

Place the pasta in a 3-quart glass casserole. Pour in the boiling water and add the salt. Cook in the center of the oven, uncovered, 3 minutes. Stir. Cook 3 minutes. Let set, covered, 10 minutes.

All pasta should be cooked *al dente,* "to the tooth," a bit chewy, with a little core remaining, especially the string or rod types, such as spaghetti, vermicelli, linguine and ziti. If you are going to cook the larger kinds, such as rigatoni, tufoli and lasagne, add one tablespoon of olive oil to the water to prevent the pasta from sticking together. Also, as in all microwave cooking, you are going to have to be alert and test. Common sense will tell you that the method of cooking pasta described here is relative. If you are going to cook a very thin and delicate type of pasta, such as vermicelli, it will cook faster than a thicker spaghetti. Thus, you reduce the cooking time by 2 minutes, and the setting time by 5 minutes. Then test. You will have to experiment, always leaning to less time, rather than more.

As delicious and versatile as pasta is, it becomes gummy and soft, almost unpalatable, if overcooked, losing all of its personality. The Italians, the most skilled pasta cooks, test the pasta while it is cooking, forking out a string and judging "by the tooth." This is an excellent idea that prevents overcooking.

The professionals, the pasta chefs in Italy, have a procedure that produces a superior pasta every time. We offer it here for your consideration. It is certainly worth the little extra effort.

When the pasta is cooked *al dente,* if it is a string or rod type, remove it from the water with pasta tongs, or with a fork. Shake off the excess water. This will leave a little coating of water on each strand of pasta that will help prevent the strands from sticking together. If you drain it, it brings it all together, and almost surely will produce a slightly gummy pasta, even if it is cooked to perfection. "Togetherness" is not recommended for pasta. Of course, if you are cooking elbow macaroni, rigatoni, etc., you cannot remove it with a fork. Use a slotted spoon, or, as a last resort, drain it, but do it quickly.

In the meantime, have a large bowl with three table-spoons of butter (for 8 ounces of pasta) in the warmer of your conventional stove. At hand have a cup of grated cheese and some black pepper; a pepper mill is preferred.

As you fork the pasta out of the water and shake off the excess moisture, place it in the warm bowl with the butter. When all the pasta is in the bowl, use a wooden spoon and fork to toss it with the butter. This will coat each strand and further protect it from becoming gummy. Add a couple of good grinds of black pepper and 2 tablespoons of the grated cheese. Toss again. Now is the time to also add 3 tablespoons of the sauce you are going to cover it with. Toss it. Serve the pasta in warm bowls or plates, with more sauce and cheese atop. Serve it quickly. Pasta should not wait for the guests. The guests should wait for the pasta.

There it is, the professionals' way. Do it any way that pleases you. But be warned: Too long under the microwaves, and pasta will return almost to its natural state.

PASTA BOLOGNESE

[Speed-cook; 13 minutes]

This, possibly the most famous of all the many pasta dishes, usually requires 22 ingredients and more than an hour to cook. By utilizing the prepared filetto *sauce in this chapter you can complete the dish in minutes.*

1 garlic clove, minced
1 tablespoon olive oil
1 pound ground beef of your choice (preferably top sirloin)
Salt and pepper to taste
2½ cups Filetto di Pomodoro (page 177)
3 medium mushrooms, thinly sliced, sautéed in butter under microwaves 2 minutes and drained
4 large chicken livers, coarsely chopped
¾ cup heavy cream
¼ cup grated Parmesan cheese
1 pound spaghettini, cooked (page 174) and drained

In a glass casserole, in the center of the oven, cook the garlic in the oil 30 seconds. Add the ground beef, seasoning with salt and pepper. Cook 2 minutes. Stir. Cook 2 minutes. Drain the oil from the beef. In the center of the oven, in a large glass measuring cup, heat the *filetto* sauce 3 minutes, or until it bubbles. Pour the hot sauce into the casserole with the beef. Stir well. Add the sautéed mushrooms and the chicken livers. Cook 2½ minutes. Stir in the heavy cream. Cook about 3 minutes, stirring after each 1½ minutes. The mixture should be bubbling. Stir. Toss half the meat sauce with the hot cooked spaghettini. Add half the cheese and toss again. Transfer to warm soup plates. Spoon the remaining sauce atop, sprinkle with the remaining cheese and serve. *Serves 4 to 6.*

FILETTO DI POMODORO
[Speed-cook; 17 minutes]

This is an elegant, light tomato sauce that restaurant owners in Italy often prepare and serve to themselves and their staff on Sundays. It freezes well, so it pays dividends to make a batch and put it in the freezer for emergencies—or for the famous Pasta Bolognese (page 176).

Use this sauce on any of your favorites: spaghetti linguine, noodles. One cup of sauce will serve two; allow 2 or 3 ounces of pasta for each serving.

1½ tablespoons olive oil
1 tablespoon butter
¼ cup minced ham or bacon fat
3 medium-size white onions, chopped
6 large fresh basil leaves, minced, or 1½ tablespoons dried basil
1 teaspoon dried oregano
Two 1-pound cans Italian plum tomatoes, put through a food mill
½ teaspoon sugar
Salt and pepper to taste

In a glass casserole, heat the oil and butter. Add the ham fat and cook in the center of the oven 2½ minutes. Stir. Cook 2½ minutes. Stir in the onions, basil and oregano. Cook 2 minutes, or until onion is soft. Add the tomatoes and sugar. Season with salt and pepper. Stir well.

Cook, uncovered, 5 minutes. Stir. Cook 5 minutes. Stir. Let set, covered, 10 minutes. The sauce is ready when you can run a wooden spoon through it without leaving a watery trail. *About 7 cups sauce.*

LINGUINE ALLA CARBONARA
[Speed-cook; 13 minutes]

This is the famous Roman dish that combines pasta with bacon and eggs.

    8 slices bacon
    2 eggs
    1 cup grated Parmesan cheese
    2 tablespoons chopped fresh parsley
    2 tablespoons pepper
    8 ounces linguine

Have four rimmed soup bowls warming in the oven of your conventional stove (200°), or in a special warmer.

Spread a double layer of paper towels on a 12-inch glass pie plate or cake dish, or on a microwave oven bacon cooker. Arrange the bacon strips on the paper, side by side, not overlapping. Cover with a paper towel. Cook in the center of the oven 3 minutes. Rotate dish half a turn. Cook 4 minutes. Remove the bacon from the paper towels. Pat any remaining fat off with fresh paper towels. Cut the bacon into pieces about half the size of a thumbnail and keep them warm. Place the eggs, cheese, parsley and pepper in a large bowl and beat with a whisk or an electric beater until well blended. Mix one tablespoon of bacon pieces into the cheese and eggs. Cook the linguine as directed on page 174 and, working quickly, take it directly from the hot water, shake off the excess water, and add the pasta to the cheese-egg mixture. The pasta must be hot to slightly set the eggs as you toss it. Using a wooden spoon and fork, toss the linguine gently, but well, with the cheese and eggs. Serve immediately in the warm soup bowls topped with the remaining crisp bacon pieces. *Serves 4.*

CLASSIC FETTUCCINE
[Speed-cook; 7 minutes 40 seconds]

For the really classic version, thinly sliced white truffles should garnish the fettuccine, but who can afford them?

1 stick butter
8 ounces fettuccine noodles, cooked *al dente* and drained (takes 6 minutes)
½ cup heavy cream, warmed
½ cup grated Parmesan cheese
Pepper to taste
1 large egg yolk

In a large glass casserole, in the center of the oven, melt the butter (it will take about one minute). Stir in the hot cooked noodles. Toss. Add half the cream and cheese. Toss. Cook 20 seconds. Add the remaining cream and cheese. Toss. Add a liberal amount of pepper. Toss. Cook 20 seconds. Add the egg yolk and toss quickly, blending it with the pasta. Serve immediately in hot bowls or plates. *Serves 4.*

WILLIAM BAUSERMAN'S MACARONI—WITH FOUR VARIATIONS ON A THEME
[Speed-cook; 15½ minutes]

2 cups elbow macaroni
4 tablespoons butter
2 tablespoons flour
2 cups medium cream
Salt and white pepper to taste
1 cup crushed saltine crackers
12 slices sharp cheddar cheese

Cook the macaroni *al dente,* as directed on page 174. Drain and rinse quickly with cold water. Add 2 tablespoons of the butter and toss. Heat the remaining butter in a glass bowl for 30 seconds, or until melted. Stir in the flour and blend into a smooth paste. Gradually add the cream, stirring until you have a smooth sauce. Cook 2 minutes. Add salt and pepper. Stir and cook one minute, or until thickened. Butter a deep glass casserole and sprinkle in a light layer of crushed crackers. Add a layer of macaroni. Sprinkle in another light layer of crackers, then a layer of the cheese. Lightly sprinkle with salt and pepper. Add the remaining macaroni and repeat the layering procedure, ending with cheese on top. Pour the cream sauce over the contents, filling to about ⅛ from the top of the casserole (you may not need all of the sauce). Cook in the center of the oven 3 minutes. Rotate casserole half a turn. Cook 3 minutes. Place under the broiler of a conventional stove until the top is golden and crusty. Serve with a side dish of well-chilled stewed tomatoes. *Serves 4.*

Variation I: Add one 7-ounce can drained, flaked, water-pack tuna to the macaroni and toss, then layer in the casserole as directed and cook.

Variation II: Cook the macaroni and toss with the butter as directed, then place in an ungreased casserole. Do not make the cream sauce. Shape a well in the center of the macaroni and fill with sour cream. Sprinkle generously with shredded, very sharp cheddar cheese and cook as directed.

Variation III: Instead of serving tomatoes separately as suggested, add one 16-ounce can drained, coarsely chopped tomatoes (mixed with ½ teaspoon dried oregano and/or basil) to the mixture. Cook as directed. If you use the tomatoes then eliminate the cream sauce.

Variation IV: Cook the basic recipe in a low-sided, flat-bottomed baking dish in a single layer, using half the cream sauce and as much cheese as you like. It cannot be too "cheesy," as cheese and macaroni are boon companions.

POLISH-STYLE NOODLES
[Speed-cook; 13 minutes]

½ pound hot Italian sausage meat
¼ cup hot water
½ small head of cabbage, shredded
Salt and pepper to taste
8 ounces egg noodles, cooked (page 174) and drained

In a glass pie plate, in the center of the oven, cook the sausage meat 2½ minutes. Stir. Cook 2½ minutes. Drain the sausage, reserving 1½ tablespoons of the fat. Place that fat in a glass casserole, add the cooked sausage, the hot water, cabbage, salt to taste and much pepper. Cover with plastic wrap, puncturing the center to permit steam to escape. Cook in the center of the oven 4 minutes. Rotate the dish half a turn. Cook 4 minutes. Let set, covered, 10 minutes. Stir in the hot noodles. Toss with the cabbage and sausage. If not hot enough, place under the microwaves 1½ minutes, or until suitably heated. *Serves 4.*

JARRATT'S RIGATONI
[Speed-cook; 1½ minutes]

This recipe comes from our friend Vernon Jarratt, who owns George's, one of Rome's most famous restaurants. It is a house specialty that has held the place of honor on the menu for many years.

4 tablespoons butter
½ pound thinly sliced prosciutto or other ham, cut into julienne strips
8 ounces rigatoni (large tubes), cooked (page 174) and drained (keep hot)
2 egg yolks
½ cup heavy cream
Pinch of nutmeg
½ cup grated Parmesan cheese

In a glass pie plate, in the center of the oven, melt half the butter and cook the ham 30 seconds. Add the rigatoni, mixing well with the ham. In a bowl, beat the egg yolks with the cream and nutmeg just enough to mix well, not until frothy. Pour it over the pasta-ham mixture. Stir it in gently, so that the pasta tubes are not broken. Stir in the remaining butter. Cook 30 seconds. Stir gently. Cook 30 seconds, or until very hot. Stir gently. Serve with the cheese sprinkled atop. *Serves 4.*

Rice

Four tips to make rice tastier:

(1) Before cooking rice in liquid, sauté it in butter with chopped onions. Use 2 tablespoons of butter and 2 small chopped white onions for one cup of rice. In a glass pie or cake plate, melt the butter and cook the onions about 2 minutes, or until soft. Stir in the rice, turning it and making certain that it is coated with the butter and well mixed with the onions. Cook 20 seconds. Then add the rice, onions and butter to 2½ cups boiling liquid. If the liquid is cold, it will take about 6 minutes to bring it to a boil under microwaves.

(2) Cook the rice in chicken broth.

(3) After the rice is cooked, do not stir it. Fluff it with a fork. This separates the grains and prevents it from massing and becoming gummy.

(4) If you are serving plain rice as a side dish, it is a good idea to blend in 2 tablespoons of melted butter and one tablespoon of chopped parsley, then fluff the rice. It improves the flavor and gives the rice interesting color.

Precooked, the minute variety, needs only to be brought to the boil, then let set, covered, 5 minutes.

COOKING LONG-GRAIN RICE
[Speed-cook; 9 minutes 20 seconds]

2 small white onions, chopped
2 tablespoons butter
⅛ teaspoon salt
1 cup long-grain rice (Uncle Ben's Converted is "never fail" rice)
2½ cups boiling chicken broth

You'll need a 2-quart casserole to make certain that you won't have a boil-over.

Cook the onions in butter 2 minutes, add the salt and rice and cook 20 seconds. Mix well, then stir all into the boiling chicken broth. Cook, covered, in the center of the oven 7 minutes. Let set, covered, 10 minutes. Remember not to stir but to fluff the rice with a fork before serving. *Makes 3½ cups rice, serving 6.*

RISOTTO MILANESE
[Speed-cook; 9 minutes]

This is a famous rice dish that will go well with any lamb, veal or poultry dish and is a table-talk combination. We are incorporating rice cooking technique described earlier, not only as a reminder, but to demonstrate that this simple mixing of flavors can raise rice to epicurean status.

1 medium-size white onion, finely chopped
1 garlic clove, minced
2 tablespoons butter
1 cup long-grain rice
2½ cups boiling chicken broth
Salt and pepper to taste
¼ teaspoon ground saffron
½ cup grated Parmesan cheese

In a glass casserole, in the center of the oven, cook the onion and garlic in the butter 2 minutes, or until soft. Stir in the rice, coating it well with the butter. Stir in the broth, salt, pepper and saffron. Cover the casserole and cook 4 minutes. Stir. Cook 3 minutes. Let set, covered, 10 minutes. Fluff with a fork, mixing in the cheese. Serve hot. *Serves 4 to 6.*

RICE WITH TUNA
[Speed-cook; 9 minutes]

1 cup long-grain rice
One 10½-ounce can condensed cream of mushroom soup, stirred until smooth
2 cups boiling chicken broth
2 white onions, chopped
½ teaspoon salt
One 10-ounce package frozen "petite" peas, thawed
One 7-ounce can fancy solid white tuna, drained and flaked

In a casserole, blend the rice, soup, broth, onions and salt. Stir well. Cook, covered, in a large casserole in the center of the oven 3 minutes. Rotate casserole half a turn. Cook 3 minutes. Stir in the peas and tuna. Cook 3 minutes, until simmering. Let set, covered, 10 minutes. *Serves 4 to 6.*

SPEEDY SPANISH RICE SUPPER
[Speed-cook; 11 minutes]

2 medium onions, chopped
1 small green pepper, cored, seeded and chopped
2 tablespoons butter
1 pound ground beef chuck
One 10½-ounce can condensed tomato soup
¼ cup water
2 teaspoons red wine vinegar
½ teaspoon salt
Pinch of dried basil
Pinch of dried oregano
2 cups hot cooked rice
1 canned pimiento, cut up

In a glass casserole, in the center of the oven, cook the onions and pepper in the butter about 3 minutes, or until soft, stirring after 1½ minutes. Add the beef and cook

2 minutes. Stir. Cook 2 minutes. Stir in the tomato soup, water, vinegar, salt, basil and oregano, blending well. Cook one minute. Stir. Cook one minute. Stir in the cooked rice and pimiento. Cook 2 minutes. Stir. Let set, covered, 5 minutes. *Serves 4 to 6.*

COUSCOUS
[Speed-cook; 5½ minutes]

This traditional Moroccan dish of crushed wheat usually is served with various vegetables and meats, especially lamb. It has a unique nutlike flavor, and offered instead of rice will mark you as a host or hostess with imagination. You can add to its personality by lightly browning chopped walnuts (or pine nuts) and raisins (or currants) and stirring them in just before serving.

    2 cups beef broth
    1 cup couscous
    1 medium-size white onion, chopped
    2 tablespoons butter
    ⅛ teaspoon salt
    ⅛ teaspoon ground cumin

In a glass casserole, heat the broth 4 minutes, or until it boils. Gradually stir in the couscous. Add the onion, butter, salt and cumin. Stir. Cook one minute. Stir. Cook 30 seconds. Let set, covered, 15 minutes, or until all the liquid is absorbed. Fluff with a fork. *Serves 4 to 6.*

BULGUR WHEAT PILAF
[Speed-cook; 10 minutes]

Long before man learned to grind wheat into flour, he parboiled it in open kettles and spread it in the sun to dry. It is crunchy, chewy, nutritious, having a delicious nutlike flavor—and few of your guests will know what it is. If you are interested in cooking one-upmanship, this is your dish. It is excellent with chicken, pork, lamb, and even the stew-type dishes.

    1 cup water
    1 cup chicken broth
    1 cup bulgur wheat
    2 tablespoons butter
    ½ teaspoon salt
    ¼ teaspoon pepper
    ¼ cup chopped scallions
    1 teaspoon chopped fresh mint
    Juice of ½ lemon

In a deep glass casserole, heat the water and broth 4 minutes, or until boiling. Stir in the bulgur wheat, butter, salt and pepper. Cover and cook 3 minutes. Stir. Cook 3 minutes. Let set, covered, 10 minutes, or until the liquid is absorbed. Just before serving, stir in the scallions, mint and lemon juice.

BARLEY IN BEEF BROTH
[Speed-cook; 15 minutes]

Barley is a cereal grass, bearing bearded flower spikes with edible seeds. These are versatile seeds, used not only for food, but to make beer, ale and whisky. If you haven't tried barley except as a drink, or in a soup such as Scotch Broth, try it as a delicious, nut-flavored change from rice, pasta or potatoes. It is also excellent with stew-type dishes, mating well with the gravy.

    3 cups boiling beef broth
    1 cup barley
    1½ teaspoons salt
    2 tablespoons butter
    ¼ cup grated sharp cheddar cheese

Pour the boiling broth into a deep glass casserole (it must be deep enough to prevent a boil-over) and stir in the barley and salt. Cover and cook in the center of the oven 5 minutes. Stir. Cook 5 minutes. Stir. Cook 5 minutes. Stir. Let set, covered, 15 minutes. Drain. Stir in the butter and cheese with a fork. The barley should be slightly chewy. *Serves 4 to 6.*

9

Leftovers

If we were asked point blank which one facet or function of the microwave oven was the best, which one accomplished what no other cooking medium could, we wouldn't hesitate to answer, even though microwaves have numerous advantages over conventional cookery. Our answer: Leftovers.

Whether you are just warming them up, or creating new dishes from leftovers, nothing—we repeat, nothing —can put life back into yesterday's dishes the way microwaves can. They reheat food without loss of flavor or quality. No other method can match this, or even come close to accomplishing it.

We offer an incident to illustrate. Pasta lovers of the fanatic type, we never throw out leftover pasta. But B.M. (before microwaves) it had to be heated in a double boiler. It was pretty good, but not great. This twice-heated pasta was apt to be gummy, and along the way it lost much of its flavor. Shortly after we acquired our first microwave oven and were still experimenting, with little confidence in ourselves or the space machine, we had an excellent dinner of linguine with white clam sauce, cooked the conventional way. As usual, eyes larger than stomachs, we overcooked by a considerable amount and ended up with a large bowl of leftover pasta. Pushed into the back of the refrigerator, it was forgotten, then accidentally discovered a week later. As suggested in the literature received with the new oven, we covered it with plastic wrap, placed the bowl of pasta in the center of the oven and heated it one minute. We stirred it and heated it another 30 seconds. The microwaves brought that week-old pasta back, tasting exactly as good as it did the night it was cooked. It seemed the impossible, made possible.

Here are two more pluses from those waves from heaven: (1) Double-duty from food, and (2) economy.

All leftovers take on a fresh personality. If you combine leftover meats, seafood, poultry and vegetables with either cooked or uncooked combinations, you'll have a taste treat that not only will surprise you but give you a new respect for leftover food.

And with the microwave oven you do not have to rush to eat those leftovers. Put them in Corning Ware cookware or Pyrex dishes that can go directly from the freezer to the oven, and have them when you please. It isn't necessary to eat turkey for a week, even though the leftovers can be planned with imagination.

Although this was mentioned previously, it is worth repeating in this section. If you are making a stew or other casserole dish, plan ahead for "leftovers" and double the amounts. After cooking, place half in a Corning Ware casserole and pop it into the freezer. These precooked dishes can then become a "just-cooked" main dish in minutes.

The magic of microwaves also permits you to use nonfrozen cooked foods by varying them in another meal thus making all your cookery "two in one," if you prefer. A good example of this is the utilization of roast leg of lamb slices (or any roast) in Leftover Lamb or Beef with Vegetables, page 195).

Do not discard leftover mashed potatoes or any leftover pureed vegetables that in the past you would not have reheated. They can be frozen, heated in the microwave oven and will taste freshly cooked.

Pat Spadaccino, an epicure and friend, recently ran a taste test. He micro-cooked, then froze, mashed parsnips. He then cooked another fresh batch on a conventional stove. He served them both, the freshly cooked ones and the microwave-heated frozen batch, and defied anyone to tell the difference. His food-knowledgeable friends could detect no difference, although two of them did think the frozen offering from the microwave oven was moister and tasted fresher.

Points to remember about leftovers:

Cover tightly with plastic wrap all food to be stored, or place it in containers with covers. This will preserve moisture and that is important.

Try to slice meats thinly and uniformly. Keep in

mind that the larger the portions, the longer the cooking time. Twelve servings are more effectively cooked in two batches; heating is faster and more evenly distributed.

If the food in large portions can be stirred, or rearranged in the casserole, it will heat, or cook, more quickly and more evenly. If it can't be stirred or have its position in the dish changed, rotate the dish half a turn after each 2 minutes.

After the cooking period, large casseroles of food should always be allowed to set, covered, at least 5 minutes.

As with all microwave cookery, watch the timing. If you are heating leftover pasta, don't let your attention wander and cook it 10 minutes or you will have rope. Also, leftover rice will become lead pellets if heated too long under microwaves. However, if prepared with other foods, cooked pasta and rice can stand more than mere heating.

If you are defrosting, pay attention. If uncertain, check the defrosting guide that came with your oven. Give the defrosted food the proper resting time, then just reheat the defrosted leftovers; do not cook. Start with 2 minutes, then check to see if the food is hot enough. This is important, for pieces of meat or poultry that have already been cooked can toughen if you leave them too long under the microwaves. Vegetables will dry out; seafood will suffer; rolls will harden.

Time: Watch it! This is quick and easy cookery, but it is not casual.

CREAMED BEEF AND PEAS WITH NOODLES
[Speed-cook; 7½ minutes]

1 large onion, chopped
2 tablespoons butter
One 10¾-ounce can condensed cream of mushroom soup
⅓ cup light cream
2 cups diced cooked beef
½ cup cooked peas
Salt and pepper to taste
2 cups cooked noodles

In a glass casserole, in the center of the oven, cook the onion in half the butter 2 minutes, or until soft. Blend in the soup and cream and stir until smooth. Stir in the beef and peas. Season with salt and pepper. Cook 2 minutes. Stir. Cook 2 minutes. Cover. Heat the noodles with the remaining butter one minute. Toss. Heat 30 seconds. Serve the creamed beef and peas over the hot noodles. *Serves 4.*

CHICKEN AND SPINACH
[Speed-cook; 6½ minutes]

This simple offering is a favorite Viennese dish. If you have the willpower, save the breast, when you broil or roast a whole large chicken, as that is generally used. This also is an excellent way to revive tired turkey.

    3 tablespoons butter
    3 tablespoons flour
 1⅛ cups chicken broth
    ½ cup heavy cream
    1 teaspoon lemon juice
Salt and pepper to taste
    2 cups cooked rice
    2 cups cooked leaf spinach
    2 cups cooked chicken, cut into bite-size slices

In a glass bowl, in the center of the oven, melt the butter. Stir in the flour and cook about 30 seconds, stirring until you have a smooth paste. Gradually pour in ½ cup of the chicken broth, stirring as it is added. Cook 30 seconds. Stir in the remaining broth; cook one minute, stirring after 30 seconds. Stir in the cream and lemon juice, season with salt and pepper and cook 1½ minutes, stirring every 30 seconds, or until you have a smooth, medium-thick sauce.

In a glass casserole, arrange the rice in an even layer. Spoon 3 or 4 tablespoons of the sauce over it. Layer the spinach evenly on top of the rice, spooning 3 or 4 tablespoons of sauce over it. Cover the spinach with the chicken slices and spoon on the remaining sauce. Cover with plastic wrap. Cook 1½ minutes. Rotate the dish half a turn. Cook 1½ minutes. Test to see if it is hot enough. *Serves 4.*

CHICKEN À LA KING
[Speed-cook; 8½ minutes]

Here's an old favorite, given a new flavor with the microwave magic.

1 medium-size white onion, chopped
2 tablespoons chopped green pepper
2 tablespoons butter
Salt and pepper to taste
1 tablespoon flour
One 10½-ounce can condensed cream of chicken soup
¼ cup heavy cream
2 tablespoons dry sherry
1 cup cooked sliced mushrooms
2 cups cubed cooked chicken
2 tablespoons diced pimiento
Pinch of nutmeg
4 slices toasted bread or 4 biscuits

In a glass casserole, in the center of the oven, cook the onion and green pepper in the butter 3 minutes, or until soft. Season with salt and pepper and stir in the flour. Blend the soup, cream and sherry; stir into the casserole with the onion and pepper. Cook 1½ minutes. Stir. Add the mushrooms, chicken, pimiento and nutmeg. Stir well. Cover loosely with waxed paper and cook in the center of the oven 2 minutes. Rotate the dish half a turn. Stir. Cook 2 minutes. Test to see if hot enough. Serve over the toast or biscuits. *Serves 4.*

CORNED BEEF AND CABBAGE
[Speed-cook; 7 minutes]

Here's a dinner that will taste as if hours instead of minutes were spent on it.

One 10½-ounce can condensed cream of celery soup
1 medium onion, chopped
4 cups shredded cabbage
1 teaspoon dry mustard
⅛ teaspoon salt
½ teaspoon pepper
¼ teaspoon caraway seeds
1½ cups diced cooked corned beef

Place all the ingredients except the corned beef in a glass casserole. Mix well. Cover with plastic wrap and cook in the center of the oven 3 minutes. Stir. Cook 2 minutes. Let set, covered, 5 minutes. Test the cabbage for tenderness. Add the corned beef, stir, and cook 2 minutes. *Serves 4.*

COUSCOUS AND CHICKEN
[Speed-cook; 6 minutes]

This dish, called Moghrabiye *in Lebanon, converts leftover chicken or lamb into an exotic dinner.*

    1 large onion, chopped
    1 tablespoon butter
 2½ cups hot chicken broth
    1 can chick-peas, drained
    1 cup couscous
    2 cups cooked chicken or lamb, cut into bite-size pieces
Salt and pepper to taste
 ½ teaspoon turmeric
Good pinch of cinnamon

In a glass casserole, in the center of the oven, cook the onion in the butter 2 minutes, or until soft. Stir in the hot chicken broth and the chick-peas. Cook 2 minutes. Stir in the couscous, chicken, salt, pepper, turmeric and cinnamon. Cook 2 minutes. Stir. Let set, covered, 10 minutes. *Serves 4.*

HURRY-UP BEEF HASH
[Speed-cook; 6 minutes]

 One 10½-ounce can condensed cream of celery soup
    ⅓ cup chopped fresh parsley
    1 medium onion, minced
 1½ teaspoons Worcestershire sauce
    1 teaspoon salt
    ¼ teaspoon pepper
    2 cups diced cooked beef
    2 cups diced cooked potatoes
    2 tablespoons butter
    2 tablespoons milk

In a bowl, mix half the soup with the parsley, onion, one teaspoon of the Worcestershire sauce, the salt, pepper, beef and potatoes. In a glass caserole, in the center of the oven, melt the butter. Stir in the beef-potato mixture. Cook 2 minutes. Stir. Cook 2 minutes. Place under the broiler of a conventional stove until brown and crisp. In a glass measuring cup, mix the remaining soup with the remaining Worcestershire sauce and the milk. Cook 2 minutes, or until bubbling. Serve as a sauce to pour over the hash. *Serves 4.*

HASTY HAM AND RICE
[Speed-cook; 4 minutes]

A baked ham hangs around quite awhile and tends to get as boring as any visitor who stays too long. Here's a refreshing change for it.

>   2 cups ground cooked ham
>   2 cups cooked rice
>   2 small ripe tomatoes, peeled, seeded, chopped and drained in a strainer
>   1 small green pepper, cored, seeded and diced
>   1 small white onion, minced
>   ⅓ cup mayonnaise
>   2 tablespoons Madeira wine
>   1 teaspoon Dijon mustard
>   2 tablespoons butter
>   ½ cup bread crumbs
>   3 tablespoons grated sharp cheddar cheese

In a bowl, thoroughly mix the ham, rice, tomatoes, green pepper, onion, mayonnaise, Madeira and mustard. Spoon evenly into a glass casserole and cook in the center of the oven 2 minutes. Rotate casserole half a turn. Cook 2 minutes. In a small glass measuring cup, melt the butter and stir in the bread crumbs, coating them well. Sprinkle the bread crumbs and cheese over the ham mixture. Place under the broiler of a conventional stove until the cheese melts and the bread crumbs are brown. *Serves 4.*

LEFTOVER LAMB WITH VEGETABLES IN THE FRENCH MANNER
[Speed-cook; 8 minutes]

Traditionally, the appeal of this dish is the contrast of the crunchy vegetables with the well-cooked lamb. The vegetables should be just tender but quite firm. Microwaves are the perfect medium for this dish.

2 tablespoons olive oil
Juice of 1 small lemon
1 garlic clove, minced
1 small white onion, finely chopped
1 sweet red pepper, cored, seeded and thinly sliced
4 small leeks (white part only), sliced
2 small zucchini (unpeeled), cut into ¾-inch slices
One 3-inch strip lemon peel, no white portion
1 teaspoon salt
½ teaspoon pepper
3 small ripe tomatoes, cut into quarters
2 cups cubed cooked lamb

In a glass casserole, combine the oil, lemon juice, garlic and onion and cook in the center of the oven 2 minutes. Stir. Add the sweet pepper, leeks, zucchini, lemon peel, salt and pepper. Cover. Cook 2 minutes. Rotate casserole half a turn. Cook 2 minutes. Add the tomatoes and the lamb. Cover. Cook 2 minutes. Let set, covered, 5 minutes. *Serves 4.*

NEXT-DAY HAM WITH NOODLES
[Speed-cook; 5½ minutes]

4 tablespoons butter
1 medium onion, chopped
⅛ teaspoon dried tarragon
Pepper to taste
One 10¾-ounce can condensed cream of chicken soup
¼ cup medium cream
2 cups cooked noodles
½ cup cut-up cooked string beans
2 cups diced cooked ham
1 garlic clove, minced
⅛ cup bread crumbs

In a glass casserole, in the center of the oven, melt half the butter and cook the onion and tarragon 2 minutes, or until the onion is soft. Season with the pepper. Blend the soup with the cream and stir into the onion in the casserole. Stir in the noodles, beans and ham. Cover loosely with waxed paper. Cook 1½ minutes. Rotate casserole half a turn. Cook 1½ minutes. In a small glass measuring cup, cook the garlic in the remaining butter 30 seconds. Stir in the bread crumbs. Sprinkle the buttered crumbs over the ham mixture and place under the broiler of a conventional stove until the crumbs are brown and crisp. *Serves 4.*

LEFTOVER LAMB OR BEEF WITH VEGETABLES
[Speed-cook; 6 minutes]

We were always glad when Joe Auer, a friend noted in the food field, roasted a leg of lamb. And we didn't care whether we were invited for that beautifully pink leg of lamb. It was the next day we were interested in, for that was when Joe served a leftover dish that he had concocted. It is memorable, especially when accompanied by plenty of lavishly buttered, crusty warm bread and washed down with a velvety red burgundy. Bravo Joe Auer!

3 medium-size potatoes, peeled, cooked and cut into
¼-inch-thick slices
1 pound broccoli, cooked
2 medium onions, thinly sliced
2 cups bite-size slices cooked lamb (see note)
Salt and pepper to taste
¼ teaspoon dried oregano
1½ cups tomato sauce
4 tablespoons butter

In a large glass casserole, alternate layers of potatoes, broccoli, onions and lamb, lightly sprinkling each layer with salt, pepper and the oregano. Spoon tomato sauce over each layer and dot with butter. The top layer should be potatoes covered with tomato sauce and dotted with butter. Cover tightly and cook 3 minutes. Rotate the casserole half a turn and cook 3 minutes, or until very hot. The onions should be slightly crunchy. *Serves 4.*

NOTE: This dish is always best if the roast lamb was cooked in the French style, the meat pink.

SHEPHERD'S PIE
[Speed-cook; 7½ minutes]

Classically, leftover lamb is used in this simple but surprisingly tasty dish, but any meat—beef, veal or pork—will do.

 1 medium onion, minced
 3 tablespoons butter
 2 tablespoons flour
 ¾ cup beef broth
 2 tablespoons minced fresh parsley
 3 cups cubed cooked lamb
 Salt and pepper to taste
 Pinch of mace
 3 cups mashed cooked potatoes
 3 tablespoons grated cheese of your choice

In a glass dish or bowl, in the center of the oven, cook the onion in the butter 2 minutes, or until soft. Stir in the flour, then, in small amounts, the beef broth, cooking 30 seconds at a time and stirring until you have a smooth sauce. This will take about 1¼ minutes. Stir in the parsley, lamb, salt, pepper and mace. Cover the bottom of a glass casserole with half the mashed potatoes. Spoon the meat mixture over the potatoes, then cover with the remaining mashed potatoes. Dot with butter. Cook in the center of the oven 2 minutes. Rotate the casserole half a turn. Cook 2 minutes or until hot. Sprinkle the cheese atop and place under the broiler of a conventional stove until brown and crusty on top. *Serves 4 to 6.*

PORK FRIED RICE
[Speed-cook; 6 minutes]

Here is a fast, Chinese-style method for creating an exotic dish from leftover pork.

- 2 tablespoons peanut oil
- 2 cups cooked rice
- 2 cups coarsely shredded cooked pork
- Salt and pepper to taste
- 1⅛ tablespoons soy sauce
- 2 eggs, lightly beaten
- 4 whole scallions, cut into halves lengthwise, then into ½-inch pieces

Pour the oil into a glass dish or a deep pie plate, and stir in the rice well, to coat the grains. Cook in the center of the oven one minute. Stir. Cook one minute. Stir in the pork. Season with salt and pepper. Cook one minute. Stir in the soy sauce. Cook one minute. Pour the eggs over the pork and rice. Stir well. Cook one minute. Stir. Cook one minute. Stir. The dish should not be dry, but if it is too moist for your taste, cook another minute or two. Before serving, garnish with the cut-up scallions. *Serves 4.*

SWIFT STEW WITH DUMPLINGS
[Speed-cook; 13 minutes]

One 16-ounce can whole white onions, drained (reserve the liquid)
Beef broth
1 tablespoon cornstarch
One 10½-ounce can condensed vegetable soup
2 cups diced cooked beef, veal or lamb
Salt and pepper to taste
1 cup prepared buttermilk biscuit mix
⅓ cup milk

Measure the onion liquid and combine with enough beef broth to make one cup. Blend in the cornstarch. In a glass casserole, mix the broth mixture, soup, onions, meat, salt and pepper. Cover and cook in the center of the oven 8 minutes, or until the edges bubble. Blend the biscuit mix and the milk, to make about 8 dumplings. Drop the dough, a tablespoon at a time, onto the bubbling stew. Cover and cook 2½ minutes. Rotate the casserole half a turn. Cook 2½ minutes. *Serves 4.*

SACHSENHAUSEN STEW
[Speed-cook; 11 minutes]

Here is a German Topf, *or stew, that uses a variety of leftover meats. Use any kind that you have.*

    1 medium onion, chopped
    1 garlic clove, chopped
    2 medium potatoes, peeled and diced
    3 tablespoons butter
    1 cup cubed cooked beef
    1 cup cubed cooked veal
    1 cup cubed cooked pork
    Salt and pepper to taste
    1 ripe tomato, peeled, seeded and chopped
    One 11-ounce can beef gravy
    ⅓ cup cider or red wine
    1 teaspoon lemon juice
    One 4-ounce can mushroom pieces, drained
    1 cup cooked peas
    2 tablespoons chopped fresh parsley

In a large glass casserole, in the center of the oven, cook the onion, garlic and potatoes in the butter 3 minutes. Stir in the meats and tomato and season with salt and pepper. Cook 2 minutes. Stir in the beef gravy, cider and lemon juice. Cover. Cook 2 minutes. Stir. Cook 2 minutes. Add the mushroom pieces and peas. Cook 2 minutes. Stir. Test to see that the potatoes are tender and the stew is hot enough. Sprinkle with the parsley before serving. *Serves 4 to 6.*

THIRD-DAY TURKEY LOAF
[Speed-cook; 9 minutes]

Have your turkey for dinner, skip two days, then have it again on the third day in this luscious loaf that will make everyone happy that you had the turkey that first day.

    ⅓ cup chopped sweet red pepper
    ⅓ cup chopped onion
    1 tablespoon butter
    6 cups chopped cooked turkey
    1 cup bread crumbs
    1 egg, beaten
    ⅓ cup chili sauce
    ⅓ cup mayonnaise
    ½ teaspoon salt
    ¼ teaspoon pepper
    ½ teaspoon Lawry's seasoned salt
    ⅛ teaspoon dried thyme

In a glass bowl, in the center of the oven, cook the sweet pepper and onion in the butter 2 minutes, then combine with the remaining ingredients in a large bowl and mix thoroughly. Spoon the turkey mixture evenly into a buttered glass loaf pan. Do not let the ends taper or they will dry out. Cook 3½ minutes in the center of the oven. Rotate dish half a turn and cook 3½ minutes. Let set, covered, 5 minutes. This is delicious either hot or cold. *Serves 6 to 8.*

TURKEY DIVAN
[Speed-cook; 4 minutes]

Here is a fast, tasty way to revive that tired holiday turkey.

    One 10-ounce package frozen asparagus spears, cooked
        and drained
    4 large slices cooked turkey breast
    Salt and pepper to taste
    One 10¾-ounce can condensed vegetable soup
    ⅓ cup heavy cream
    ½ cup grated Romano or Parmesan cheese

Arrange the asparagus spears in a single layer in a shallow glass casserole. Cover them with the turkey slices and sprinkle lightly with salt and pepper. Blend the soup and cream into a smooth sauce and pour it over the turkey. Cover loosely with waxed paper. Cook in the center of the oven 2 minutes. Rotate casserole half a turn. Cook 2 minutes. Sprinkle with the cheese. Place under the broiler of a conventional stove until the cheese and sauce are bubbling and brown. *Serves 4.*

VEAL PAPRIKASH
[Speed-cook; 7½ minutes]

Leftover veal is worth doing something special with, especially when you have microwaves as a helpmate.

1 medium-size white onion, finely chopped
1 small green pepper, cored, seeded and cut into thin slivers
3 tablespoons butter
2 tablespoons flour
1 tablespoon paprika (preferably Hungarian)
1 cup chicken broth
⅛ teaspoon sugar
½ teaspoon salt
½ teaspoon lemon juice
2 cups small cubes cooked veal
1 egg yolk
⅓ cup sour cream
2 tablespoons chopped fresh parsley

In a glass casserole, in the center of the oven, cook the onion and green pepper in the butter 2 minutes, or until soft. Blend the flour and paprika and stir into the vegetables. Gradually stir in the chicken broth, cooking 30 seconds, adding more, and stirring until you have a smooth sauce. This whole process should take about 1½ minutes of cooking time. Stir in the sugar, salt, lemon juice and veal. Cook 3 minutes. Stir. Blend the egg yolk and sour cream and stir into the casserole ingredients, a tablespoon at a time. Cook 30 seconds. Stir. Cook 30 seconds. The dish should be just heated through. Before serving, sprinkle the paprikash with the parsley. This is excellent with buttered noodles. *Serves 4.*

10

Vegetables

Over 15 percent of Japanese households have microwave ovens, which means that Japan leads the world in microwave cookery.

Why do so many Japanese favor the microwave oven? There are several reasons. Space. Energy. Speed. Without question, however, the most important one is the manner in which microwaves cook. The Japanese diet consists mainly of seafood and vegetables, with vegetables in the lead. Like all Orientals, they cook their vegetables fast and like them crunchy. Microwaves accomplish this better than any other medium.

Microwave vegetable cookery offers many advantages. By now you probably take the speed for granted, but we want to point out again two astounding facts that we ourselves never can seem to assimilate: You can bake a potato in 4 minutes, an acorn squash in 7. Both vegetables require approximately one hour in a conventional oven. Using gas or electricity, that has to make a baked potato or squash an expensive item to serve your family.

But besides saving time, thus energy and expense, microwaves also bring beauty to vegetable cookery. Natural colors are not only retained but enhanced. You will be startled and pleased by the green of cooked zucchini.

As very little water is used, there is virtually no loss of vitamins and nutrients. In conventional cooking, these are lost in the water. Microwave vegetables are good for your health.

In addition to these factors, add one that is more important to most of us than any other: Taste. Vegetables cooked by microwaves are fresh-tasting and delicious. In fact, once you've eaten properly micro-cooked vegetables, you probably will not like them cooked any other way. Many of the vegetables cook in their own moisture; others need only a touch of butter.

Cooking vegetables, however, is no more casual than any other facet of microwave cooking. They quickly can be overcooked. And, as with grades and textures of meats, there is a variance in cooking time, depending upon what kind of vegetables you are using. Pat Spadaccino, a microwave fan, found that cooking a vegetable fresh from the home garden was quite different from cooking one purchased in a market. The fresh-picked one cooks more quickly.

The watchword again is *test*. Test frequently during the cooking. For example, if the cooking time given for a squash is 7 minutes, test it after 5 minutes and again at 6.

Results are better if the vegetables are covered while cooking. A little water should be added to some vegetables, about a tablespoon. But this will be absorbed and usually no draining is necessary. Cooking with the utensil covered retains the steam which helps cook the vegetables more evenly.

Any vegetable with a skin, such as a potato, should be pricked in several places to prevent it exploding. This also holds true for frozen vegetables in plastic packages. Prick the packages.

Stir, in order to distribute the heat evenly, making sure that you start stirring from the outer edge of the dish, so that the portions there will be moved towards the center and those near the center will be moved to the outer edge.

Any vegetable that ends up dry and tough has been overcooked. Unlike vegetables cooked conventionally, those cooked by microwave will be crunchy. Thus, when you take vegetables from a microwave oven they should be firm. If they aren't, you have cooked them too long. If you want to keep them crunchy, remember that they will cook for a few minutes after they are taken from the oven. Allow for this while cooking, and give the vegetable a setting period of about 3 or 4 minutes to finish cooking.

Don't mix frozen, fresh or canned vegetables together. Cooking times differ for each.

We do not cook frozen vegetables in their containers, but it can be done (unless the containers are aluminum foil). Halfway through the cooking period they must be stirred, or shaken, to rearrange the position so they will cook evenly.

If cooking solid-pack frozen vegetables in a dish, the icier side should be up. This permits an even distribution of heat as the water from the melted ice passes through the vegetables. If frozen vegetables are taken from a loose pack, 2 tablespoons of hot water should be added, and they should be stirred halfway through the cooking period.

Canned vegetables just need to be heated in only half of their liquid.

Cooked vegetables need only to be reheated, usually about 1½ minutes, depending upon the size of the portion being reheated. Add no liquid and heat them covered. Because they heat internally, and not upon the surface, the fresh color will remain, as will the flavor, and, if you watch carefully, they will not dry out.

There is no doubt that the microwave oven is the best vegetable cooker in existence, worth its price for just that alone. But cook with caution.

The timing rule of thumb, as we have stated, for converting recipes from conventional cooking to the microwave is about a fourth of the conventional time. *This is not true for vegetable cookery.* For example, that much discussed baked potato that takes one hour in the conventional oven cooks in 4 minutes, or only 1/15 of the conventional time. Many of the vegetables cook in a surprisingly short time. Thus, you have the same old problem that confronts you in every phase of microwave cookery: You will be tempted to overcook, to give the peas, squash or cabbage "another minute or two." Don't do it.

ACORN SQUASH WITH MADEIRA AND BUTTER
[Speed-cook; 7 minutes]

One 1-pound acorn squash
2 tablespoons butter
1 tablespoon Madeira wine
Salt and pepper to taste

Cut the squash in half, but do not scoop out the seeds and the stringy fibers. Cook on a paper towel in the center of the oven 4 minutes. Remove the seeds and fibers. Place one tablespoon of butter and ½ tablespoon Madeira in each squash half. Cook 3 minutes. Season with salt and pepper. (When cooking 2 squash, cook about 13 minutes.) *Serves 2.*

Variation: This easily can be turned into a unique accompaniment to the Thanksgiving turkey. Just before serving, half fill the squash cavities with canned, drained whole cranberries.

HONEY ACORN SQUASH
[Speed-cook; 7 minutes]

One 1-pound acorn squash
½ teaspoon salt
¼ teaspoon mace
1 teaspoon brown sugar
2 teaspoons honey

Pierce the whole squash straight through in several places with an ice pick or skewer. Place on a paper towel. Cook 3 minutes. Turn the squash over and cook 2 minutes. Cut the squash in half and remove the seeds and stringy fibers. Blend the salt, mace, brown sugar and honey and spoon into the squash cavities. Cook one minute. Turn position of the squash. Cook one minute. *Serves 2.*

BUTTER BEANS IN TOMATO SAUCE
[Speed-cook; 6 minutes]

1 small green pepper, cored, seeded and chopped
1 small white onion, chopped
1 tablespoon butter
One 10¾-ounce can condensed tomato soup
¼ cup water
1 teaspoon prepared mustard
1 tablespoon vinegar
1 tablespoon brown sugar
Two 16-ounce cans butter beans, drained
Salt and pepper to taste

In a glass casserole, cook the green pepper and onion
in the butter in the center of the oven 2 minutes, or
until soft. Stir in the soup, water, mustard, vinegar and
brown sugar. Cook 3 minutes, or until hot. Stir in the
butter beans. Cook one minute, or until hot. Season with
salt and pepper. *Serves 4 to 6.*

ITALIAN GREEN BEANS
[Speed-cook; 10 minutes]

1 large onion, chopped
1 garlic clove, minced
1 small green pepper, seeded, cored and chopped
2 tablespoons olive oil
4 small ripe tomatoes, peeled, seeded, chopped and
drained in a strainer
1 pound green beans, cut into 1-inch pieces
½ teaspoon sugar
¼ cup chicken broth
Salt and pepper to taste

In a glass casserole, in the center of the oven, cook the
onion, garlic and green pepper in the oil 2 minutes or
until soft. Stir in the tomatoes, beans, sugar and chicken
broth. Cook, covered, 4 minutes. Stir. Cook 4 minutes.
Let set, covered, 3 minutes. Season to taste with salt
and pepper. *Serves 4 to 6.*

WAX BEAN CASSEROLE
[Speed-cook; 15 minutes]

Two 10-ounce packages frozen wax beans
½ teaspoon pepper
⅛ teaspoon dried thyme
One 10½-ounce can condensed cream of chicken soup
1½ teaspoons soy sauce
One 3½-ounce can French fried onions

In a glass casserole, place the frozen beans, icy side up. Sprinkle with pepper and thyme. Cook, covered, in the center of the oven, 6 minutes. Stir. Cook 6 minutes. Blend the soup and soy sauce and stir into the cooked beans. Stir in half the French fried onions. Cook 2 minutes, or until hot. Sprinkle on the remaining French fried onions. Cook one minute. *Serves 4 to 6.*

BROCCOLI WITH GRUYÈRE
[Speed-cook; 9 minutes]

1 pound fresh broccoli (about ⅔ of a bunch)
3 tablespoons water
Salt and pepper to taste
2 tablespoons butter, melted
⅛ cup grated Gruyère cheese

Divide the thick stems of the broccoli by cutting from the top down, right through the stems, so you will have thin-stemmed (about ½ inch in diameter) stalks of broccoli. Peel the stems and score the ends. Arrange them in a glass baking dish with the buds in the center, stems pointing outward. Add the water and cook, covered, in the center of the oven 8 minutes, turning the broccoli over after 4 minutes. Let set, covered, 3 minutes. Test for tenderness. It should be crisp but tender. Sprinkle the salt, pepper and melted butter over the broccoli, then the cheese. Cover and cook one minute or until the cheese melts. *Serves 4.*

Variations: Substitute white wine for the water for an interesting flavor. Another simple, tasty sauce for broccoli is make by blending ½ cup mayonnaise, the juice of ½ lemon and ½ teaspoon Lawry's seasoned salt. Spoon over hot or cold cooked broccoli.

BRUSSELS SPROUTS WITH TOASTED ALMONDS
[Speed-cook; 8 minutes]

1½ pounds (2 pints) brussels sprouts, cleaned
3 tablespoons water
3 tablespoons butter
1 tablespoon lemon juice
¼ cup toasted slivered almonds
Salt and pepper to taste

Place the brussels sprouts in a glass casserole. Pour in the water, cover and cook in the center of the oven 4 minutes. Stir. Cook 4 minutes. Let set, covered, 5 minutes. Drain well. Stir in the butter, lemon juice, salt and pepper and sprinkle with the toasted almonds. *Serves 4 to 6.*

CAULIFLOWER IN QUICK CHEESE SAUCE
[Speed-cook; 7 minutes]

½ teaspoon salt
1 medium head of cauliflower (about 1 pound), cut into flowerets
2 tablespoons water
One 11-ounce can condensed cheddar cheese soup
3 tablespoons heavy cream
½ cup buttered bread crumbs

Sprinkle the salt into a glass casserole, then add the cauliflower flowerets. Add the water, cover and cook in the center of the oven 3 minutes. Rotate the casserole half a turn. Cook 2 minutes. Drain. In a large glass measuring cup, blend the soup and cream. Cook 2 minutes, or until hot. Pour the sauce over the cauliflower. Sprinkle with the bread crumbs and place under the broiler of a conventional stove until the crumbs are brown. *Serves 4 to 6.*

CARROTS IN CONSOMMÉ
[Speed-cook; 10 minutes]

1 medium onion, chopped
2 tablespoons chopped fresh parsley
2 tablespoons butter
⅛ teaspoon mace
8 medium carrots, scraped, cut into ½-inch pieces
¼ cup canned condensed consommé

In a glass casserole, cook the onion and parsley in the butter 2 minutes, or until the onion is soft. Stir in the mace, carrots and consommé. Cover and cook in the center of the oven 4 minutes. Stir. Cook, uncovered, 4 minutes. Let set, covered, 5 minutes. *Serves 4.*

CARROTS MARSALA
[Speed-cook; 6 minutes]

3 tablespoons butter
Pinch of dried thyme
Salt and pepper to taste
10 small, slender carrots, scraped and cut into 1-inch pieces
¼ cup Marsala

Put the butter, thyme, salt and pepper in a glass casserole. Place the carrots on top of the seasonings. Cook, covered, in the center of the oven 2 minutes. Stir, coating the carrots with the butter. Pour in the wine. Cover. Cook 2 minutes. Stir. Cover and cook 2 minutes. Let set, covered, 3 minutes. *Serves 4.*

EASY CREAMED CELERY
[Speed-cook; 8 minutes]

4 cups 1-inch celery pieces (scraped; cut on the diagonal)
2 tablespoons beef broth (beef bouillon cubes dissolved in hot water make a quick broth)
One 10½-ounce can condensed cream of celery soup
Salt and pepper to taste

In a glass casserole, combine the celery and beef broth and cook, covered, in the center of the oven 4 minutes. Drain. Stir in the soup; cook 4 minutes. Season with salt and pepper. *Serves 4.*

CORN ON THE COB

This summertime American favorite is spectacular cooked by microwaves. We use three techniques, all equally good:

(1) Carefully strip back the husk (do not tear it off) and remove all the silk. Brush the corn liberally with melted butter and sprinkle with salt. Pull the husks back into place. Tie with string around the tip to keep the husks intact. Cook.

(2) Place buttered, salted ears in a large glass casserole. Add a tablespoon of water. Cover with plastic wrap. Cook.

(3) Wrap each buttered, salted ear securely in waxed paper and place in a spoke fashion on paper towels in the oven. Cook.

Cooking Times

2 ears of corn: 4 to 6 minutes; turn corn over at 2 minutes, or halfway through the cooking time.

4 ears of corn: 8 to 10 minutes: turn corn over at 4 minutes, or halfway through the cooking time.

6 ears of corn: 9 to 11 minutes; turn corn over at 4½ minutes, or halfway through the cooking time.

Very large ears will need extra cooking time. The corn should set, covered, 3 to 5 minutes after cooking.

CORN PUDDING
[Speed-cook; 10 minutes]

1 egg
1 tablespoon sugar
Salt and pepper to taste
1 heaping tablespoon cornstarch
One 16-ounce can cream-style corn
1 cup milk

In a bowl, beat together the egg, sugar, salt, pepper and cornstarch. Add the corn and milk and blend well. Pour the mixture into a buttered deep glass baking dish. Cook, uncovered, in the center of the oven 5 minutes. Stir well, from the outside in. Cook 5 minutes, or until nearly set in the middle. Let set, covered, 3 minutes. This will have a surprising soufflé consistency. *Serves 4.*

OUT-OF-THE-CUPBOARD CORN SCALLOP
[Speed-cook; 4 minutes]

One 10¾-ounce can condensed cream of vegetable soup
1 small onion, minced
½ teaspoon pepper
One 16-ounce can whole kernel corn, drained
1½ cups crushed saltine crackers
2 tablespoons butter

Blend the soup, onion and pepper. In a glass casserole, alternate layers of corn, the soup mixture and crushed crackers. Dot with butter. Cook in the center of the oven 2 minutes. Rotate casserole half a turn. Cook 2 minutes, or until hot. *Serves 4 to 6.*

CREAMED PEAS AND ONIONS
[Speed-cook; 7 minutes]

One 10-ounce package frozen peas
One 16-ounce can small white onions, drained
One 10¾-ounce can condensed cream of mushroom soup
3 tablespoons heavy cream
¼ teaspoon pepper
¼ teaspoon dried tarragon
Salt to taste

In a glass casserole, place the peas, icy side up. Cook 4 minutes. Drain. Stir in the onions. Blend the soup, cream, pepper and tarragon. Stir the soup mixture into the peas and onions. Cook in the center of the oven 2 minutes. Stir. Cook one minute, or until hot. *Serves 4 to 6.*

FAST ONIONS AMANDINE
[Speed-cook; 5 minutes]

One 10½-ounce can condensed cream of mushroom soup
Two 16-ounce cans small white onions, drained
½ cup grated sharp cheddar cheese
¼ cup toasted slivered almonds

Stir the soup in its can until smooth. In a glass casserole, place the onions and stir in the soup. Cook, covered, in the center of the oven 2½ minutes. Rotate the casserole half a turn. Sprinkle on the cheese, then the almonds. Cook 2½ minutes, or until hot. *Serves 4 to 6.*

FRESH GREEN PEAS IN WINE AND BEEF BROTH
[Speed-cook; 6 minutes]

2 pounds fresh peas (about 2 cups shelled peas)
2 medium celery ribs, scraped and thinly sliced
4 whole scallions, minced
½ teaspoon pepper
Pinch of dried thyme
2 tablespoons beef broth
1½ tablespoons dry white wine
3 tablespoons butter
2 teaspoons cornstarch
Salt to taste

In a glass casserole, place the peas, celery and scallions. Sprinkle with the pepper, tarragon and beef broth. Cook, covered, in the center of the oven 3 minutes. Stir in one tablespoon of the white wine, and the butter. Cook 2 minutes. Blend the remaining wine and cornstarch and stir it in. Cook one minute. Let set, covered, 3 minutes. Add salt to taste. *Serves 4 to 6.*

SAUTÉED PEPPERS, ONIONS AND MUSHROOMS
[Speed-cook; 6 minutes]

Here's a way to relieve the boredom of serving the same old vegetables the same old way. See Variation (below) to convert into a main dish.

> 2 small green peppers, cut into thin rings
> 2 small sweet red peppers, cut into thin rings
> 2 medium onions, sliced
> 2 tablespoons olive oil
> ½ pound fresh mushrooms, sliced
> ¼ teaspoon dried oregano
> 1 teaspoon salt
> ⅛ teaspoon pepper

In a glass casserole, in the center of the oven, cook the green and red peppers and onions in the olive oil 4 minutes, stirring after 2 minutes. Stir in the mushrooms, oregano, salt and pepper. Cook one minute. Stir. Cook one minute. Let set, covered, 3 minutes. *Serves 4 to 6.*

Variation: A unique main-course dish also can be built on this recipe. Allow one hot and one sweet Italian sausage per serving. Prick the sausages. Cook for 2½ minutes on each side in half the oil, covered with waxed paper to prevent splattering. Add the remaining vegetables in order and cook as directed above.

BAKED POTATOES

Everyone loves baked potatoes. They are nutritious and delicious, and they go with just about any main dish. The only problem is that with conventional cookery it takes at least one hour to bake them. If they are cooked ahead, wrapped in foil and kept warm (as the restaurants prepare them), they become soggy and lose much of their flavor.

Baked potatoes, then, are the speedy show-off microwave vegetable. We confess that, any time we are demonstrating our microwave oven and its miraculous speed, we always bake a potato and offer it to the guest who is seeing the oven in operation for the first time. Beforehand we ask the guest to time the cooking. He or she is tasting the potato in less than 5 minutes. We also are able to sit down to a fish or steak dinner and decide at the last minute that a baked potato would taste just right. We can have it in minutes.

Try to select blocky, nontapered, uniform-in-size baking potatoes (we like Idahoes), each about 7 ounces, which is considered a medium-size potato. If the potatoes aren't all the same size some will be over-cooked. The cooking times here are for potatoes of even dimension that weigh exactly 7 ounces. Scrub them well, and pierce both sides in several places with a fork. No cooking dish is necessary. Place the potatoes in the oven, one inch apart, on double folds of paper towels. The towels will absorb some of the moisture from the potatoes and help prevent oversteaming.

To cook a single potato, place it in the center. Arrange 3 or more like the spokes in a wheel (with none in the hub or center position), one inch apart. Cook-

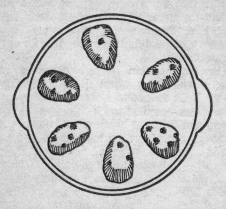

ing time depends upon the size and variety of the potatoes. We have found that a New York State potato cooks faster than the russet, or so-called Idaho. Most important: When half the cooking time has elapsed, turn the potatoes over and rearrange their position. If you are cooking a potato 4 minutes, remind yourself to turn it by cooking just 2 minutes; when the buzzing stops, turn the potato and cook it another 2 minutes.

Use the same method of selection and cooking for baked sweet potatoes or yams, but reduce the time by one minute.

Time

1 potato:	4 to 5 minutes
2 potatoes:	6 to 7 minutes
3 potatoes:	8 to 9 minutes
4 potatoes:	10 to 11 minutes
6 potatoes:	14 to 15 minutes

If cooking the shorter time, let set 10 minutes before serving.

These are estimated times. You will have to experiment to your satisfaction. according to how well you like your potato cooked. Again we remind you that the potato will cook after it is removed from the oven. Thus, they should be firm at the end of the cooking time. If they are withered-looking before you take them from the oven, they are overcooked. To be on the safe side, the shorter cooking time should be favored; we use it and find it exactly right for our tastes and our oven.

With the speed cooking of the baked potato you will find that a whole new world of potato cookery has opened up. Bake the potatoes, then dice them, melt butter in the browning skillet and hash-brown the potatoes. Slice them and fry them in butter for cottage potatoes. Cream them. Scoop out the baked potato, place in a bowl , add butter and cream and beat into fluffy mashed potatoes. Add cheese and minced onion to the mashed potatoes, place the mixture back in the potato shells, sprinkle a little more grated cheese atop, then place the stuffed shells in the oven until the cheese melts. Make potato salads. Potato pancakes. There is almost no limit to what you can do with that 4-minute baked potato.

GERMAN POTATO SALAD
[Speed-cook; 11 minutes]

4 slices bacon
2 medium onions, chopped
One 10½-ounce can condensed cream of celery soup
2 tablespoons water
2 tablespoons vinegar
¼ teaspoon celery seed
½ teaspoon sugar
⅛ teaspoon pepper
4 medium (7-ounce potatoes, baked, (page 212), peeled and sliced
2 tablespoons chopped fresh parsley

In a glass casserole, arrange the bacon slices, cover with a paper towel to prevent splattering and cook 4 minutes. Remove the bacon, blot grease from the slices with a paper towel and let cool. Crumble the bacon and set aside. In the bacon fat in the casserole, cook the onions 2 minutes, or until soft. Stir in the soup, water, vinegar, celery seed, sugar and pepper. Cook 2 minutes. Stir. Cook 2 minutes. Add the potato slices, parsley and crumbled bacon. Cook 30 seconds. Stir. Cook 30 seconds. Stir. Serve hot. *Serves 4.*

LYONNAISE POTATOES
[Speed-cook; 9 minutes]

3 tablespoons butter
½ teaspoon salt
¼ teaspoon pepper
¼ teaspoon dried marjoram
4 medium-size white onions, thinly sliced
4 medium potatoes, peeled and thinly sliced
2 tablespoons hot chicken broth (a quick broth can be made by dissolving 1 chicken bouillon cube in 1 cup hot water)

Place the butter in the bottom of a glass casserole and sprinkle in the salt, pepper and marjoram. Arrange the onions in a layer on top of the butter and seasonings.

Cover and cook in the center of the oven 3 minutes. Arrange the potatoes in a layer atop the onions and sprinkle the chicken broth over them. Cook, covered, 3 minutes. Stir well. Cook 3 minutes. Let set, covered, 5 minutes. Test for tenderness and seasoning. The potatoes and onions should be crisp, yet tender. *Serves 4.*

SWIFT BUT SAVORY SCALLOPED POTATOES
[Speed-cook; 4 minutes]

One 10½-ounce can condensed cheddar cheese soup
¼ cup heavy cream
½ teaspoon pepper
Small pinch of cayenne
4 medium potatoes, peeled, cooked and sliced
2 medium-size white onions, minced
1 tablespoon butter
Paprika

Blend the soup, cream, pepper and cayenne thoroughly, making a sauce. In a glass casserole, arrange alternate layers of potatoes and onions, spooning some of the sauce on each layer. Dot the top layer with the butter and sprinkle with paprika. Cook, uncovered, in the center of the oven 2 minutes. Rotate casserole half a turn. Cook 2 minutes, or until hot. *Serves 4.*

POTATOES WITH BROCCOLI
[Speed-cook; 12 minutes]

⅓ bunch (about ½ pound) broccoli
One 8-ounce potato
1 medium onion, chopped
1 garlic clove, minced
3 tablespoons olive oil
Salt and pepper to taste

Divide the thick stems of the broccoli by cutting from the top down, right through the stems, so you will have thin-stemmed (about ½ inch in diameter) stalks of broccoli. In the center of the oven, cook the potato in its jacket 4½ minutes. Arrange the broccoli in a glass casserole with the buds in the center and the stems near the edge of the dish, and cook in the center of the oven 2½ minutes, rotating the dish at 1½ minutes. Transfer the broccoli to a bowl. Pour off any liquid in the casserole. Add the olive oil and cook the onion and garlic 3 minutes, stirring at 2 minutes. Cut the broccoli into bite-size pieces. Peel and slice the potato when it is cool enough to handle. Add the potato and broccoli to the onion in the casserole and cook 2 minutes, or until hot, stirring after one minute. Season with salt and pepper. Serve hot or cold. If it is served cold, stir in the juice of half a lemon. *Serves 2.*

RATATOUILLE
[Speed-cook; 12 minutes]

This is said to be a French dish, originating in southern France where many of the cooks are Italian, a fact the French find forgettable. We suspect that this, like the fork, was first popularized by the Italians, who are masters of many zucchini and eggplant dishes. We like it either hot or cold, and serve it with many of our meat dishes, from lamb to duck. On a hot summer day a dish of cold Ratatouille, with bread and beer, makes a superb supper.

2 cups unpeeled zucchini cubes (½-inch pieces)
2 cups peeled eggplant cubes (½-inch pieces)
Flour
1½ teaspoons salt
4 garlic cloves, minced
⅓ cup olive oil
½ teaspoon dried oregano
3 medium onions, thinly sliced
2 medium green peppers, seeded, cored and cut into thin strips
½ teaspoon dried basil
3 large ripe tomatoes, peeled, seeded and thinly sliced

Separately toss the zucchini cubes and the eggplant cubes with flour to coat them lightly. In a large buttered glass casserole, arrange a layer of zucchini cubes and sprinkle with a third each of the salt, garlic and oil. Cover the zucchini with a layer of eggplant cubes, sprinkle with a third each of the salt, garlic and oil, and all of the oregano. Make a third layer with the onion slices, sprinkling on the remaining salt, garlic and oil. Arrange a layer of pepper strips over the onions, and sprinkle on half the basil. Cover and cook in the center of the oven 4 minutes. Stir. Cook 4 minutes. Stir. Arrange a layer of tomato slices on top and sprinkle with the remaining basil. Cover and cook 4 minutes. Let set, covered, 5 minutes. *Serves 4 to 6.*

ROEDKAAL (DANISH RED CABBAGE)
[Speed-cook; 17 minutes]

1 head red cabbage (3 to 3½-pounds)
1 small onion, minced
2 tablespoons butter
1 small tart apple, peeled, cored and minced
1 tablespoon flour
2 tablespoons sugar
¼ cup cider vinegar
½ teaspoon caraway seeds
2 tablespoons currant jelly
Salt and pepper to taste

Remove the outside tough leaves of the cabbage, then quarter, core and shred the vegetable. In a glass casserole, in the center of the oven, cook the onion in the butter 2 minutes. Stir in the cabbage and apple, sprinkle with flour, stir and cook 2 minutes. Stir in the sugar, vinegar and caraway seeds. Mix well. Cook, covered, 8 minutes, stirring after 4 minutes. Stir in the currant jelly. Cook 5 minutes. Let set, covered, 5 minutes. Season with salt and pepper. *Serves 4 to 6.*

SPEEDY SUCCOTASH
[Speed-cook; 12 minutes]

History tells us that this tasty dish was created by the American Indians, who also gave us corn. It is one of our favorite vegetable combinations, which we like with micro-cooked Milano Meat Loaf (page 119) and a baked potato (page 212).

One 10-ounce package frozen whole-kernel corn
One 10-ounce package frozen Fordhook lima beans
2 tablespoons butter
1 tablespoon flour
½ cup heavy cream
⅛ teaspoon paprika
Salt and pepper to taste

Place the frozen vegetables in a glass casserole, icy side up. Cook, covered, in the center of the oven 7 minutes, stirring at 4 minutes. Drain well. Stir in the butter until it melts, then stir in the flour. Cook one minute. Stir in the cream and paprika. Cook 4 minutes, stirring at 2 minutes. Let set, covered, 5 minutes. Season with salt and pepper. *Serves 6.*

SWISS CREAMED FRESH SPINACH
[Speed-cook; 4 minutes]

2 pounds fresh spinach
3 tablespoons butter
1 medium onion, chopped
1 garlic clove, minced
2 tablespoons flour
⅛ teaspoon nutmeg
½ cup heavy cream
Salt and pepper to taste

Wash the spinach, drain well and chop. In a glass casserole, in the center of the oven, cook the onion and garlic in the butter 2 minutes. Stir in the chopped spinach. Sprinkle with the flour and nutmeg and stir. Pour in the cream and mix well. Cover, cook 2 minutes and stir. Season with salt and pepper. *Serves 4 to 6.*

ZESTY ZUCCHINI
[Speed-cook; 6 minutes]

4 medium zucchini (unpeeled), cut into ¼-inch rounds
One 8-ounce can Hunt's seasoned tomato sauce
¼ teaspoon salt
⅓ cup grated Swiss cheese
1 cup crisp garlic croutons

Place the zucchini slices in a glass casserole. Cover and cook in the center of the oven 3 minutes. Drain. Stir in the tomato sauce and salt. Sprinkle with the cheese. Cover and cook 3 minutes, or until the zucchini is tender but still crunchy. Let set, covered, 5 minutes. Sprinkle with the croutons just before serving. *Serves 4.*

SWEET-AND-SOUR ZUCCHINI STRIPS
[Speed-cook; 8 minutes]

This tasty Italian squash is universally loved, and its ways of preparation are endless. There even is a zucchini cookbook. Here's one dish few will have had.

  1 large onion, chopped
· 1 tablespoon butter
  1 tablespoon olive oil
  1½ pounds small, firm zucchini (unpeeled), cut into strips the size of French-fried potatoes
  1 teaspoon Hungarian paprika
  1 tablespoon butter blended with 1 tablespoon flour
  ¼ cup cider vinegar
  ¼ teaspoon dill weed
  1 teaspoon sugar
  ½ teaspoon salt

In a glass casserole, in the center of the oven, cook the onion in the butter and olive oil 2 minutes. Add the zucchini strips, sprinkle with paprika and cook 2 minutes, turning the zucchini strips twice. Stir in the blended butter and flour until well mixed, then add the vinegar, dill weed, sugar and salt. Cover and cook 2 minutes. Stir. Cook 2 minutes or until the zucchini is tender but still crisp and crunchy. *Serves 4.*

ZUCCHINI ABRUZZI STYLE
[Speed-cook; 9 minutes]

  1 medium onion, chopped
  2 tablespoons butter
  8 small slender zucchini, cut into ½- to ¾-inch equal-size pieces
  2 eggs
  Salt and pepper to taste
  ¼ cup grated Parmesan cheese

In a glass casserole, cook the onion in the butter 2 minutes, or until soft. Add the zucchini, cover and cook 3 minutes. Stir. Cook 2 minutes. Let set, covered, 3 minutes. Drain off all liquid. Beat the eggs, salt, pepper and cheese together. Stir into the casserole with the zucchini. Cook 2 minutes, stirring after each minute, or until the eggs have set. Serve immediately. *Serves 4.*

11

Desserts

It won't brown cakes or pies, but the microwave oven will take the drudgery out of cooking all desserts, and is so good at cooking everything from a cake to a custard almost "instantly" that the wonder will not be about the oven itself, but how you ever got along without it. You'll also find that fruits and fruit desserts have an incomparable fresh fruit flavor that is lessened, if not lost, in conventional cookery. You can cook a cake in 5 minutes, 6 cupcakes in 3 minutes. But there are rules to review, and points to consider:

Custards

Custards are quick and easy—but also easy to overcook (they will curdle and separate). We prepare individual custard cups, and set them in a glass baking dish in one inch of water. This seems to equalize the cooking. It also is a good idea to stir custards from time to time to prevent them from boiling over. Undercook all custards, as they will continue to cook out of the oven.

Fruit desserts

Test fruits and fruit desserts when half the cooking time has elapsed. Times will vary, depending upon the ripeness of the fruit and what variety it is. For example, apples take longer than peaches. Remember, too, that during the setting time the fruits will continue to cook. When using cut-up fruit, even cooking is assured if pieces are the same size.

Cakes

Cake pans should be greased only on the bottom. An even crust will result if you let the cake set 10 minutes in the pan before cooking it. They rise quickly, and higher, in the microwave oven, so only half fill the pan. The extra batter can be used for cupcakes.

Just before you pour the batter into the pans, pass a knife through it several times to release the air bubbles. We find that doughy centers in cakes can be eliminated by setting the cake pan on an inverted saucer.

Cook just one cake layer at a time, about 5 minutes. Even cooking is also obtained by rotating the cake pan a quarter turn every 2 minutes.

It is also pertinent to note that cakes baked in differently shaped utensils have different cooking times. Here's the way we time our cakes:

> 8- or 9-inch round pan: 5 minutes
> 8x8x2-inch square: 7 minutes
> 9x13-inch rectangular: 10 minutes
> Deep bundt dish: 12 minutes

The cake is cooked when a toothpick inserted in the center emerges clean. The cake surface probably will be moist after cooking. Do not be tempted to cook it longer to reduce the moisture. That will result in overcooking other parts of the cake. After a brief setting period the moisture will disappear.

Let the baked cake set 5 minutes, then invert on a wire rack and let cool about 10 minutes.

We find that layer cakes are easier to ice if they are first refrigerated one hour. Do not try to frost or ice a cake right after cooking. The trapped heat in the cake will melt it.

All packaged cake mixes have a basic recipe, which reads approximately like this: "Combine cake mix, 1⅓ cups water, 2 eggs." It then goes on to instruct how to mix, beat and bake. By using ingenuity, you can improve the flavor of an ordinary mix, converting it into a cake no one would believe came from a package. To stir your imagination, here are a few ideas: Instead of using water, use wine, rum, liqueurs, fruit juice, buttermilk; also add butter, flavorings, vanilla extract, almond, peppermint, grated lemon or orange rind, instant coffee, chopped nuts, chocolate chips, an extra egg. If you use sour cream, add ¾ cup plus ½ cup of water, no other liquid.

When using cake mixes, simply line the bottom of the baking dish with "brown-in" paper or waxed paper and butter the paper lightly if you are going to remove the cake. If you are going to serve the cake from the pan or dish, instead of lining the dish with waxed paper butter it. Peel the paper from the bottom after the 10-minute cooling period.

We've also discovered that it is wise to eat microwave cakes sooner than those cooked conventionally. They dry out a little faster. You'll have to experiment with your own oven to get the timing exactly right. We cook our cakes 5 minutes per layer, but you might be better off cooking just 4 minutes. Play it safe and slightly undercook to allow for that carry-over cooking time. With a couple of cakes you'll have the hang of it and turn out masterpieces in minutes.

Cupcakes

Speaking of minutes, cupcakes are a sensation if you want to show off the speed of your oven.

> 1 cupcake: 30 seconds
> 2 cupcakes: 60 seconds
> 6 cupcakes: 2½ minutes

Cook the cupcakes in paper baking cups placed in glass custard cups. They should be filled only ⅓ full. When baking three or more cupcakes, place them in a circle for even cooking. Results are better if you do not cook more than 2 at a time. Overcooking can readily occur. Time is so short that it is a simple matter to bake a couple dozen in about 10 minutes.

We've discovered that once cupcakes are baked they should be removed from the glass custard cups. If they aren't, condensation formed while the cupcakes are cooling collects and can make the bottom of the cupcakes soggy.

Pies

Although pies do not brown under microwaves, they do cook well and their crusts are flaky.

Precook pie shells before filling, or they will be soggy. Flute the edges higher than you usually do. This enables the pie to hold a larger amount of filling. It also makes the stirring of the filling easier. Place the pie plate on another inverted pie plate to prevent doughy crusts. Stirring is necessary for even cooking. Stir gently from the outside (where the waves cook first), moving the cooked portion in toward the center. Stir after 2½ minutes of cooking time.

Cook the pie 2 minutes, then rest the pie one minute. This should be repeated until the pie is cooked. Rotate the pie a quarter turn every 2 minutes.

You'll probably have your own recipe for making a pie shell, but here's ours, with the timing. There are excellent frozen pie crusts on the market. But your own will be better.

PASTRY SHELL
[Speed-cook; 3 minutes]

1 cup all-purpose flour
½ teaspoon salt
½ cup shortening
4 tablespoons milk

Sift the flour and salt together. Place in a bowl and cut in the shortening with a pastry blender until you have a mixture resembling cornmeal. Sprinkle in one tablespoon of milk at a time, gently tossing it into the mixture with two forks. When all the milk is incorporated and the mixture well moistened, form it into a firm ball with your hands. On a lightly floured board, roll out the pastry to ⅛ inch thickness, rolling from the center to the edge. Let set 10 minutes.

Shape into a 9-inch pie plate, fluting the edges with your fingers or a fork. Cover with a paper towel, then insert an 8-inch glass pie plate, which will hold the pastry flat and prevent shrinkage.

Bake in the center of the oven 3 minutes, rotating a quarter turn every minute. Remove the paper towel and 8-inch pie plate, and let the pie shell cool before filling it.

Here are some hints to help in heating up desserts:

Rewarming one serving of pie, cake or coffee cake takes exactly 15 seconds.

A trick that we have found helpful in serving ice cream: If the ice cream is brick-hard from the freezer, place it right in its container in the oven and heat 15 seconds for one pint, 30 seconds for one quart. Careful —the ice cream should be softened just to the scoopable, not soupable, stage.

All the sundae toppings—butterscotch, pineapple, caramel, chocolate, etc.—can be placed under microwaves 15 seconds, just to soften. They must, however, be in a glass container. If you wish to heat them longer and serve them hot, transfer them to a measuring cup for the additional heating; otherwise, the glass containers that they are sold in might break.

To defrost and warm convenience or commercial desserts will take varying lengths of time, depending upon thickness. Most should be heated uncovered. You'll learn this quickly. For example, six 15-ounce frozen blintzes should be placed in a circle, heated 5 minutes, then turned and heated another 5 minutes. A frozen 32-ounce peach or cherry cobbler, removed from its aluminum foil, should be placed in a glass container, heated 20 minutes and rotated a quarter turn every 5 minutes. Many convenience food packagers and manufacturers are printing microwave defrosting, heating and cooking times on their wares.

But, as somebody's grandmother said, "Why buy it when you can make it?" And, with microwaves, you can make it in minutes.

GEORGE HERZ'S LEMON CUSTARD FLUFF
[Speed-cook; 7 minutes]

3 tablespoons butter
1 cup sugar
4 eggs, separated
¼ cup flour
¼ cup lemon juice
2 teaspoons grated lemon rind
½ teaspoon vanilla
1 cup milk

In a large bowl, cream the butter; add the sugar and cream the butter and sugar together thoroughly. In another bowl, beat the egg yolks well until light and fluffy, then add them to the butter and sugar, along with the flour, lemon juice, lemon rind and vanilla. Add the milk and mix thoroughly. Beat the egg whites until stiff and fold into the other ingredients. When well mixed, pour into a glass baking dish. Place that dish in a larger glass dish containing hot water about one inch deep. Cook in the center of the oven 7 minutes, stirring from the outside in towards the center at 3 minutes and at 6 minutes. Let cool and serve right from the baking dish or, if you like, just before serving invert on a serving dish so the lemon custard will be on top and the fluff on the bottom. *Serves 6.*

BAKED APPLES
[Speed-cook; 5 minutes]

4 large apples (unpeeled), cored
¼ cup brown sugar
1 tablespoon butter
Sugar cinnamon, ground

Place one tablespoon of the brown sugar in the cored cavity of each apple. Top each apple with ¼ tablespoon of butter. Sprinkle with cinnamon. Place the apples in a circle in a round glass dish. Cook in the center of the oven 2½ minutes. Rotate the dish half a turn. Cook 2½ minutes. Let set 10 minutes. *Serves 4.*

BUTTERSCOTCH RUM BANANAS
[Speed-cook; 3 minutes]

½ cup butter
½ cup brown sugar
¼ cup dark Rum
4 small ripe (but not overripe) bananas, cut into halves
    lengthwise
4 large scoops hard-frozen vanilla ice cream

Combine the butter and sugar in a glass measuring cup
and cook in the center of the oven 1½ minutes, stirring
after each 45 seconds. Stir in the rum. Pour the mixture
into a shallow glass baking dish. Arrange the banana
halves in the sauce in the baking dish. Cook 45 seconds.
Turn the bananas over and cook 45 seconds. Place the
ice cream on four dessert plates. Spoon the sauce over
the ice cream and arrange 2 banana halves on either
side of the scoop of ice cream. *Serves 4.*

QUICK ELEGANT POACHED PEARS
[Speed-cook; 13 minutes]

1 cup sugar
2 cups white wine
¼ teaspoon allspice
1 cinnamon stick
1 small piece fresh gingerroot
4 firm ripe Bartlett pears (unpeeled) cut into halves and
    cored

In a glass baking dish large enough to hold the 8 pear
halves, place all the ingredients except the pears. Cook
in the center of the oven until the mixture almost simmers and the sugar is dissolved. Stir. Cook 8 minutes,
stirring at 4 minutes. The mixture should be syrupy.
Place the pears in the syrup. Cook 2½ minutes. Rotate
the dish half a turn. Cook 2½ minutes. Chill before
serving. *Serves 4.*

RAPID RHUBARB
[Speed-cook; 5 minutes]

That fresh rhubarb from your garden can be on the table as a sweet-tart dessert minutes after you have cut it.

  2 cups chopped fresh rhubarb
  ⅛ teaspoon salt
  ½ cup sugar

Place the rhubarb and salt in a glass casserole. Cover and cook in the center of the oven 2 minutes. Stir. Cook 2 minutes. Stir in the sugar. Cover and cook one minute. Let set, covered, until cool. *Serves 4.*

CHOCOLATE CAKE SURPRISE
[Speed-cook; 10 minutes]

When your guests ask you what makes this delicate chocolate cake so light and so moist, your answer is the surprise: "Mayonnaise!"

  2 cups unsifted all-purpose flour
  1 cup sugar
  1 teaspoon baking soda
  ¼ cup unsweetened cocoa
  ⅛ teaspoon salt
  1 cup mayonnaise
  1 cup water

In a mixing bowl, blend the flour, sugar, soda, cocoa and salt. Stir in the mayonnaise and the water. With an electric beater, beat on low speed until all the ingredients are mixed and moistened. Beat at high speed 1½ minutes. Grease the bottom only of a glass baking dish deep enough that the batter will fill it only halfway. Cook in the center of the oven 10 minutes, rotating the dish a quarter turn every 2 minutes. Let the cake set 10 minutes to finish its carry-over cooking. The cake is done if a toothpick stuck in the center comes out clean. Let it cool completely before frosting. *Serves 6 to 8.*

MINA THOMPSON'S SOUR CREAM COFFEE CAKE
[Speed-cook; 10 minutes]

Topping Mixture:

¼ cup white sugar
⅛ cup brown sugar
1 teaspoon ground cinnamon
1 cup chopped pecans or walnuts

Batter:

½ cup butter
1 cup white sugar
2 eggs
1 cup sour cream
1 teaspoon pure vanilla extract
2 cups all-purpose flour
1 teaspoon baking soda
1 teaspoon baking powder
½ teaspoon salt

In a bowl, combine the topping ingredients and mix thoroughly. Set aside. In another bowl, make the batter. Cream the butter and sugar, add the eggs, sour cream and vanilla and mix well. Stir in the flour, baking soda, baking powder and salt until well blended. Butter the bottom only of a 9-inch square glass baking dish. Pour in half the batter. Sprinkle on half the topping mixture. Add the remaining batter and sprinkle on the rest of the topping. Cook in the center of the oven 10 minutes, rotating the dish half a turn at 5 minutes. The cake is done when a toothpick inserted in the center comes out clean. *Serves 8.*

FUNG CHAN CHIN'S CLASSIC CHEESECAKE
[Speed-cook; 9 minutes, 10 seconds]

Crust:

    32 single graham crackers, crushed
    ¼ cup sugar
    6 tablespoons butter, melted (about 40 seconds under
       microwaves)

Filling:

    4 eggs, separated
    ½ cup sugar
Four 3-ounce packages cream cheese, heated in a bowl
       30 seconds under microwaves
    2 teaspoons pure vanilla extract
Dash of almond extract

Topping:

    2 cups sour cream
    3 tablespoons sugar
    1 teaspoon almond extract
    ⅛ teaspoon ground cinnamon

Blend the cracker crumbs, ¼ cup sugar, and the butter. Pack evenly onto the bottom and sides of a 9-inch glass deep-dish pie plate, making a shell. Refrigerate. In a large bowl, beat the egg yolks until light and fluffy. Add the ½ cup sugar and blend well. Beat in the softened cream cheese, one package at a time. Blend in one teaspoon of the vanilla, and the almond extract. In another bowl and with clean, dry beaters, beat the egg whites until stiff. Mix in the remaining vanilla extract and fold the egg whites into the egg yolk-cream cheese mixture. When well blended, turn into the chilled graham cracker shell. Cook in the center of the oven 6 minutes, rotating the dish half a turn every 2 minutes. Let cool 45 minutes.

To make the topping, blend the sour cream, 3 tablespoons sugar and the teaspoon of almond extract. Spread over the cool filling. Dust with the cinnamon and cook the cheesecake in the center of the oven 2 minutes, rotating half a turn at one minute. Let cool and place in the refrigerator to chill overnight. *Serves 8.*

JAMAICAN CHEESECAKE
[Speed-cook; 6 minutes, 10 seconds]

⅓ cup butter
24 single honey graham crackers, crushed
Two 8-ounce packages cream cheese
3 eggs, beaten
¾ cup sugar
1 teaspoon pure vanilla extract
2 tablespoons dark rum

Heat the butter in an 8-inch round glass dish or pie plate in the center of the oven 40 seconds, or just until the butter melts. Blend the butter and the cracker crumbs in the glass dish. Pack evenly onto the bottom and sides of the dish, making a shell. Place the cream cheese in a bowl and heat 30 seconds, or just until softened. Beat the cream cheese until smooth. Stir in the eggs, sugar, vanilla and rum, and beat until the mixture is smooth. Pour into the graham cracker shell. Cook in the center of the oven 5 minutes, rotating the dish half a turn every 2 minutes. The center will be soft. Refrigerate overnight; the pie will set as it chills. *Serves 8.*

DORIS L. MAYS' FRENCH STRAWBERRY GLACÉ PIE
[Speed-cook; 10¾ minutes]

1 unbaked 9-inch pie shell, frozen or your own
1 quart ripe strawberries, washed, drained and hulled
One 3-ounce package cream cheese, softened 15 seconds under microwaves
1 cup sugar
3 tablespoons cornstarch
1 pint heavy cream, whipped

Cover the prepared pie shell with a paper towel. Place an 8-inch glass pie plate on top of the paper towel.

Cook in the center of the oven 3 minutes. Remove the 8-inch pie plate and the paper towel. Cook the pie shell 1½ minutes. Let set 15 minutes before filling to cool.

Spread the softened cream cheese evenly over the bottom of the pie shell. Place half the strawberries on the cream cheese, distributing them evenly. In a bowl, place the remaining berries and cook 3 minutes. Mash and strain them. Return the juice to the bowl. There should be 1½ cups of strawberry juice. If necessary, add a little water to increase to this amount. Blend the sugar with the cornstarch and gradually stir into the juice. Cook in the center of the oven 1½ minutes. Stir. Cook 1½ minutes, or until the mixture simmers and is thickened. Let cool. Pour the cooled thickened juice over the strawberries in the pie shell. Refrigerate 2 hours. Decorate with the whipped cream.

PIE À LA MODE

Place one piece of peach or apple pie (at room temperature) on a serving plate. Top with a scoop of hard-frozen vanilla or peach ice cream. Heat 15 seconds. The pie will be warm, the ice cream only slightly softened. *Serves 1.*

HUGHBERTA NEERGAARD'S PARTY-TIME ICE CREAM PIE
[Speed-cook; 6 minutes, 40 seconds]

1 stick butter
1 cup all-purpose flour
¼ cup brown sugar
1 cup finely ground pecans
2 quarts ice cream of your choice

In a bowl, heat the butter about 40 seconds or until melted. Stir in the flour, brown sugar and half the pecans, stirring until well blended. Pat the mixture onto the bottoms and sides of two 9-inch glass pie plates, forming shells. Cook one shell at a time in the center of the oven 2¼ minutes, rotating the plate half a turn at one minute. Let cool. One at a time, place each quart of ice cream in its container on a plate and heat in the oven half a minute, or until slightly soft. Fill the cooled pecan shells evenly with the softened ice cream. Sprinkle with the remaining ground pecans. Freeze and serve at your leisure. *Makes 2 pies, serving 12.*

ALICE VAUGHN'S CHOCOLATE SAUCE
[Speed-cook; 2 minutes, 20 seconds]

No longer do you have to melt chocolate in a double boiler!

    2 ounces unsweetened chocolate
    1 cup sugar
    ⅛ teaspoon cream of tartar
    One 6-ounce can evaporated milk
    1 teaspoon pure vanilla extract
    Pinch of salt

Place the chocolate in a large glass measuring cup. It is not necessary to heat the chocolate until it is completely melted (carry-over heat will continue to melt it). Just heat it in the center of the oven 1⅛ minutes, or until the chocolate begins to melt. Remove and stir well until it is thick and creamy. Blend in the sugar and cream of tartar. Add the milk gradually and heat for 30 seconds. Stir. Heat for 10 seconds. Stir. Heat for 10 seconds. Stir until well blended. Remove from the oven and stir in the vanilla and salt. Let cool. *Makes about 1⅛ cups sauce.*

Variation: This can be converted into a different and rich sauce for desserts by using ½ can of evaporated milk and 3 ounces of dark rum.

MEXICAN SUNDAE

This is an old favorite with people in upstate New York, but seems to be unknown elsewhere. Try it; your guests will love it.

  1 very generous scoop of vanilla ice cream
  2 tablespoons Alice Vaughn's Chocolate Sauce (above)
  2 tablespoons Spanish peanuts

Place the ice cream in a serving dish. Cover with chocolate sauce. Sprinkle with the peanuts. *Serves 1.*

HOT FUDGE SUNDAE

This is an appreciated mid-winter dessert.

  1 generous scoop chocolate or vanilla ice cream
  3 tablespoons Alice Vaughn's Chocolate Sauce (page 233), heated
  2 tablespoons whipped cream (not from a push-button can!)

An easy way to heat the chocolate sauce is to place it in a measuring cup, heat 30 seconds; stir; heat 40 seconds. Stir and pour over the ice cream, then add the dollop of whipped cream. *Serves 1.*

INDEX

DISH	OUTSIDE DIMENSIONS HT.	OUTSIDE DIMENSIONS TOP DIM.	OUTSIDE DIMENSIONS TOP DIM. W/HANDLES	INSIDE DIMENSIONS DEPTH	INSIDE DIMENSIONS TOP DIM.	CAPACITY LEVEL FULL	CAPACITY WORKING
PYREX® ware Clear Ovenware							
No. 221—1½ qt. Round Cake Dish	2″	8¾″	10½″	1¾″	8¼″	48 oz.	34 oz.
No. 222—2 qt. Square Baking Dish	2¼″	8⅝″	10¼″	2″	8″	68 oz.	49½ oz.
No. 232—2 qt. Oblong Baking Dish	2″		13½″ x 7⅞″	1¾″	11¾″ x 7½″	78 oz.	57 oz.
No. 463D-N— 6 oz. Custard Cup	1⅞″	3¾″		1¾″	3½″	6¾ oz.	4 oz.
No. 532—1 qt. Liquid Measuring Cup	5¼″	5½″	7⅛″	5″	5″	39 oz.	39 oz.
No. 683—1½ qt. Covered Casserole	3⅞″	7⅞″	9⅜″	2½″	7½″	53 oz.	41 oz.
(ht. without cover)	2⅞″						
No. 684—2 qt. Covered casserole	4⅛″	8¾″	10¼″	2¾″	8¼″	71 oz.	57 oz.
(ht. without cover)	3⅛″						

DISH	OUTSIDE DIMENSIONS			INSIDE DIMENSIONS		CAPACITY	
	HT.	TOP DIM.	TOP DIM. W/HANDLES	DEPTH	TOP DIM.	LEVEL FULL	WORKING
PYREX® ware Bakeware in Color: the following items are available							
Spring Blossom Green (-1) Butterfly Gold (-4) Old Orchard (-47) Homestead (-48)							
No. 480—3 pc. Covered Casserole set (Dimensions for 3 bowls with covers)							
1 qt. casserole	3¾"	6¼"	7½"	3"	5⅞"	36 oz.	30 oz.
1½ qt. casserole	4¼"	7½"	9¼"	3¼"	7"	57 oz.	47 oz.
2½ qt. casserole	4¼"	8¾"	10⅝"	3½"	8¼"	86 oz.	75 oz.
No. 500—4 pc. Oven, Refrigerator & Freezer set (Dimensions for vessels with covers)							
1½ cup dish (set contains 2)	3¼"	4¼" x 3⅜"		2½"	4" x 3"	11 oz.	8 oz.
1½ pt. dish	3¼"	6¾" x 4¼"		2½"	6¼" x 3¾"	25 oz.	19½ oz.
1½ qt. dish	3¼"		9½" x 6⅞"	2¼"	8¼" x 6½"	55 oz.	40 oz.

INSTRUCTIONS FOR USING
MICROMATE® BROWNING DISHES

Micromate® browning dishes are glass-ceramic dishes with special coatings on the outside bottom of each dish that permits browning, searing, grilling and frying during microwave cooking. When the empty coated dish is preheated in the microwave oven, the special coating absorbs the microwave energy becoming very hot. Browning begins when food is placed on the preheated surface and continues throughout the cooking cycle.

Preheating the dish is important because it permits the browning of foods, while the microwave does the cooking. Preheating times vary depending upon the type of food to be browned. See general cooking chart on next page for specific preheating times.

To preheat:

1. Place empty coated dish in the center of the microwave oven shelf without its cover.
2. Close oven door; turn on microwave power using accompanying chart as a general guide for preheat times.
3. Hot and cold spotting on the inside surface of the dish is a function of the microwave oven resulting from the microwave oven heating pattern and not the dish.

To brown foods:

4. Open oven door and without removing dish, place food on heated surface. Smoking and spattering will occur as in any pan-broiling or broiling situation. The PYREX® brand cover may be used on the dish to reduce spattering but will hold the steam in the dish producing "steam-flavored" food. If a dry, crispy surface is desired, do not use a cover.

   Paper toweling may be used in place of the glass cover. This will reduce the spattering while allowing the steam to escape from the dish. Do not allow paper toweling to touch bottom heated surface of the dish or it may char.
5. Close oven door; turn on microwave power following cooking guidelines as suggested on the chart.
6. If both sides of the food are to be browned, open over door, turn food, close door and cook on second side for suggested time (see chart). To obtain extra browning on the second side, place the food on an unused portion on the bottom inside surface of the dish.
7. Open oven, remove dish using pot holders. Food may be served directly from the micromate browning dish.
8. When cooking food consecutively, the dish should be preheated a shorter period of time (usually about one half original preheat time) after removing food but before adding additional food.

**General Cooking Chart for
Corning Micromate® Browning Dishes**

This chart should be used only as a guide since desired pre-heat time and cooking time will vary with each microwave oven. Degree of doneness is a matter of personal preference and can be regulated by decreasing the cooking time.

| | | | COOKING TIME | |
FOOD	QUANTITY	*PREHEAT TIME	FIRST SIDE	SECOND SIDE
Steak	(1) 7 oz. ¾ inch thick	4 min.	1 min.	30-45 sec.
Hamburgers	1 or 2 patties	4 min.	1½ min.	1½ min.
	3 or 4 patties ¼ lb. each pattie	4 min.	3 min.	1½-2½ min.
Pork Chops	1 or 2 chops	4 min.	3 min.	1-3 min.
	3 or 4 chops ½ to ¾ inch thick	4 min.	6 min. cover, if desired	4-6 min.
Chicken	3 or 4 pieces 8 to 12 oz. total, floured	4 min. add ½ tbsp. fat after preheat	4-5 min. cover, if desired	3-4 min.
French Toast	1 slice	3 min.	30 sec.	30 sec.
	4 slices	3 min.	1 min.	1 min.
Grilled Cheese Sandwiches	1 or 2 buttered lightly	3 min.	30-45 sec.	30-45 sec.
Eggs, Fried Sunny Side Up	1 or 2	1-1¼ min. add 1 tbsp. fat after preheat	cover, 1¼ min.	

For additional foods not listed on the general cooking chart, consult specific recipes in *Mastering Microwave Cooking*.

*Degree of browning is a personal preference. Browning will begin at the preheat time given, however, increasing the preheat time (up to 8 min. for hamburgers) will give a greater degree of browning.